To Nicholas [illegible]
with fond regards

Tom [illegible]

PREVIOUS PRAISE FOR JONATHAN R. DULL'S

The French Navy and the Seven Years' War

"A magnificent book, another tour de force in combined diplomatic, political, and naval history."—N. A. M. RODGER, author of *The Safeguard of the Sea: A Naval History of Britain*

"Dull has written a magisterial history of the war and the role of the French Navy. . . . This history will long stand as the definitive work on the French Navy of the period."—HAROLD N. BOYER, *Sea History*

"This book is not merely a history of the French Navy but a step-by-step exposition of a hugely complex war, laid out by a single historian whose starting point is the diplomacy and politics of the protagonists, and who fits the French Navy into this framework. . . . Dull skillfully places the last piece in the jigsaw and constructs a sophisticated view of the war from the perspective of Versailles, while at the same time presenting a patient and detailed analysis of the British war effort."—ROGER KNIGHT, *Mariner's Mirror*

"Those interested in learning the inside story of how governments actually conduct war will find this a fascinating work, and a sobering reflection of how they probably still carry on today."
—ROBERT GUTTMAN, *Military History*

"This excellent book deserves a wide audience. It far surpasses most histories of the Seven Years' War. . . . This book belongs on the shelf of anyone seriously interested in early American and Atlantic history, French maritime and naval history, and in the history of international relations in the eighteenth century."
—JAMES PRITCHARD, *Journal of Military History*

“Dull’s book is a monument to careful scholarship. With clear, concise prose, he navigates deftly through a complex tale of war, diplomacy, and politics. His book is the definitive work on this topic.” —*Canadian Journal of History*

“With the publication of Jonathan R. Dull’s *The French Navy and the Seven Years’ War*, we at last have an accessible, brisk, and erudite narrative of this global struggle.”—RAFE BLAUFARB, *Journal of Modern History*

“An impressive and an important addition to the literature. *The French Navy and the Seven Years’ War* will for years to come be an essential addition to the library of specialists and students of eighteenth century naval (and diplomatic) history alike.” —OLAF UWE JANZEN, *Northern Mariner*

“There are a great many books for English-speaking readers concerning the British Royal Navy in the 18th century, but not many that provide solid, well-researched material concerning its greatest rival, the French Navy. Dull helps fill in that gap and provides some much-needed balance with this work. Overall, this is a much-needed study for any scholar interested in this time period or in western naval and maritime history.”—*Choice*

The Age of the Ship of the Line

THE AGE OF THE Ship *of the* Line

THE BRITISH & FRENCH NAVIES, 1650–1815

JONATHAN R. DULL

University of Nebraska Press ✻ *Lincoln and London*

Manufactured in the
United States of America

Library of Congress Cataloging-
in-Publication Data

Dull, Jonathan R., 1942–
The age of the ship of the line:
the British and French navies,
1650–1815 / Jonathan R. Dull.
p. cm. — (Studies in war, society,
and the military)
Includes bibliographical references
and index.
ISBN 978-0-8032-1930-4 (cloth: alk. paper)
1. Great Britain. Royal Navy—
History—18th century. 2. Great
Britain. Royal Navy—History—17th
century. 3. France. Marine—History—
18th century. 4. France. Marine—
History—17th century. 5. Ships of the
line—History—18th century. 6. Ships
of the line—History—17th century.
7. Warships—Great Britain—History.
8. Warships—France—History. 9. Great
Britain—History, Naval. 10. France—
History, Naval. I. Title.
DA87.D85′ 2009
359.00941′09033—dc22
2008051658

Set in Scala by Bob Reitz.

Contents

Maps and Battle Diagrams

Maps

Battle Diagrams

Preface

Between 1689 and 1815 the British (or initially the English allied with the Scots) fought seven wars against France. Their navies played an important, sometimes critical, role. The power of the rival navies was based chiefly on their ships of the line, great wooden warships carrying two or three tiers of iron or brass cannon. The age of the ship of the line is largely the story of the navies of Britain and France, the two powers best able to afford the massively expensive fleets of ships of the line. Although Spain and the Netherlands maintained good sized navies throughout the period, by the early eighteenth century they had become subordinate players in the naval rivalry of Britain and France. Other navies, such as those of Russia, Denmark, Sweden, Naples, and Venice, were regional powers, largely restricted to the Baltic or Mediterranean Seas. The goal of this book is to explain the background, course, and results of the seven wars between the British and French, particularly the causes of the final British triumph.

By treating the British and French navies in tandem I hope to give a balanced account of their rivalry; I confess to loving both countries and warmly supporting their friendship. The statesmen of the eighteenth century generally saw war not primarily as a contest of societies but more as a contest of economies, in which victory went to the strongest, not to the "best," and in which the chief virtue was endurance. I approach these wars in much the same way, using ships of the line as the measure of strength. Thus this book pays as much attention to the number of ships of the line engaged in the various campaigns as to the admirals and statesmen who directed them. In all the Franco-British wars of the period, including the one Britain lost, the War of American Independence, the side that could put the most ships of the line to sea was successful.

I have learned much by conversations with historians more knowledgeable than I am in nautical matters. I am particularly grateful to Daniel Baugh, Richard Harding, John Hattendorf, Roger Knight, Nicholas Rodger, Patrick Villiers, and Clive Wilkinson; the mistakes I have made are totally my responsibility. Some of these conversations took place during either a 2005 trip to Paris or a 2006 trip to Greenwich, England, made possible, respectively, by the Association France-Amériques and the National Maritime Museum. I am extremely grateful to the members of both organizations for their generosity, hospitality, and kindness, particularly to Patricia Cédelle and Janet Norton, who handled the respective arrangements.

In the interest of saving space I will not repeat the acknowledgments to friends and colleagues that I made in my last book, *The French Navy and the Seven Years' War*. I am still indebted to all of them for their help or encouragement. I must, however, again thank my sister, Caroline Hamburger, for her hospitality during the times I was in London, and my wife, Susan Kruger, for her constant helpfulness and support. I dedicate this book to my children, Veronica Lamka, Robert Dull, Max Kruger-Dull, and Anna Kruger-Dull, in the hope that someday they will live in a world without war.

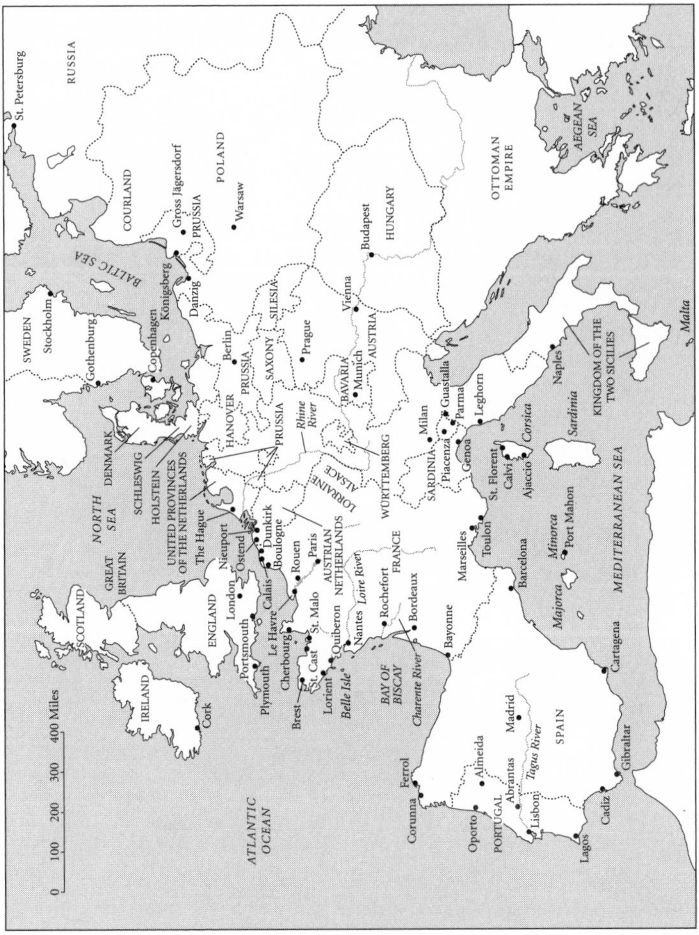

MAP I. Europe in 1750

From Dull, *The French Navy and the Seven Years' War* (Nebraska, 2005).

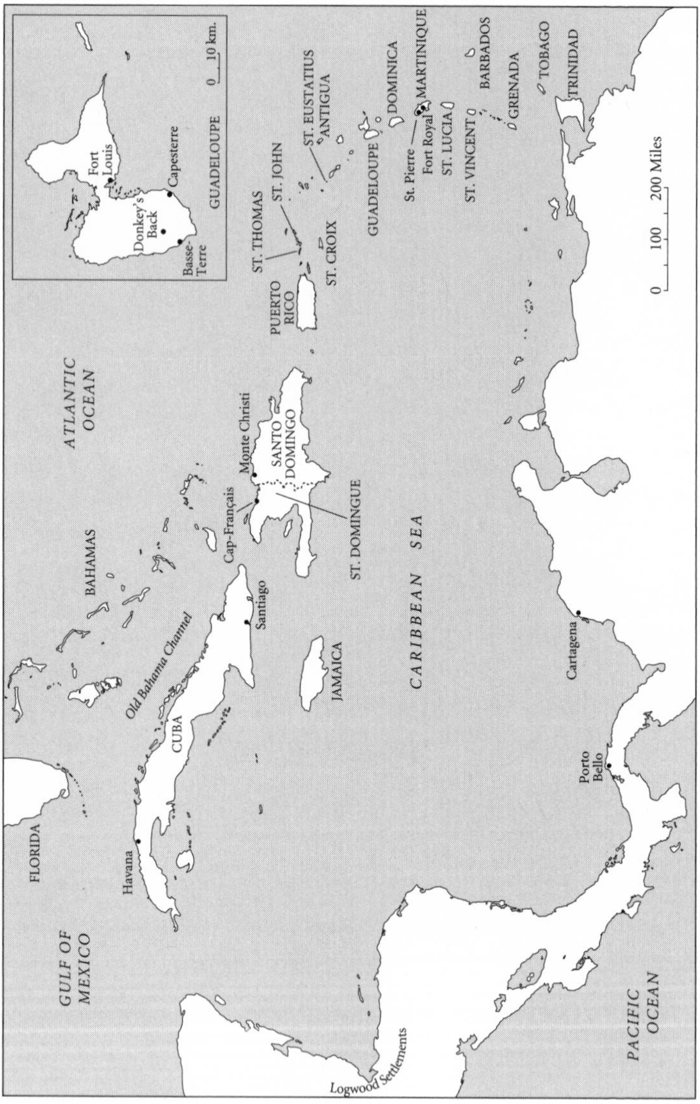

MAP 2. The Caribbean

From Dull, *The French Navy and the Seven Years' War* (Nebraska, 2005).

The Age of the Ship of the Line

1. The Ship of the Line Begins Its Reign

I

Between the 1650s and the 1850s, naval warfare was ruled by the ship of the line and the line of battle after which it was named. These huge three-masted wooden ships were some 120 to 210 feet long with a beam (width) of 30 to 60 feet. They carried between 40 and 130 cannon mounted along two, three, or, in the case of the Spanish ship of the line *Santísima Trinidad,* four decks.[1] The ship of the line was the most expensive, technologically advanced, and visually impressive weapon of its day. It also was the measure of national naval power, like the dreadnought of World War I or the aircraft carrier of World War II. The line of battle—a string of warships following each other bow to stern—was the best way to bring its power to bear, as each ship thus could give support to neighboring ships. Only in shallow or poorly charted waters, like the eastern Baltic, was the ship of the line not dominant; there the galley, a shallow-draft oar-powered warship, continued to play a major role throughout the eighteenth century.

The era of the ship of the line began when its two components, the ship of the line and the line of battle, were combined. That time was long in coming. The line of battle is so logical an arrangement that the earliest groups of European ships carrying cannon sometimes made use of it. A Portuguese fleet commanded by Vasco da Gama seems to have employed a line of battle off the coast of India in 1502.[2] Its use was intermittent, however, because its main advantage was mutual support in an artillery duel. Some naval battles consisted of such duels; the English, for example, foiled the Spanish Armada of 1588 by the use of cannon. Until the middle of the seventeenth century, however, naval warfare often involved either boarding (ships grappling an opponent and then dispatching a boarding party) or the use of fire ships (setting ships on fire in order to ram them into enemy vessels). The Dutch, who by the 1640s had become the greatest naval power in Europe, were masters of a variety of tactics. In 1639, they used both a line of battle and fire ships against a huge Spanish fleet off the English coast.[3]

The use of great ships of 50 or more cannon also was long established by 1650. Most major naval powers had one or more of these ships, such as the English *Prince Royal* of 55 cannon, launched in 1610, and the *Sovereign of the Seas*, 90 cannon, launched in 1637, or the French *Couronne*, 68, launched in 1638. These ships, however, were clumsy to sail and expensive to build, man, and maintain. As an admiral's flagship they could be useful in a battle, but without other ships of similar size they could not alter the disorganized melee of a naval battle based on boarding or the use of fire ships. Fleets during the first half of the seventeenth century were very heterogeneous, moreover, frequently consisting mostly of converted merchant ships.

A turning point came in 1649 when the Parliament of England decided to build a group of very large and heavily armed frigates (fast, medium-sized warships usually carrying 20 or more cannon) that was the predecessor of groups (or "classes") of ships of the line of a standard size. The thirteen ships of the *Speaker* class, launched between 1650 and 1654, were of roughly similar size (about 750 tons) and carried 48 to 56 cannon; in tonnage and armament they were similar to a very large galleon, the chief warship of the late sixteenth and early seventeenth centuries and still the mainstay of the Spanish navy, but they were longer, lower, and faster than galleons. No other navy had a group of ships to match them; the Dutch navy, hitherto Europe's best, continued to rely chiefly on taking merchant ships into naval service.[4]

The line of battle first was used, however, before most of the *Speaker* class were launched. Both England and the United Provinces of the Netherlands were republics, Charles I of England having been executed in 1649. Both were Protestant, too, although different enough in persuasion to create tension. It could be argued that they were natural allies against Catholic monarchies such as Spain and France; at any rate, geography did not automatically make them enemies. They were bitter trade rivals, however. Outside of Europe, trade rivalry, particularly for spices in Asia or slaves in Africa, frequently involved the use of force. As there were no effective international means of mediating disputes, the Netherlands and England were unable to resolve their trading disputes, and each feared domination by the other. As the crisis worsened, each tried to intimidate the other, leading in 1652 to a war that could have been avoided.[5]

Although the new English battle fleet temporarily disrupted Dutch shipping and fought several battles, the first campaign of the war was indecisive. On 29 March 1653 the three officers jointly commanding the English navy issued instructions that guaranteed its fleets henceforth would fight in a battle line. Two months later the English won a smashing victory off the Gabbard shoal in the North Sea, largely due to their use of the line of battle.[6] This marriage of ship and tactics endured for two centuries. The sailing ship line of battle dominated naval warfare through the Battle of Sinope in 1853, in which a line of Russian ships of the line destroyed a group of Turkish frigates. During the ensuing Crimean War of 1854–56, ships of the line, including some equipped with auxiliary steam power, were the chief naval weapon, although by now they were vulnerable to explosive shells. The death blow to the ship of the line, however, was the launching of the first iron warships in the early 1860s.[7] The line of battle persisted through the age of iron and steel battleships, though, until the last great fleet action, the 1944 Battle of Leyte Gulf.

II

What accounts for so enduring a marriage between this weapon and these tactics? In part, both were the product of the same technological advances, the creation of large cannon firing extremely heavy cannonballs and the development of gun ports, openings cut in the sides of ships through which cannon could fire. It took a very large ship to carry banks of cannon weighing several tons apiece. Equally important the ship needed great strength to withstand the impact of cannon balls sometimes weighing as much as 42 pounds; in the late eighteenth century, the British even developed cannon firing a 68-pound ball. Ships needed as many cannon as they could carry, using equal numbers on both sides, starboard and port. Moreover, ships needed large crews to work their sails and fire their cannon; a French cannon firing a 36-pound ball, for example, weighed more than four tons and needed fourteen men to fire it.[8] Although crew members slept and ate among the guns, ships needed space for water, food and drink, munitions, and various spare parts and supplies.

The ship of the line was like a floating fortress, but it had points of weakness that a fortress did not. Its bow and stern could not be as strong and straight as its sides if it were to maneuver through the water, and it had room for only a few cannon facing directly ahead or astern. This made it vulnerable to a volley of cannon balls fired from directly in front or behind it. Not only could these penetrate more easily, but also once inside an enemy ship they would find little resistance, since the ship of the line was not divided into compartments like a modern steel ship. Such an attack, called "raking," usually inflicted heavy casualties and damage. A lone ship had only its speed and maneuverability to protect it from raking; on its own a ship of the line was vulnerable even to frigates, which were smaller but more nimble except in a heavy wind. The best protection for a ship of the line was having other ships of the line just ahead of and just behind it. This mutual support against raking depended on the ships sailing together in as close and straight a line as possible. This line of battle also had offensive advantages. If fleets were passing in opposite directions, each ship could pound the hulls or fire into the masts of several opponents in succession.

The line of battle also was effective, particularly as a defensive tactic, because of other limitations of wooden sailing warships. There were two major ways of overcoming a line of battle. The first was "doubling" one of the ends of the line, that is, placing warships on both sides of the enemy ships at either the front or back end of the line. The second was to break the line by a concentration of force somewhere in its middle. Both tactics were very difficult unless the attacker had a considerable advantage in numbers or skill, because it was much easier for sailing ships to keep formation and maintain mutual support while on the defensive. Difficulties in communicating between ships and in maneuvering in unison made coordinating an attack so challenging that decisions in battle usually had to be left to individual ship captains.

Throughout most of the late seventeenth and eighteenth centuries it was rare for a fleet of superior size to suffer a decisive defeat. Sir Cloudesley Shovell, one of the leading admirals at the beginning of the eighteenth century, claimed that without a miracle, numbers would gain the victory.[9] Although generally British warships were sturdier and their crews better trained that were the French, the differences in quality between them usually were not enough to produce a major victory unless there was a substantial difference in numbers. Most battles ended with few ships being lost, and generally casualties were fewer than those in land battles involving similar numbers of men. Captured French ships served alongside British ones and vice versa. Decisive battles, such as the 1759 Battle of Quiberon, usually came after the quality of French crews had drastically declined. After the onset of the French Revolution, however, the French navy underwent a rapid decline, largely due to shortages of funds, sailors, and supplies. Admiral Horatio Nelson's defeat of a larger Franco-Spanish fleet at Trafalgar was due less to his genius than to the poor quality of the fleet opposing him. Such a battle was unusual. In most cases the key factor in a battle was numerical superiority.

In spite of Nelson's victories there was relatively little evolution in naval tactics between 1660 and 1815. Similarly the evolution of the ship of the line was gradual and unspectacular until the nineteenth century. The maximum size of a ship of the line increased slowly over the seventeenth and eighteenth centuries; the 120-gun *Nelson* of 1805 was only 70 percent larger than the *Sovereign of the Seas* of 1637.[10] Vital components such as sternposts and mainmasts were best constructed from a single tree, whose maximum size was limited by nature. The British navy tried to compensate by packing more guns on the decks of its vessels, but this did not work very well;

an 80-gun French ship was almost as large and as powerful as a 100-gun British ship. The first "revolution" in the design of the ship of the line did not occur until near the end of its existence with the invention of the screw propeller and the use of steam. Admittedly the ship of the line did benefit from continual improvements such as the development in the late eighteenth century of copper plating for hulls, which retarded the growth of marine organisms.

Such improvements, even if gradual, had some effect on naval warfare. A major difference between seventeenth- and eighteenth-century navies was their endurance. The former was generally held in port during winter weather while the latter could fight year-round; the newer ships were less top-heavy and more maneuverable thanks to larger and better designed hulls and improvements in rigging and sails.[11] A second difference was a large increase in the number of seamen per ship; for example, in 1690 a French 80-gun ship carried a crew of 600, a 74-gun ship a crew of 500, and a 64-gun ship a crew of 400. By 1759 an 80-gun ship required 860 men, a 74-gun ship required 695, and a 64-gun ship required 500. Slightly more than half of the crews were petty officers and trained sailors. The remainder were ship's boys, marines, and various landsmen. The same development occurred in the British navy.[12]

The requirements for a ship to serve in the line of battle also increased. In the middle of the seventeenth century, a ship with 40 cannon qualified as a ship of the line, but by the beginning of the eighteenth century at least 48 or 50 were needed. At the Battle of Beachy Head in 1690, for example, half of the French line of battle of seventy ships were ships mounting 50 to 58 cannon, although only one had fewer than 50. By the middle of the eighteenth century, 64 cannon generally were needed, and in the 1780s, the French navy began phasing out ships carrying fewer than 74. The cumulative effect was navies of bigger ships and more crewmen, which cost much more money. Louis XIV's navy of 1692 had ninety-five ships of the line plus half a dozen warships of 44 or 46 cannon, but only forty-nine ships carried 64 or more cannon; in 1782 the French navy had seventy-two ships of the line, of which sixty-seven carried 64 or more.[13]

III

Although the English had a head start over the Dutch in the development of both the ship of the line and the line of battle, the first war between the two states (1652–54) was not decisive. During the war, power in the Commonwealth passed from Parliament to Oliver Cromwell. Faced with other threats, he did not choose to exploit the naval supremacy gained by the English navy. He signed a compromise peace with the States General, the ruling body of the Netherlands. After Cromwell's death in late 1658, public support for the republic collapsed, in large part because of an expensive war against Spain begun in 1655. In 1660 the Stuart monarchy was restored. Naval construction slowed temporarily, largely because Parliament did not trust the new king, Charles II, but it did not completely stop.[14] Charles II was a strong supporter of the navy, and his brother James served as lord high admiral between 1660 and 1673. The navy continued to have a strong influence on British politics and diplomacy. For James and Charles, the Dutch were still the enemy, and the efforts to crush them had the potential side benefit of strengthening the monarchy against Parliament. As we shall discuss in the next chapter, England fought two more wars against the Netherlands (1665–67 and 1672–74), but they were less successful than the first had been. The Dutch learned from their shortcomings in the first war. They built larger ships and eventually adopted the line of battle.[15] They also benefited from excellent political leadership and superb admirals. During the last of these wars, however, the Dutch were fighting for survival against another rival, one that had a far larger population than England as well as a huge army and a large navy. The English, too, soon realized that the Dutch were no longer their chief rival. A new competitor for both their navies had arisen: the navy of France.

2. Louis XIV and His Wars

I

During the 145 years before the French Revolution, France was ruled by only three kings, Louis XIV, Louis XV, and Louis XVI. They were different in personality and abilities, but early in their reigns each made the same mistake, attacking a neighboring state without just cause. Each enjoyed some initial success but then was trapped in a cycle of violence and financial expense that he came to regret.

One of the problems of Louis XIV's successors was living up to the image of the French monarch he established. Their reigns can be understood only in relationship to his.[1] Louis XIV began his direct rule of France at age twenty-two in 1661. He was trained by his mother's chief advisor and perhaps secret husband, Cardinal Jules Mazarin (or Giulio Mazzarini in his native Italian). Although the French public distrusted and disliked him, Mazarin was one of the greatest of French statesmen. He exercised wide powers granted him by Louis's mother, serving as regent for her son after the death of her husband, Louis XIII, in 1643. Mazarin brought to a successful conclusion a lengthy war against France's hereditary enemies, the Habsburgs. The Austrian branch of the Habsburg family had wished to turn the Holy Roman Empire, containing not only Germany but also much of central Europe, into a unitary state instead of a loose confederation of hundreds of largely independent principalities. Many of the rulers of those principalities resisted, particularly German Protestants fearful of the Habsburgs' aggressive Catholicism. The resistance of one such principality, the Kingdom of Bohemia, precipitated the Thirty Years' War of 1618–48. During the war the opposition against the Habsburgs was supported by outside rulers such as the kings of Denmark and Sweden; the Austrian Habsburgs in turn received aid from their Spanish cousins, also members of the House of Habsburg.[2] France joined the war against the Habsburgs in 1635. Although Louis XIII was a Catholic, he put interests of state ahead of religion by helping the Protestants against their Catholic overlord.

The war was difficult. Spain still had a powerful army and navy. In 1636 a Spanish army operating from the Spanish Netherlands, the area which today is Belgium, advanced as far as Corbie, near Amiens, only seventy miles from Paris. It soon retreated, however, and gradually the increasingly competent French army asserted itself.[3] The war in Germany ended favorably for France in 1648. The Peace of Westphalia not only preserved the independence of the myriad principalities that made up the Holy Roman Empire but also gave France and its ally Sweden the right henceforth to intervene on behalf of the small princes. The French war against Spain lasted for another eleven years. Often a better alternative to a peace treaty that crushes an enemy is one that permits befriending it. The 1659 peace settlement with Spain negotiated by Mazarin was a relatively moderate one that encouraged reconciliation; one of its key elements was the arrangement of a marriage between the young king of France and his cousin Maria Teresa, the eldest daughter of Philip IV of Spain.

The treaties with Spain and the Holy Roman Empire gave France considerable security. The economy of Spain had virtually collapsed, Portugal had established her independence from Spain, and the Spanish army and navy were shells of their former selves, although the extent of the Spanish decline was not immediately obvious. The Holy Roman Empire was divided and powerless, and even the core Habsburg possessions in central Europe were economically, administratively, and militarily underdeveloped. France had little reason to fear invasion, even from the Spanish Netherlands. After the restoration of the Stuart dynasty in 1660, England was not a threat; Charles II was a cousin of Louis XIV and soon gave proof of his goodwill by selling France the important port of Dunkirk, recently captured from Spain. The Dutch, although commercially powerful, had a relatively small army and posed little military threat. In effect France was virtually surrounded by a network of weak buffer states that would protect it in the event of a revival of the Habsburgs.

Louis now had the option of concentrating his attention on increasing the power of the crown and the prosperity of his people, thereby reverting to the policy followed before France's entrance into the Thirty Years' War.[4] Louis, however, tried to increase royal power and French wealth, while simultaneously pursuing an aggressive foreign policy. Doubtless he did not see these goals as contradictory. Stimulating French prosperity meant that he could increase taxes, enabling him to better administer his realm and expand his army and navy. His armed forces could be used not only to extend France's borders but also to provide employment for the nobility, the monarchy's chief political rivals. (Among France's 20 million people, some 100,000 families were considered to possess noble blood and enjoyed many social, political, and financial privileges.)[5] Successful wars would increase the king's prestige and would frighten potential rivals, both domestic and foreign.

Louis chose to extend France's borders by force, thereby forestalling another option, that of reducing (or at least not expanding) the size of the army and following the example of England and the Netherlands, who gave priority to colonies, trade, and naval strength. Following such a policy would have required considerable political skill, as there was little potential support for it among the great nobles, some of whom had challenged Mazarin during the 1648–52 insurrections known as the Fronde. Initially Louis tried to make France both Europe's leading military power *and* Europe's leading naval power. Once he began ruling France directly in 1661, one of his first projects was strengthening the navy. That year the energetic Jean-Baptiste Colbert became intendant of finances and took control of the French navy, even though he did not officially become secretary of state for naval and colonial affairs until 1669. Colbert quickly took steps to expand French commerce and to build up the navy in order to provide protection for French shipping. The navy built by Louis XIII and his chief minister, Cardinal Richelieu, had suffered badly during the lengthy war with Spain, particularly after its Dutch allies left the war in 1648.[6] When Louis XIV assumed direct rule of France, the French navy possessed only five warships carrying 50 or more cannon. Over the next dozen years, it placed in service eleven ships carrying 72–120 cannon and fifty-two carrying 48–70 cannon. By 1670 the French navy had more tons of ships than the navies of either England or the Netherlands.[7]

France did not do as well as England, however, at establishing a network of colonies to provide consumer products like tobacco to the mother country and to foster trade, thereby training sailors for its navy. Colbert's colonial policies, based on patronage and slanted toward short-term financial gain, were contradictory and shortsighted. French colonies were underpopulated and isolated from each other. Not until the 1720s would the French colonial empire be put on a sound footing, chiefly by the growth of West Indies sugar production, based, like that of the British West Indies, on the merciless exploitation of slave labor.[8]

Colbert began building an infrastructure in France, however, to support the navy. Central to that infrastructure were the great shipyards of Brest and Rochefort along the Atlantic coast and Toulon in the Mediterranean. Here the navy constructed, repaired, and based its warships and assembled naval supplies from anchors to masts. The most problematic of the dockyards was Rochefort, constructed on a marshy and unhealthy site on the Charente River, some ten miles from the sea. Its roadstead, where fleets assembled after leaving harbor, was superb, but the passage from river to roadstead was so shallow that larger ships had to remove their cannon to enter it. The port of Brest, near the western end of the English Channel, had a superb harbor, although the passage to it from the ocean was dangerous and the necessity of an easterly wind to leave port restricted its usefulness. France had no deep natural harbor east of Brest, whereas England had four dockyards—Chatham, Sheerness, Woolwich, and Deptford—on the Thames or near its mouth. These dockyards were close to the Straits of Dover at the Channel's eastern end. Another dockyard at Portsmouth on the south coast of England lay directly on the Channel.

Unlike the English, the French had a permanent fleet in the Mediterranean. It was based at Toulon, where another large dockyard was built. The division of the French navy between Toulon and the Atlantic ports presented both advantages and disadvantages. Toulon could draw on the resources of the Mediterranean, such as wood from the shores of the Adriatic, and could use the sailors of southern France, such as those from the nearby port of Marseilles.

Toulon was difficult to blockade, so the French Mediterranean fleet could be used for surprise attacks, particularly at the beginning of a war, as happened in 1756 and 1778. On the other hand, the Mediterranean fleet was exposed to capture should it try to join the Atlantic fleet at Brest, or the Atlantic fleet could be defeated before the Mediterranean fleet arrived.

The great French and English dockyards, with their building slips, dry docks, storehouses, and manufacturing facilities, became the largest industrial establishments in Europe. By 1814 the British royal dockyards, which had employed 2,000 to 3,000 workers in 1688, employed more than 15,000 workers, including more than 4,200 at Portsmouth and more than 3,800 at Plymouth.[9]

The English and French navies demanded not only dockyards but also cannon, food, naval supplies of all sorts, and sailors. These cost huge sums of money and required highly organized bureaucracies. The French, largely starting from scratch, created a centralized system, with a single naval minister and a series of bureaus devoted to such tasks as overseeing shipbuilding or personnel. It was an organization not unlike the U.S. Navy during World War II. Within the dockyards, however, power was divided between civilian administrators and naval officers as a means for the naval ministry to exercise control; this led to conflicts that were even worse than those between English dockyard officials and naval officers. The more haphazard English system depended on cooperation between various boards, the most important of which was the Board of Admiralty. After its establishment in 1689, the admiralty made regulations, appointed officers, supervised the other boards, and shared with the cabinet, particularly the secretaries of state, the control of naval operations. (Until 1782 there were two secretaries of state who advised the king on foreign policy: the northern secretary, theoretically responsible for *eastern* Europe, and the southern secretary, theoretically responsible for *western* Europe.) The Navy Board was responsible for shipbuilding and repair, finance, and personnel, including noncommissioned (warrant) officers. The Victualing Board collected and distributed biscuit, salt meat, cheese, dried peas and beans, oatmeal, sugar, butter, and other foodstuffs. Another board was responsible for the care of the sick and wounded sailors. The system of multiple boards provided continuity and experience and proved quite flexible, although its cumbersome structure could create problems when fleets had to be outfitted quickly. In particular, the Ordnance Board, which provided cannon to both the army and navy, often posed a problem. The French and English systems both involved a mixture of public and private enterprise. Both navies, for example, sometimes purchased warships from private dockyards, although the practice was much more common in England.

Another similarity was that each naval establishment had only a limited impact on strategy. The heads of the French and English navies were only one voice on the councils that advised their respective kings on major foreign policy decisions. The French naval minister was usually but not always a member of the king's Council of State (Conseil d'Etat), which generally consisted of half a dozen or so senior advisors. The English first lord of the admiralty served on an informal "inner cabinet" of about the same size. The major difference between the two navies was in the level of financial support each received. The English navy was considered vital to national security and was always well funded, while the French navy, usually considered less crucial to French security than was the French army, generally lived a hand-to-mouth existence, a major source of the difficulties it faced throughout most of the age of sail.[10]

This financial uncertainty also was one of the differences between life aboard a French ship of the line and life aboard an English (or later, British) ship of the line. The French developed a system of "classes" by which sailors in a given area served aboard naval warships in rotation, giving them a chance to earn a living aboard better paid and safer merchant ships when not serving in the navy. In practice, however, the system often broke down. The French navy usually was desperate for crewmen and like the English navy was willing to take them by compulsion if necessary. Because it often had great difficulty in paying its crewmen, service was unpopular. The English filled part of their crews by using the dreaded "press gangs" to force merchant seamen into naval service. The English, however, at least were able to pay their crewmen, although wages were usually tardy and did not rise to meet inflation. Both navies were willing to use foreigners; the French Mediterranean fleet, for example, frequently hired Italians.

Life aboard ship was harsh by today's standards, but less so by the standards of the seventeenth and eighteenth centuries. Food and drink were plentiful aboard ship, and work was less difficult than aboard merchant ships. As warships needed large crews to man the gun decks in case of battle, there were plenty of men for daily tasks. On the other hand, large crews made for severe crowding and lack of privacy. In both navies, discipline was harsh, but relations were mitigated by professional camaraderie and shared pride in the ship's sailing and fighting ability. Many crewmen aboard a given ship in either navy were from the same area, which was a source of unity. In the French navy, regional differences were particularly important. Ships in the Mediterranean fleet were manned by crewmen from Provence and southern France, while in the Atlantic fleet crewmen generally came from Brittany and other regions along the Atlantic coast. This made for tension when ships from the Mediterranean had to serve alongside ships from the Atlantic. The gulf between officers and men was somewhat wider in the French navy because officers did not help to raise their own crews and usually spoke only French, while crews spoke Breton or Provencal. Moreover, promotions to the highest ranks in the French navy were reserved for members of the nobility, at least after 1715, whereas many British admirals came from a middle-class or even working-class background. Also, all British officers of lieutenant's rank and higher had received practical training in seamanship and had passed an examination to prove their competence.

Life in both navies was less dangerous than army life because battles were less frequent. On the other hand, the crowded conditions aboard ship fostered the spread of disease. In spite of repeated attempts by French naval ministers to improve the health of crewmen, French ships were more prone than were English ships to epidemics such as typhus, probably because standards of cleanliness on most of its ships were much inferior to British. The French navy was more interested than was the British in the application of science in areas such as ship design; for example, the concept of the metacenter (the basic measurement of stability) was the work of a French scientist, Pierre Bouguer. French theoreticians also were the first to devise a signaling system using flags to represent numbers. The French navy, however, made little use of these breakthroughs and generally was more conservative in regard to technology, at least until the French Revolution. At the end of the eighteenth century, for instance, the British greatly reduced scurvy aboard ships by the frequent, although not universal, use of lemon or lime juice, while the French navy persisted in using vinegar, which the British tried but rejected. On the other hand, the French navy experimented with canned food in 1803, a decade before the British, although its general use awaited the mass production of tin cans.

On balance, life aboard a ship of the line was determined by the nature of the ship itself. An English sailor would have found the routine aboard a French ship reasonably familiar except for not often having his beloved beer to drink. French crews usually drank wine, which English crews drank in the tropics or when beer wasn't available (although wine eventually became common aboard British ships). He would not have eaten quite as well on a French ship, but he probably would have had less difficulty obtaining shore leave.[11]

II

Until 1672 the new French navy did little fighting. Louis XIV's father-in-law, Philip IV of Spain, died in September 1665, leaving his only surviving son to inherit the throne as Charles II. The new king was only three years old and very unhealthy. Surprisingly, he lived another thirty-five years, but he had no children from either of his marriages. Although his eldest sister had renounced any claims to inherit the throne of Spain when she married Louis XIV, the renunciation was contingent upon the payment, never made, of a large dowry. Louis did not wait, however, for the demise of his young brother-in-law to claim an inheritance for Queen Marie-Thérèse (Maria Teresa). The traditional property laws used in the Spanish Netherlands were applied to support a highly dubious claim that she, rather than her younger half-brother, had a right to inherit this portion of the Spanish Empire. First, however, Louis chose in 1666 to comply with a Dutch request for assistance in their second war with England. He sent a fleet to help the Dutch but made sure it kept clear of the fighting. The following year, with the Dutch and the English still at war, he sent a large army to occupy the Spanish

Netherlands. He was foiled, however, when his nominal ally, the Dutch, made peace with England and then became its ally; the Swedes joined the alliance as well. Facing the danger that the new allies would come to the assistance of Spain, Louis XIV was forced to make peace in May 1668. The Treaty of Aix-la-Chapelle gave him relatively minor gains in the Spanish Netherlands, although they did include the important city of Lille.

Louis's first war, known commonly as the War of Devolution, had no major battles and lasted little more than a year, but it had great consequences. Loving the panoply of war and possessing a large, newly rebuilt army, Louis was unwilling to settle for the relative security France enjoyed as a result of the work of Mazarin. He used violence in an attempt to protect France from the hypothetical danger that the Spanish Netherlands might again pose. He treated Spain as if it were France's natural enemy, partly no doubt because the Spaniards insisted that Louis's wife had renounced her claims to the Spanish throne, but even more because he did not have the imagination to escape from conventional wisdom. As a result he became caught in a cycle of wars, each wider, more dangerous, and more expensive than its predecessor.

Had Louis been wiser, the cycle could have been broken. In early 1668 Emperor Leopold I, the head of the Austrian branch of the Habsburgs, agreed to a treaty by which the empire of Spain would be partitioned upon the death of Charles II. Either Louis, as the husband of Maria Teresa, or their children would receive the Spanish Netherlands, the provinces of Franche-Comté and Navarre, plus Naples, Sicily, and the Philippine Islands. Leopold, as the husband of Maria Teresa's sister, Margareta Teresa, would receive the Spanish crown and the rest of Spain's possessions. Once again all that was needed was patience for France to gain secure borders without the danger and expense of war.[12]

Louis, however, was unwilling to obtain by peace what he could gain by war. He eventually decided to attack the Dutch, who had opposed his gaining the Spanish Netherlands by arms and might oppose his gaining them by partition.[13] In 1670 he broke apart the Dutch-English alliance by reaching an agreement with Charles II of England. By the Treaty of Dover Louis promised a subsidy to Charles, thereby helping him to escape his financial dependence on Parliament. In return he obtained the promise of English help in his planned war on the Netherlands. Charles hoped to win a quick victory over the Netherlands without needing any parliamentary assistance.

The English public had little enthusiasm for another war against the Dutch. England had seen few benefits from the two previous wars. The second of these trade wars (1665–67) had ended with a great humiliation. To save money Charles II had decided not to arm the main English fleet. The English thus had no defense when the Dutch appeared in the Medway, part of the Thames estuary, in June 1667. The Dutch burned part of the English fleet and carried back to the Netherlands the great 80-gun ship of the line *Royal Charles*, the second largest ship in the English navy.[14]

The new war began in 1672 when a huge French army invaded the United Provinces of the Netherlands via the German states along the Rhine. The French bypassed the Spanish Netherlands, although Louis hoped the Spaniards soon would become involved in the war so he could seize more land from them. The French and English navies combined forces against the Dutch navy. The French sent a fleet of thirty warships (thirteen full-sized ships of the line of 54–78 cannon, thirteen small ships of the line of 46–50 cannon, and four large frigates of 38 cannon) to join fifty British ships of the line in order to support an invasion by sea. Surprisingly, the attacks on the Netherlands failed. The Dutch had the greatest admiral of the century, Michiel Adriaanszoon de Ruyter. Although badly outnumbered by the combined Anglo-French fleet, he fought them on equal terms in several battles in 1672 and 1673. In the process he poisoned relations between England and France, as the English public blamed the French navy for failing to share equally in the great battles of the war, Solebay (28 May 1672) and the Texel (11 August 1673). In the latter battle sixty Dutch ships of 40 or more guns held their own against eighty-six British and French ships of a similar size. Meanwhile a squadron of Dutch frigates captured New York, which had been obtained by the English in the previous war. Parliament, as suspicious of its own king as it was of the king of France, forced Charles to make a separate peace with the Dutch in early 1674.[15]

The Dutch successfully resisted their enemies on land, too. By opening their dikes the Dutch turned the province of Holland into an island that the hitherto successful French army could not penetrate. Moreover, they found a dynamic and popular leader in William, the young Prince of Orange, who was appointed captain general and admiral general of all Dutch forces, as well as stadholder (chief magistrate) of most of the provinces of the Netherlands.

In 1673 both branches of the Habsburgs entered the war on the side of the Dutch. The partition treaty was put aside, although attempts were made later to arrange another. Under pressure from the emperor's army along the Rhine, the French army was forced to retreat from the Netherlands. Eventually, however, the war turned in France's favor. The French beat back an attack by seventeen ships of the line under de Ruyter and 7,500 troops on Martinique, their most important Caribbean colony. A French army captured the province of Franche-Comté from Spain, and in the

Spanish Netherlands, where most of the fighting occurred, the French army outclassed the armies of the Netherlands and Spain. The French navy supported an expeditionary force that was sent to Sicily to support an uprising against Charles II of Spain. Although the French eventually had to abandon the island, their squadrons held their own in several battles against the Spaniards and Dutch, in one of which the great de Ruyter was mortally wounded. The war finally ended in late 1678, barely forestalling the entrance of England into the war on the side of the Netherlands and Spain. The Treaty of Nymwegen (Nijmegen) gave France the province of Franche-Comté as well as some territory along the border with the Spanish Netherlands. These gains were small recompense for the huge cost of the war and the widespread hatred and distrust that Louis inspired in the rest of Europe. The war ruined any French hopes of renewing the English alliance; France's only remaining ally was Sweden, by now only a minor power.[16]

Louis XIV, however, continued his aggressive behavior, adding territory along his border, such as Strasbourg, and bullying his neighbors. During a brief war with Spain in 1683–84, for example, a French squadron bombarded and partially destroyed the city of Genoa for helping the Spaniards. In response to this aggressiveness, Emperor Leopold I, the Austrian ruler, founded a league of German princes, the League of Augsburg. More ominous from a French standpoint, he not only repulsed a Turkish attack on Vienna but also captured Hungary and then advanced on Belgrade. In response Louis decided to strike at the League of Augsburg before Leopold could force the Turks to make peace, a demonstration of how secular was Louis's diplomacy; he was willing to help not only non-Catholics but even non-Christians. In September 1688 he ordered the French army to attack the fortress of Philippsburg near the

Rhine and to occupy the Palatinate, a strategically important nearby area. He believed this would frighten the League of Augsburg into accepting both a treaty incorporating his recent acquisitions and the selection of a pro-French candidate as archbishop of Cologne; this in turn would encourage the Turks to continue fighting the emperor and thereby prevent Leopold from shifting his troops to western Europe.

Louis discounted the threat posed by his bitterest enemy, Prince William of Orange. William was the son-in-law of James II of England, who had succeeded his brother Charles upon the latter's death in 1685. James retained his post as lord high admiral, which he had exercised intermittently since his brother's accession in 1660; day-to-day operations were left to the brilliant administrator Samuel Pepys, secretary of the admiralty from 1673 to 1679 and from 1684 to 1689, a parliamentary commission serving in the interim.[17]

As a convert to Catholicism, James was anxious to establish religious equality for his fellow Catholics and to place them in key posts in the English government and army. He thus far had had limited success. Until 1688 he posed only a minor threat to Protestantism in England, particularly since his immediate heirs, his daughters Mary (married to William of Orange) and Anne (married to the amiable but lackluster Prince George of Denmark) both were Protestant. In 1688, however, James's second wife gave birth to a male heir, James prepared for the autumn election of a new Parliament, and the army began accepting Catholics, particularly from Ireland. William of Orange now saw the chance of gaining the support of the English army and navy against the French. He solicited a secret invitation from seven prominent Englishmen to intervene on behalf of his wife, and he began preparing a Dutch fleet and army to invade England. Louis's spies learned of the preparations, but James refused naval French assistance; therefore, the French fleet at Brest was not mobilized. Louis was not concerned, as he expected that a Dutch invasion would lead to civil war in England, thus immobilizing both countries while he dealt with the League of Augsburg.

William had a narrow window of opportunity before the coming parliamentary election in England. His first attempt to sail was foiled by bad weather, but, ignoring the dangers of autumn weather in the North Sea, he made a second try. On 11 November 1688 he sailed again. The transports carrying his 20,000 troops were escorted by thirty-two Dutch ships of 40 or more guns and twenty-one smaller ones. The Dutch fleet was commanded by Arthur Herbert, an English admiral who had been smuggled into Amsterdam. James, finally realizing his danger, outfitted thirty-eight ships carrying 40 or more guns to intercept the invasion flotilla. The English commander, George Legge, Earl of Dartmouth, was unsure of the loyalty of his captains and crews and acted indecisively. With the aid of some fortunate shifts of the wind, Herbert eluded him and brought William's troops safely to Torbay on the south coast of England. James had an army of some 30,000 men, but failed to make use of it. When his officers began deserting to the advancing Dutch, James, no longer the confident leader he had been during the Second and Third Dutch Wars, lost his nerve. He sent his wife and baby ahead to France and then was permitted by William to flee.[18] In early 1689 a newly summoned Parliament ruled that the throne was vacant and offered it to William and Mary jointly. They accepted, and William became King William III. Queen Mary acted essentially as a regent when William was conducting military campaigns outside of England, but she deferred to her husband's wishes. With the deposing of James and the resignation of Pepys, the navy needed to be placed in reliable hands. Rather than appoint a new lord high admiral, William established a Board of Admiralty with two admirals and five members of Parliament, including Herbert as its head.

In 1689 England and Scotland joined the growing Austrian-Dutch alliance against France. They were followed by Spain and the key Italian principality of Savoy along France's eastern border. The French navy now was outnumbered. It had seventy-four ships of the line of 48–110 cannon compared with eighty-eight English and fifty-three Dutch ships of similar size.[19] Moreover, the French navy was unprepared for war. Its dockyards were short of naval supplies, and many of its ships needed overhauls or major repairs. Perhaps even worse, Louis XIV had deprived French Protestants of their rights in 1685, causing widespread emigration and costing France at least 5,000 trained sailors. By an estimate made the following decade, only 36,000 or 37,000 sailors remained. This was so inadequate to the navy's needs that, when war came, it quickly abandoned its system of "classes" and resorted to conscription.[20]

Louis, however, made a major effort to help his cousin James. Between 1689 and 1691 the key battleground was Ireland, where James arrived to lead a rebellion against William and Mary, hoping eventually to recover his English throne. Although a fleet of twenty-four French ships of the line successfully landed troops at Bantry Bay in 1689 and defeated an English fleet of eighteen ships of the line and a 36-gun frigate, the French did not follow up their victory. Although William's grasp of naval strategy was little better than Louis's, the English soon gained control of the Irish Sea and poured troops into Ireland. The French fleet at Brest, commanded by Lieutenant General of the Fleet Anne-Hilarion de Cotentin, comte de Tourville, did little to contest British control of Irish waters, although 6,500 French troops were convoyed to Cork in the spring of 1790 by a French squadron. Tourville's main fleet did win a clear victory over Herbert, now the Earl of Torrington, at the Battle of Beachy Head on 10 July 1690. Torrington's thirty-four British and twenty-two Dutch ships of the line were outnumbered by Tourville's great fleet of seventy ships of the line (not counting five ships of 50 guns or fewer that did not fight in the line). Tourville drove the English and Dutch fleet from the English Channel, but his pursuit was cautious, and he had no troops to make a landing. Instead of collecting troop transports, French naval minister Jean-Baptiste Colbert, marquis de Seignelay and son of the great Colbert, had built fifteen galleys in Rochefort to attack shipping in English ports. Ironically, Tourville's victory occurred the day before William III's greatest triumph, the Battle of the Boyne, a squadron of French frigates arriving in Ireland too late to help James. That autumn the English captured the ports of Cork and Kinsale, leaving only Limerick in the hands of the Jacobites (those loyal to James).

In 1691 Tourville's outnumbered French fleet avoided combat but provided a screen to protect the French coast and supply convoys to Limerick. Nevertheless the Irish port surrendered in October. The following year the French did collect troops to invade England. Tourville was forced by Louis to sail before the arrival of thirty-five ships of the line from Toulon in hopes that a landing could be made before the Dutch fleet joined the British. The allied fleet, commanded by Admiral of the Fleet Edward Russell, was assembled with exceptional speed; fifty-six British and twenty-six Dutch ships of the line intercepted Tourville's forty-four ships of the line off Cape Barfleur near the Norman port of St. Vaast-la-Hougue, where the troops had assembled. Tourville had been personally ordered by Louis XIV to fight, much as Torrington had been ordered in 1690 by Queen Mary; he did so in spite of the odds against him. He lost no ships at the subsequent Battle of Barfleur, but in its aftermath the British trapped and destroyed at Cherbourg and St. Vaast-la-Hougue fifteen French ships of the line, using boarding parties and fire ships, while a sixteenth was shipwrecked. The French saved most of the crews of the stranded ships, so the defeat was not catastrophic, as the French had more ships than they could man effectively.

Tourville won a great victory in 1693 by taking his entire fleet into Spanish waters, where he captured ninety merchant ships from a huge British and Dutch convoy for the Mediterranean and two Dutch ships of the line from its escort. France now had ninety-nine ships carrying 48 or more guns, the English navy had eighty-nine, and the Dutch had fewer than seventy-two.[21] A disastrous harvest in 1693, however, helped cause a diversion of French strategy toward capturing enemy merchant ships, particularly those carrying food. Some 340,000 soldiers were serving in the French army, about 75,000 more than during the height of the Dutch War. They required large expenditures, while French economic troubles caused a 25 percent drop in royal revenues. With armies to support in Spain, Italy, Germany, and the Spanish Netherlands, Louis could no longer afford his huge fleet, even though the French navy was approaching the combined strength of the British and Dutch navies.

In 1694 a squadron from Brest joined the Toulon fleet to support operations against Barcelona, but a large British-Dutch fleet arrived in the Mediterranean in time to foil them; this was the last major French fleet operation of the war. The French naval budget for 1691, 1692, and 1693 had averaged about 33 million livres per year. In 1694 Louis cut it to about 24 million livres and began loaning many of his warships to investors to act as privateers, attacking the trade of England and its allies. In 1697 a joint venture between the king and private investors even led to a squadron of seven of the line capturing Cartagena de Indias, the main Spanish port on the southern shore of the Caribbean, and bringing back more than 7.5 million livres worth of booty. In contrast Parliament voted an average of £2.45 million, equivalent to about 32 million livres, from 1694 through 1697.[22] Even so, the British fleet was reduced in size in 1696 and 1697, partly for financial reasons and partly because, with the main French fleet demobilized, there was little use for it except for convoying. The French war on trade (*guerre de course*) became a model for subsequent navies too weak to risk fleet encounters, but it was adopted not for strategic reasons but to save money.

Even with Louis concentrating his financial resources on the army after 1693, a military solution to the war proved impossible. To break the stalemate, the French turned to diplomacy. By making substantial concessions, they persuaded Savoy to abandon the war in 1696, soon leading to the end of fighting in Italy. The following year the French finally captured Barcelona and then negotiated the Treaty of Ryswick. Except for minor gains in North America and the sparsely populated western portion of the Spanish Caribbean island of Santo Domingo, they had to abandon the conquests made during the present war, although they did keep most of those made prior to 1688. Unexpectedly, the new Caribbean colony, which was named St. Domingue, would become the richest possession in the West Indies in the eighteenth century.

III

The war was a sobering experience for Louis, who was anxious to avoid another conflict. The greatest danger point was Spain, where

Charles II remained in extreme ill health and without children. Louis tried to make a new partition treaty with Emperor Leopold, but was unsuccessful, although he did reach agreement with England and the Netherlands. In 1700 Charles II finally died. To the amazement of Europe, his will left all his domains to a younger grandson of Louis rather than a son of Leopold. Given the Spanish desire to preserve their empire intact, the choice was logical; the Austrian Habsburgs had no navy with which to protect the overseas part of the Spanish Empire.

Louis had little choice but to accept the Spanish crown for his grandson, who became Philip V. War between Louis and Leopold probably was inevitable, no matter who received the Spanish inheritance. Leopold was not prepared to compromise. Had his family received the crown, it is unlikely Louis would have stood by, as the union of Spain and Austria would have posed great risks to France, particularly given the recent growth of Austrian power.

The accession of Philip V was an even worse threat to the European balance of power. It made it probable that England and Holland eventually would become involved in any hostilities, because of the danger to them of a union between France and Spain. Louis increased the likelihood of war by demonstrating that the division between his France and his grandson's Spain was artificial. He sent French troops to take over the forts of the Spanish Netherlands and had Philip award to French firms the contract for supplying slaves to Spanish America. Thus it took only a year from the outbreak of an Austrian-Spanish war in Italy in 1701 (with the French as auxiliaries) for the war to become general. With a weakened army, France now faced war against most of the powers of Europe, a war with fronts in Germany, the Spanish Netherlands, Italy, and eventually Spain. When war began with England in 1702, the navy had only about ninety-five ships of the line, about a dozen fewer than in 1694.[23]

During previous wars the French army had faced serious problems but had not suffered major defeats. Now facing great soldiers like the Duke of Marlborough and Eugene, Prince of Savoy, it endured a string of defeats with terrible casualty lists: 40,000 at Blenheim in 1704, 15,000 at Ramillies in 1706, 13,000 at Oudenarde in 1708, and 17,000 at Malplaquet in 1709. The naval war was hopeless.[24] The previous war had greatly strengthened the English navy, which was better administered during the present war than during the last war and could use the expanded base of Portsmouth and the newly established base of Plymouth on the south coast of England to support operations. Most of the fighting, however, occurred in the Mediterranean. On 24 July 1704 the English and Dutch captured lightly defended Gibraltar. The French navy then won the war's only major action between lines of battle, the Battle of Malaga (13 August 1704), even though its fifty ships of the line were outnumbered by a combined fleet of forty-one English and twelve Dutch ships of the line commanded by Admiral of the Fleet Sir George Rooke. The French commander, Admiral Louis-Alexandre de Bourbon, comte de Toulouse, an illegitimate son of Louis XIV, failed, however, to follow up his victory by recapturing Gibraltar.

Faced with massive military expenses, Louis again cut his naval budget. By 1709 it probably was little more than half the roughly 21 million livres appropriated in 1704; meanwhile Parliament voted at least £2 million (roughly 30 million livres) every year from 1702 through 1714. Short of funds, the French navy began renting warships to private contractors as it had during the previous war. The number of ships of the line armed by the French navy declined from sixty-nine in 1706 to thirty-three in 1707, to twenty-seven in

1709, and to thirteen in 1711.[25] Although France fought no more great fleet actions, privately financed French squadrons played a key role in keeping communications open to the French and Spanish possessions in the Western Hemisphere. They also supported combined operations in the Atlantic and Caribbean and in South America, including the captures of Santiago in the Portuguese Cape Verde Islands, Montserrat and St. Eustatius in the Caribbean, and Rio de Janeiro. Their attacks on English trade, the so-called guerre de course, tied down much of the English fleet, as during the previous war, and brought in thousands of prizes. The French navy did maintain a fleet in the Mediterranean in support of Louis's grandson in his war in Spain against the Austrian claimant. This theater of operations attracted large English and Dutch fleets, too. By 1706, fifty-six of the eighty-eight English ships carrying 48 or more cannon were in the Mediterranean as well as sixteen of the twenty-eight Dutch.[26] During the following year, the port of Toulon was besieged and the French Mediterranean fleet had to be scuttled. After the enemy was driven off, the ships were raised, but at least ten ships of the line were ruined.[27] The island of Minorca, possessing the finest port in the western Mediterranean, was captured in 1708 by the navy of Great Britain. (England and Scotland had agreed to an act of union the previous year, thereby transforming the English navy into the British navy.)

Louis was saved by two factors. First, the British and Dutch war efforts were dependent on continued financing by merchants and landowners who elected Parliament and the States General of the Netherlands. These taxpayers lacked patience for wars of attrition with limited and possibly unattainable objectives, long casualty lists, and high taxes, as would also be the case in later British wars with France. Louis, humbled by defeat, demonstrated in adversity great fortitude and patience. He was finally able to detach Great Britain and the Netherlands from their alliance with the Habsburgs. The Austrians, British, and Dutch did not send their best troops to Spain; thus Philip V, with French help, was able to prevail.[28] The War of the Spanish Succession was ended in 1713–14 by the Peace of Utrecht and the Peace of Rystadt. Philip retained the Spanish throne, although Spain lost Minorca and Gibraltar to Britain, Sicily to the Duke of Savoy, and Milan, Sardinia, Naples, and the Spanish Netherlands to Austria. France lost its colonies at Hudson Bay and Newfoundland and the part of its colony of Acadia that now is Nova Scotia, although Louis retained some of his earlier territorial gains in Europe. Of even more importance to French security, the treaties assigned the Spanish Netherlands to Austria, which had no navy and whose army was mostly based far to the east. This neutralized the area's threat to either France or Britain and made possible a reconciliation between France and Britain and an era of peace for all of Europe.

3. Foolish Wars End an Age of Peace

I

Although the War of the Spanish Succession did not eliminate France as a competitor, it still was a major British triumph. The British now had the world's most powerful navy, as the French had been beaten and heavy military expenses had forced the Dutch to abandon naval competition. The acquisition of Gibraltar and Minorca, where dockyards were built, permitted Britain to intervene in the Mediterranean whenever it wished. The lessons learned in twenty-five years of war had vastly improved naval administration. With more seaworthy and better provisioned ships, it was easier to conduct overseas operations. In the 1720s Britain established dockyards at Jamaica and Antigua, followed in 1749 by Halifax. This provided an important advantage over France for conducting naval operations in the Western Hemisphere.[1] The increase of trade during the recent wars led to an expansion of merchant shipping and hence to a larger number of sailors for when the navy needed them. The incorporation of the privately financed Bank of England in 1694 provided the navy an efficient and reliable source of loans. Although the bank had some early difficulties, it soon helped the British government gain a reputation for trustworthiness. This permitted it to borrow money at home and abroad at reasonable interest rates; until 1797, the bank's notes could be exchanged for coin. The British government also established a permanent national debt whose interest was guaranteed. In contrast, the French government repudiated part of its debts, undermining its reputation and forcing it to pay higher interest rates. Moreover, its attempts to establish a national bank ended in a 1720 bankruptcy so spectacular that no further attempt was made during the seventy years before the French Revolution.[2] During the eighteenth century, power—including sea power—was based on credit, so the French were at a severe disadvantage.

Queen Anne, the ruler of Great Britain since the death of her sister, Mary, in 1694 and brother-in-law, William, in 1702, had little time to enjoy Britain's triumphs. She died in August 1714, leaving no children. The throne passed to her closest Protestant relative, her distant cousin George, elector of Hanover, a great-grandson of James I of England. George was experienced in both government and war. For the previous sixteen years he had ruled Hanover, a medium-sized principality in northwestern Germany; he also had commanded an army in Germany between 1707 and 1709. Even more important than his experience were his character and ability. Wise, moderate, decisive, and subtle, he proved an able monarch.

His accession created a problem for Louis XIV of France, who had given exile and recognition to the deposed James II of England and, after James's death in 1701, to his heir, James Edward Stuart. Louis's sense of moral obligation to the Stuarts conflicted with his reluctance to lead France into yet another war. He was willing to provide covertly muskets and gunpowder to supporters of James Edward Stuart, but to go no further. On 1 September 1715 Louis died; two weeks later, the Earl of Mar, a Scottish supporter of the

Stuarts, raised the standard of rebellion. The Jacobites (supporters of a Stuart restoration) managed to gain initial control of much of Scotland, but their rebellion was badly led and received virtually no help from France. George I, in contrast, received the assistance of 6,000 Swiss and Dutch troops and deployed thirty warships to seal off the rebels. By early 1716 the rebellion was defeated.[3]

The French had their own dynastic problems. Louis XIV's son, the dauphin, was dead, and the Treaty of Utrecht prevented Louis's grandson, Philip V of Spain, or Philip's heirs from assuming the French throne. Instead, first in line of succession was Louis XIV's five-year-old great-grandson, also named Louis, who was in fragile health. Louis XIV's will provided for a council of regency until the young king was able to govern for himself. The regency council's nominal head was Philippe, duc d'Orléans, son of Louis XIV's younger brother, but the late king had wished a major role in the council for his own illegitimate sons. Orléans moved quickly to forestall his rivals by quashing the late king's will and taking control of the French government as regent on behalf of his young cousin.[4]

Orléans, although dissolute in his personal life, was as shrewd, moderate, and peace loving as was George I. He also was a kind and respectful protector of the young Louis XV. Moreover, Orléans had a family bond with the king of England, as his mother was the niece of George's beloved late mother. Cooperation promised political benefits for both men. There also were solid diplomatic reasons for an alliance between Britain and France. Although war had ended in western Europe, it continued in the region of the Baltic contested by Sweden and Russia. As elector of Hanover, George joined in the coalition against Sweden, making use of the British fleet and the diplomatic skills of Admiral Sir John Norris, but he feared the growth of Russian power. France also was concerned about the

Baltic region, which supplied both the British and French navies with iron, masts, timber, and naval materiel such as hemp, pitch, tallow, and tar. A British-French alliance might permit a compromise peace and establish a balance of power in the Baltic.[5]

Two superb diplomats, James Stanhope and Guillaume Dubois, conducted the negotiations for an alliance. Britain and France reached agreement in the autumn of 1716; soon thereafter the Dutch joined the alliance. It permitted a common front that finally led to a compromise peace in the Baltic in the summer of 1721. It also allowed France and Britain to check the aggression of Philip V of Spain, who in 1717–18 attacked Sardinia and Sicily in hopes of regaining some of Spain's lost territories. In response, a French army invaded Spain while a fleet of twenty British ships of the line commanded by Admiral Sir George Byng defeated a Spanish fleet of eleven ships of the line off Cape Passaro, Sicily, capturing seven of them.[6] In early 1720 a chastened Spain joined the Franco-British-Dutch alliance.

Orléans died in late 1723, just after the coronation of Louis XV, who had reached the age of majority. Orléans's distant cousin, Louis-Henri, duc de Bourbon and prince de Condé, served as Louis's chief minister for two and a half years. He did not challenge the British alliance, but concentrated on finding a wife of marriageable age for the young king. Before he was removed from office in June 1726, he succeeded in marrying Louis to Marie Leszczynska, daughter of the deposed king of Poland, Stanislas Leszczynski.

Bourbon's successor was the wise and moderate tutor of the king, Archbishop (and soon Cardinal) André-Hercule de Fleury. Already seventy-six years old, he served as unofficial chief minister until his death in 1743.[7] He continued the French partnership with George I until the latter's death in mid-1727. George's son and successor, George II, begrudgingly accepted the continuation of the alliance.

Never had Europe seen a period of peace as wide-ranging and long-lasting as that which endured from late 1721 to late 1733, a peace that largely was the product of the alliance between Britain and France, the only states wealthy enough to make a lengthy war on their own or to subsidize other states to make war. Brief hostilities between Britain and Spain did occur in 1727, but largely were restricted to artillery exchanges at Gibraltar. Except for it and a Russo-Persian war in 1722–23 that reached as far north as Tbilisi, the guns of Europe remained silent, even though sometimes violent colonial disputes continued in Africa, the Caribbean, and the fisheries off North America.[8] There even was a mechanism, although somewhat primitive, for preventing disputes from degenerating into war: the congresses held at Cambrai and then at Soissons, which were attended by representatives of the major powers.

Peace brought economic growth to both Great Britain and France.[9] It also brought greatly diminished naval rivalry. Orléans presided over the liquidation of much of the great fleet built by Louis XIV. The expenses of the massive wars of the last decades of Louis's life had forced the curtailment of naval construction. From 1696 through 1715 the French navy launched only about thirty ships of the line, none carrying more than 76 cannon. At this time all French ships of the line were built of oak; only the Spanish dockyard at Havana had access to tropical hardwoods such as Cuban cedar or mahogany, while ships of the line built of teak did not appear until the nineteenth century. As few ships of oak survived more than twelve to sixteen years of normal service before having to be rebuilt or scrapped, most of the French navy was ready for demolition.[10] This took place ruthlessly once the War of the Spanish Succession was ended. By 1720 only twelve ships of the line that had served in Louis XIV's navy remained on the navy's active roll.[11] Although the British navy also reduced its strength somewhat, it still contained over 100 ships of the line in 1720.[12] From 1720 through 1728 the French navy undertook a moderate building program, launching twenty-five ships of the line, while the British launched thirty. Ten of the French ships were of a new type carrying 74 cannon that were more powerful than the 70's and 60's that composed the bulk of the British fleet. The French building program was large enough to maintain a fleet in being, but not so large as to menace Britain. By 1728 all of the ships of 80–110 cannon built by Louis XIV had been demolished, and only one new one had been built.[13]

Tension in North America also diminished. Louis XIV's last two wars had seen heavy fighting there, including unsuccessful English attacks on Quebec in 1691 and 1711. After 1714, hostilities ceased, although New France (Canada and all the other French possessions north of Louisiana) and various British colonies such as New York competed for the Indian fur trade. No firm agreement was reached by Britain and France at Utrecht on the boundaries between New France and the neighboring British colonies. Resolution of territorial issues, such as what was included in the French cession of Acadia, was left to a bilateral boundary commission, but it proved an ineffective mechanism for adjudicating disputes. Meanwhile the rivals reinforced their claims by building forts in disputed areas such as the British American fortified trading post at Oswego on Lake Ontario (1727) and the more substantial French fort of St. Frédéric on Lake Champlain (1737). They also competed by proxy through seeking influence over the Indians nations who continued to dominate the area. Sometimes they fought those nations they considered hostile, such as the bloody French war against the Fox.

The powerful Iroquois confederacy, however, served in effect as a neutral buffer state between them. The Franco-British frontier, however, was less tense than the border between the new British colony of Georgia and Spanish Florida or possibly even the border between the French colony of Louisiana and the neighboring Spanish colony of Texas.[14]

In spite of the advantages of the alliance to both parties, the relationship between Britain and France was an uneasy one, particularly after the deaths of George I and the duc d'Orléans. George II, the pugnacious new British king, did not wish to play a subordinate role to France, and beneath his mild manners Fleury was equally domineering. In early 1731 Britain and the Netherlands signed a defensive alliance, the Treaty of Vienna, with France's rival, Austria. Two years later Louis XV made an alliance with his uncle, Philip V of Spain, the so-called Family Compact.[15] For practical purposes the Franco-British alliance was dead, although neither Fleury nor the British prime minister, the peaceable Robert Walpole, wished relations to deteriorate further.

The dozen years of European peace finally ended soon after the death of Augustus II of Poland on 1 February 1733. The Polish monarchy was elective, and it was inevitable that Louis XV would support the election of his deposed father-in-law. It was also inevitable that this would be opposed by Russia and Austria, allies since 1726. They supported the son of the late Augustus. The French candidate, Stanislas Leszczynski, was elected king on 12 September 1733; ten days later, advancing Russian troops forced him to flee Warsaw. The following month, France declared war on Austria and Russia.

Fleury took extraordinary steps to keep Britain out of the war. By promising not to invade the Austrian Netherlands (now Belgium) he ensured the neutrality of the neighboring United Provinces of the Netherlands. This gave the British a reason for remaining neutral as well; moreover, George disliked the Austrians as much as he disliked the French and was willing to evade his obligations to them. The French government made sure he would not change his mind. It refrained from mobilizing a major fleet at Brest and sent only a token force of two ships of the line, one frigate, and a few thousand troops to Danzig where Stanislas had taken refuge. This tiny force was easily overwhelmed by the Russians. Meanwhile larger French armies were fighting successfully against the Austrians in Germany and, with Spanish help, in northern Italy.[16]

The defeat of Stanislas served Fleury's diplomatic purposes. In an elaborate series of exchanges that ended the War of the Polish Succession in 1735, Stanislas was awarded the duchy of Lorraine in compensation for the loss of Poland. Upon his death in 1766, this vital principality, which during part of Louis XIV's reign had been French, reverted to France. This ended a grave danger to France as the previous duke, Francis Stephen, was engaged to be married to Maria Theresa, the daughter and designated heir of Emperor Charles VI, the archduke of Austria. Had Lorraine passed into Austrian hands, French security would have been severely compromised. In compensation, Francis received the right to inherit the duchy of Tuscany in northern Italy. Spain also benefited. Austria gave Prince Charles (Don Carlos), a younger son of King Philip, the Kingdom of the Two Sicilies (the Kingdom of Naples and the Kingdom of Sicily) in exchange for the small duchy of Parma in northern Italy and the relinquishing of Charles's claims to Tuscany. The various exchanges were made in 1737 when the final Austrian-French treaty was signed and when France took over administration of Lorraine on behalf of Stanislas.[17]

There, however, had been a price to pay for France's gains in territory and prestige. That price was neglect of the French navy. From 1729 through 1737 France launched only four ships of the line and purchased a fifth; during the same years the British navy launched thirty-three.[18] The French navy was not able to recover from those lost years for decades to come.

II

In the aftermath of the War of the Polish Succession, many Britons seem to have suffered a crisis of confidence. Walpole's neutrality during the war had helped France to increase its relative strength on the European continent and thus potentially to weaken Britain's security. As long as Fleury maintained his power, Britain had little to fear, but his age and frailty were a source of concern. Equally concerning was the growth of French trade. Britons commonly perceived Britain's power to stem from its prosperity. French economic growth seemed almost as threatening as French military power.[19] Luckily few areas of direct confrontation menaced the fragile peace between the two countries, as rivalry in India was regarded chiefly as a matter for their respective East India companies and rivalry in America as being mostly of local concern. The same could not be said of relations between Britain and France's ally Spain.

According to the 1713 Treaty of Utrecht, modified in 1716, the South Sea Company of Great Britain had the right, called the asiento, to provide 4,800 slaves to the Spanish colonial empire for each of the next thirty years. It also had the right to send a ship each year to participate in trade fairs in Spanish Central America. The South Sea Company used these privileges to engage in massive smuggling to the heavily regulated but undersupplied Spanish colonies of the Caribbean. Spain retaliated by establishing patrols, using ships called guarda costas, to repress the smuggling. Claiming the right to inspect British ships, they engaged in their own abuses, seizing ships and imprisoning sailors, sometimes even innocent ones. Between 1725 and 1737 several dozen ships were taken by the guarda costas. In 1731 a guarda costa captured the *Rebecca*, and its crew cut off the left ear of the *Rebecca*'s master, Robert Jenkins. In October 1737 the merchants of London petitioned the king to procure satisfaction for such Spanish abuses and to prevent British ships from being visited and seized illegally.[20]

To the great discomfort of Sir Robert Walpole and his ministry, the London press and public opinion took up the merchants' cause. Relations with Spain were part of the responsibilities of Thomas Pelham-Holles, Duke of Newcastle, the secretary of state for the southern department and the senior and more influential of the two secretaries of state. Newcastle soon began negotiations with Spain. Unfortunately, Philip V of Spain was even touchier about his honor than was George II. It took until the beginning of 1739 to arrange a compromise agreement, the Convention of the Pardo. As part of the agreement, the Spanish government agreed to pay £95,000, perhaps equivalent in today's terms to $10 million. Of this sum, £68,000 would be paid by the South Sea Company in compensation for taxes not hitherto paid to Spain.

The English public was disappointed, believing that a war with Spain would be both quick and profitable, especially considering there was an enormous disparity between the British and Spanish navies. At sea or in port, Britain had about 100 warships of 50 or more cannon, a third of them carrying 80, 90, or 100 cannon. Some needed repair, and when war broke out, it would be difficult to find crewmen to man them, but even so the British navy dwarfed the Spanish navy, which contained about forty-two ships of the line, only two of which carried more than 70 cannon, the *Real Felipe,* 112, and the *Santa Isabel,* 80.[21]

Walpole's hopes for a peaceful resolution of British-Spanish disputes, seemingly on the verge of fulfillment, were foiled, however, and the public finally got the war it wished, the so-called War of Jenkins's Ear. This reversal of fortune was caused by the greed of the South Sea Company, which refused to pay its share of the settlement, the opportunism of Newcastle, who in order to court popularity decided to keep a British fleet of ten ships of the line in the Mediterranean even though the Spaniards had demobilized their fleet, and the pride of Philip V, who responded to this insult by breaking off negotiations, thereby making war inevitable.

Britain was provocative toward France, too. Its Mediterranean fleet began a blockade of Cadiz in June 1739, stopping ships of neutral countries, including France. When the French protested, Newcastle responded in a conciliatory manner, and the crisis passed. Soon, however, Britain would threaten French interests in a manner to which even the cautious Fleury had to respond.

Britain officially went to war against Spain on 19 October 1739. The navy already was well on its way to being fully manned as sailors arriving on merchant ships were pressed into service: by August 1739 forty-eight ships of the line (including 50-gun ships) were in sea pay. By September sixty-eight were in service, and by January 1740 there were seventy-seven.[22] The question facing Walpole, Newcastle, First Lord of the Admiralty Sir Charles Wager, and their colleagues was how best to use them.[23] Britain hoped that the blockade of Cadiz, the chief Spanish naval port, would interrupt Spain's trade with its Caribbean colonies. The blockade was not very successful, however, because Spain was able to divert its shipping to other ports. Parliament and the public expected the

British navy to capture Spanish treasure ships bringing gold and silver to Cadiz. Given the uncertainty of such a success, however, the British government decided to capture, and perhaps retain, one or more of the ports from which the treasure ships departed. It initially planned to capture Manila, from which the famed Manila galleons sailed for Acapulco.[24] The Walpole government realized, however, that to capture distant Manila and have the news reach England would take too long to satisfy the public. Soon after war was declared, it shifted its objective to the Caribbean, particularly to the great port and shipbuilding center of Havana. It hoped by the summer of 1740 to send 8,000 marines and soldiers to the British West Indies to rendezvous with 3,000 soldiers raised in the British colonies of North America. From there they would proceed to attack Havana. In March 1740 news arrived that Vice Admiral Edward Vernon, commanding the British West Indies squadron, had successfully raided Porto Bello, an important Spanish port in Central America. Vernon became a national hero, and British expectations of further successes rose.[25]

It was impossible to keep secret the preparation in England of the large number of transports, supply ships, and escorting warships needed for so large an expedition and easy to guess that the expedition would be sent to the Caribbean. The English preparations presented a challenge to Cardinal Fleury. Although he was reluctant for war, he could not permit the British to make any conquests that would upset the balance of power or threaten France's commercial interests. Fortunately the French had colonies in the area, particularly the wealthy colony of St. Domingue (now Haiti) near Cuba, and the islands of Martinique and Guadeloupe to the south, not far from the Spanish Main, the Spanish possessions along the northern coast of South America. Short of an act of war, Great

Britain could not prevent France from sending warships to its own colonies, from where they could sail to help the Spaniards.

Fleury's strategy was even more successful than expected, accomplishing its objectives without even having to resort to hostilities. It took many months for the British to assemble its ships and troops for the Caribbean. The troops were not embarked aboard transports until August 1740. By then the French navy was ready. On 25 August a dozen ships of the line sailed from Toulon, and a week later another fourteen sailed from Brest. This represented virtually the entire effective strength of the French navy, which had only thirty-five ships of the line, including those not in condition to serve. The Spanish navy sent a dozen ships of the line to reinforce its small squadron in the Caribbean.[26]

In December 1740 the troop convoy from England reached its rendezvous point, the island of Dominica, and then proceeded to Jamaica. By now the entire French fleet was at St. Domingue, in position to help protect Havana or to threaten Jamaica. It was so weakened by disease, however, that on 27 January 1741 all but seven ships of the line sailed for France.[27] Nevertheless it accomplished its mission. Vernon, commanding the thirty British ships of the line collected at Jamaica, decided that Havana was too strong to be attacked with the 8,500 British and American troops at his disposal, particularly since more than a third of them were needed to fill out the crews of his warships. He persuaded Major General Thomas Wentworth, commanding the army detachment, to switch his target to the rich port of Cartagena de Indias on the Spanish Main, which the French had raided in 1697. Before sailing there, however, Vernon felt it necessary to deal with the French fleet at St. Domingue. By the time he arrived, most of the French fleet was gone. A probable war with France was averted, but Vernon's futile voyage to St. Domingue took several weeks during which disease continued to erode the number of Vernon's crewmen and Wentworth's troops.

Vernon and Wentworth did not reach the area of Cartagena until 4 March 1741. They then had a series of obstacles to overcome. To reach the harbor of Cartagena, they had to reduce several Spanish forts. After they secured the harbor, they still had to capture the city of Cartagena, which was protected by other forts. After neutralizing several forts, the British finally were able to enter the harbor on 26 March. They either captured or forced the Spaniards to scuttle all their naval forces in the harbor, including six ships of the line. Before Cartagena could be attacked, however, the main fort covering the approaches to the city had to be taken, a fort that was out of reach of the guns of the British fleet. Vernon, frightened by the number of crew members' deaths from disease, demanded that the fort be stormed rather than besieged in order to save time. Wentworth agreed to the demand, but the attack was repulsed on 9 April, with almost 600 casualties. A week later the British began evacuating their army. The defeat at Cartagena cost the British their best opportunity for a victory in the Caribbean. Later operations on the east coast of Cuba and in Central America were total failures.

The Cartagena operation illustrates a major problem in British amphibious operations during the age of sail: the conflicting demands of naval and army commanders. The British government generally was unwilling to place one in command of the other. Only when one was unselfish enough to subordinate his wishes to the other's were combined operations successful.[28]

III

While the French fleet was in the Caribbean, the entire course of French diplomacy changed. On 20 October 1740 Charles VI died.

Like every other Holy Roman Emperor over the previous three centuries, Charles was a member of the House of Habsburg. As such he was the archduke of Austria, king of Hungary, king of Bohemia, and ruler over the other lands of the Habsburg patrimony. Charles, having no male heir, left his lands to his daughter Maria Theresa, although as a woman she was not eligible for election as Holy Roman Emperor. By the treaty that had ended the War of the Polish Succession, France had recognized Maria Theresa's rights of inheritance, the so-called Pragmatic Sanction. Since the end of that war Fleury had been working for a French-Austrian alliance; this should have been the moment to complete it. On the other hand, France had considerable temptations to disregard its obligations to Maria Theresa. A century earlier the Habsburgs had failed to turn the Holy Roman Empire into a modern unified state like France or Spain. Since then, however, they had rebuilt their strength by expanding to the east and south against the Ottoman Empire, which included most of the Balkans as well as Turkey and much of the Middle East. By stripping the Habsburgs of much of their territory, the Habsburg threat, which had dominated French diplomacy for centuries, could be ended.

The most tempting reason for war against Austria, however, was not Austrian strength but Austrian weakness. The treaty that ended the War of the Polish Succession had diminished the Austrian threat by turning Lorraine into a French client state, depriving Austria of a prime invasion route into France. Moreover, in 1739 the Austrian army had been defeated by the lightly regarded Turkish army, and Austria was forced to surrender Belgrade, with France mediating the peace.[29] Finally the young and inexperienced Maria Theresa did not appear a formidable opponent.

As Louis XV hesitated, Frederick II, the new ruler of Prussia (a medium-sized state mostly in northeastern Germany), acted. In December 1740 he invaded the rich Habsburg province of Silesia, which today forms the southwestern portion of Poland.[30] In the jungle of eighteenth-century European diplomacy, weakness invited predators like Frederick. Would the young and naïve Louis XV join the pack?

Fleury did his best to restrain Louis. Inadvertently, however, he had created a rival for the king's attention. Maria Theresa wished her husband, Francis Stephen, Grand Duke of Tuscany, to be elected Holy Roman Emperor, succeeding his father-in-law. Fleury was unwilling to see another Habsburg, even one only by marriage, elected Holy Roman Emperor, particularly since before becoming Grand Duke of Tuscany Francis Stephen had been Duke of Lorraine. Fleury long had feared Francis's candidacy; even now Francis might wish to regain his former duchy, overturning the most important French gain from the War of the Polish Succession. The French candidate was its ally, Charles Albert, ruler of Bavaria and holder of one of the nine electoral votes. To win the support of the other electors, Fleury selected as his envoy one of the heroes of the last war, Lieutenant General Charles-Louis-Auguste Fouquet, comte (later duc) de Belle-Isle. A week after Belle-Isle was selected, Frederick II invaded Silesia. In this new environment, Belle-Isle now urged the king to use military means to support the candidacy of Elector Charles Albert.[31]

Louis now became caught up in the enthusiasm of some of the leading noblemen at court for a war that would provide them employment and potential glory. In June 1741 Belle-Isle, now a marshal of France, the highest rank in the French army, signed a treaty with Frederick that promised French military intervention in Germany in exchange for Frederick's support as an elector for the candidacy of Charles Albert. The other electors soon joined in. George, elector of Hanover and king of England, promised to abstain from voting in exchange for Hanover's neutrality being respected in case of war. Fleury could not even delay the outbreak of war. Bavaria attacked Austria late in July 1741, and two weeks later a French army crossed the Rhine, acting as auxiliaries to Charles Albert. The year ended in triumph as on 26 November Prague was captured by a brilliant general, comte Maurice de Saxe, an illegitimate son of the ruler of Saxony who had chosen to serve in the French army. (Archduchess of Austria Maria Theresa also was queen of Bohemia, whose capital was Prague.) On 12 February 1742 Charles Albert was elected emperor.

Philip V of Spain also became involved in the search for plunder. Ferdinand, his son by his first marriage, was heir to the Spanish throne, but Philip's Italian-born second wife wished their own two sons to be rulers, too. The elder, Charles, had gained the throne of the Kingdom of the Two Sicilies as a result of the last war. By attacking Maria Theresa's possessions in northern Italy, the Spanish royal couple hoped to obtain a principality for their younger son, Philip, to rule, which would please France, too, because Philip had just married Louis XV's eldest and favorite daughter, Louise-Elisabeth. Although the French navy was not needed for a war in Germany, a war in northern Italy was different. In November and December 1741 the French navy helped the Spanish navy escort two great troop convoys to Italy with 25,000 troops from Barcelona. The British Mediterranean fleet was too weak to interfere.[32]

For the next two years the French navy served as an auxiliary to the Spanish navy. It had several skirmishes with the British navy, but they did not lead to war.[33] Meanwhile the British sent an army of 16,000 men to the continent to serve as auxiliaries to the army of Maria Theresa. On 27 June 1743 British, Austrian, and Hanoverian troops under the personal command of George II defeated the French in a major battle in Germany, the Battle of Dettingen; France and Britain technically remained at peace, however. By now the French and Spanish military position had gravely deteriorated. Maria Theresa proved brave, smart, and charismatic. The Austrians drove the French not only out of Prague but also back across the Rhine. Prussia, having gained Silesia, dropped out of the war, while the Spanish army in northern Italy was forced to retreat to the Adriatic. Finally in September 1743 the Kingdom of Sardinia (comprising the island of Sardinia and the Italian provinces of Piedmont and Savoy) allied with Britain and Austria.

France responded to adversity by expanding the war. On 25 October 1743 it formally allied with Spain in support of Prince Philip's claim to the northern Italian territories of Milan, Parma, and Piacenza. In addition to their joint war against Austria, France joined Spain in declaring war on Sardinia and promised Spain that it also would declare war on Britain. At the end of 1743 Louis XV and his chief advisory body, the Royal Council of State, decided that France would attack the Austrian Netherlands, attempt to gain control of the Mediterranean in conjunction with Spain, and invade England in order to replace George II with James Stuart, the son of the former king and French ally, James II.

These plans grossly overestimated the capabilities of the French navy. At the beginning of 1744 the French navy contained only thirty-eight ships of the line, some of which needed repair. It could fit out (prepare for sea) only fifteen ships at Toulon to help the Spaniards gain control of the Mediterranean and another fifteen at Brest and Rochefort to assist in the invasion of England.[34]

Not surprisingly, both operations failed miserably. Sending a fleet to the stormy English Channel in the middle of winter was enormously risky.[35] The fleet that sailed from Brest on 6 February 1744 took until 5 March to reach the Straits of Dover. Its commander, Lieutenant General of the Fleet Aimard-Joseph, comte de Roquefeuil, detached two ships of the line and two frigates to Dunkirk to provide close escort for 10,000 troops under the comte de Saxe, who intended to land them near the mouth of the Thames. As Roquefeuil awaited pilots for the final stage of his voyage, Admiral of the Fleet Sir John Norris's fleet of twenty ships of the line (including one of 100 guns and four 90's) appeared. Only by good fortune did the French fleet escape almost certain destruction. The wind died down before the British could attack. During the night Roquefeuil fled to the south. A fierce storm began the following day, sinking almost a dozen of the transport ships at Dunkirk, but saving the French fleet from its pursuers.[36]

The Mediterranean fleet, commanded by Lieutenant General of the Fleet Claude de Court de La Bruyère, was no more successful than was the Atlantic fleet. On 19 February 1744, its fifteen ships of the line sailed from Toulon in company with twelve Spanish ships of the line, although another six Spanish ships of the line had to be left behind because of a shortage of crewmen. They expected to crush the British Mediterranean fleet, which was anchored near Toulon in Hyères roadstead. This would open the Mediterranean for the passage of Spanish troops to Italy. The French and Spaniards, however, had underestimated the size of the British fleet, which contained thirty-four ships of the line. Even though generally Spanish and French ships were larger and better armed than British ships carrying an equal number of guns, the odds were against them. Although the British fleet included six 50's, it also had four 90's and eight 80's; the Franco-Spanish fleet had a

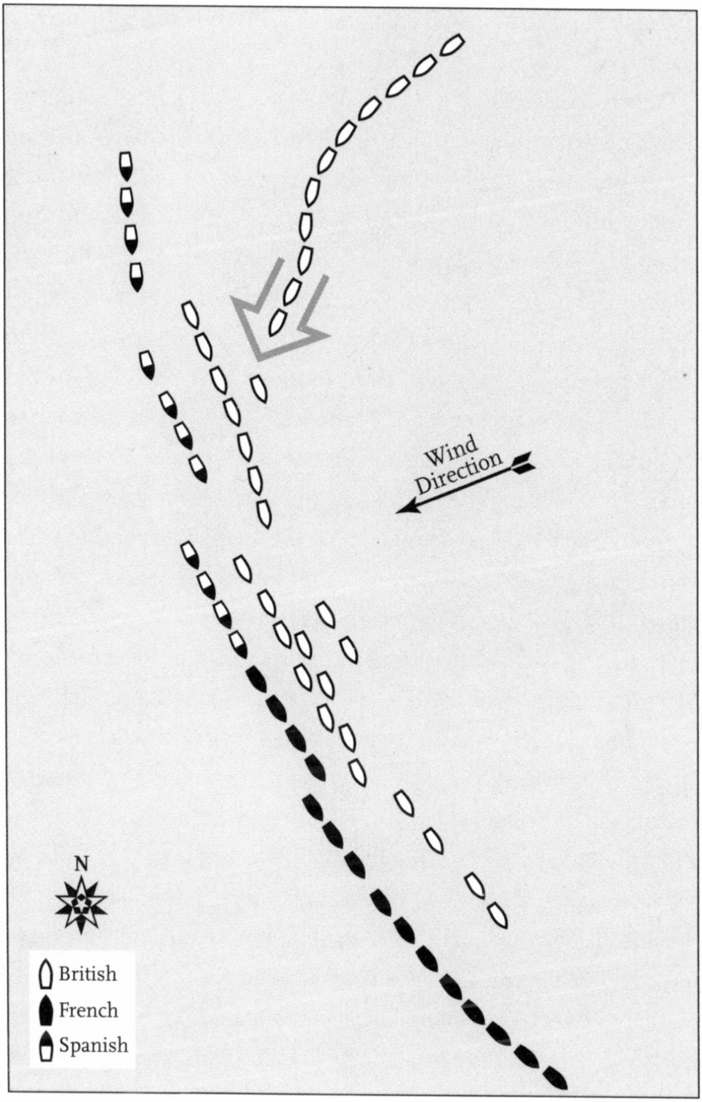

1. Toulon, 22 February 1744

Spanish 114-gun ship and a Spanish 80, but no other ship carried more than 74 guns.

Again, the French navy was fortunate to escape a crushing defeat. The British commander, Vice Admiral Thomas Mathews, fearing the enemy fleet would try to escape, set out in pursuit without putting his own fleet in alignment. On 22 February he caught and attacked the Franco-Spanish fleet. Standard practice was for each attacking ship to select its opposite number in the enemy fleet, but it also was traditional for a flagship (a ship carrying an admiral) to attack the enemy's flagship. To accomplish both, a fleet needed to be placed in the proper order. Mathews had not taken the time to do so. The British fleet became bunched around the center of the enemy line, leaving the enemy van (the head of the line of battle) without opponents. Fortunately for the British, several of their warships stationed themselves to prevent the ten leading enemy ships, all French, from doubling back so as to attack the British from its port side while it was fighting the center of the enemy Fleet line from starboard. The eleven rearmost British ships, under Mathew's second-in-command, Vice Admiral Richard Lestock, lagged behind and did not fully engage the enemy rear. Several captains of individual ships also did not closely engage the enemy. Thus the bulk of the fighting fell on only a dozen British ships of the line, which fought five French and a dozen Spanish ships of the line. The British were successful in forcing the enemy to flee, but only one enemy ship, the Spaniard *Poder*, 66, was destroyed. Mathew's pursuit was halfhearted, as he feared the enemy would use his absence to move troops. The French and Spaniards escaped to the Spanish port of Cartagena (not to be confused with the Caribbean port of Cartagena de Indias). Spaniards and French had faced the same difficulties in operating together as had the British and French in the 1670s and the British and the Dutch in the wars against Louis XIV. As was usual after a battle, one of the allies, in this case Spain, was resentful that the burden of fighting had fallen on its ships. As a result, joint operations between the French and Spanish navies ceased.[37]

Mathews had feared that the Brest fleet was en route to the Mediterranean, but these fears proved groundless. By failing to combine their Atlantic and Mediterranean fleets, the French navy launched each of its attacks with too few ships to be effective. During the summer of 1744, the French divided their two fleets into squadrons of four to six ships of the line apiece in order to intercept British convoys and to protect French trade with Canada and the West Indies.

The French army was more successful, particularly in the Austrian Netherlands. It captured a number of the so-called barrier fortresses near the French border, garrisoned by Dutch troops, although these victories were due more to Dutch incompetence than to French skill. Meanwhile an Austrian army crossed the Rhine and invaded Alsace. France was saved by Prussia, which on 14 August 1744 reentered the war by invading Bohemia, causing the Austrians to recall their troops from Alsace. The Prussian offensive also was unsuccessful, as were an Austrian attack on Naples and a Franco-Spanish attack on Piedmont. Regardless of nationality, rarely could any offensive overcome the advantages of the side on the defensive, which almost always had shorter supply lines.

After 1744 the French navy was starved of funds, so the French army could act on the offensive.[38] The navy played little role during the Scottish uprising of 1745. Disillusioned by their failure to invade England, the French government largely lost interest in establishing James Stuart on the British throne. James's twenty-four-year-old son, Charles Edward Stuart, took matters into his own hands. He was assisted by a group of shipowners from the ports of Nantes and St. Malo who chartered an elderly French navy ship of the line, the *Elisabeth*, 64. With the *Elisabeth* as an escort, he sailed on a privateer to Scotland, possibly with the connivance of the French government. Although the *Elisabeth* was forced to put back after a fight with an English ship of the line, Prince Charles Edward arrived safely. He was able to win enough Scottish support to capture Edinburgh, whereupon he led a small army into England. French interest in invading England now revived. Fearful of the British navy, the French refused, however, to commit any ships of the line. Instead they hoped to slip an invading army across the Strait of Dover by stealth, relying on privateers for escort. They assembled troops between Dunkirk and Boulogne, but surprise was lost when the British intercepted a group of supply ships off Boulogne in mid-December 1745. Charles Edward's army retreated from the English city of Derby, which was the closest it got to London. As British troops converged on the coast of England and British warships massed along the French coast, the slim chances of a successful landing faded. The only direct French military support that reached Charles Edward were 1,000 or so troops sent piecemeal to Scotland. In 1746 the rebellion was crushed, although Charles Edward was rescued by two privateers from St. Malo.[39]

The navy also could not prevent another major French failure in 1745, the loss of the fortified city of Louisbourg on Isle Royale (Cape Breton Island). Soon after the beginning of open warfare against Britain, French forces in Canada mounted an attack on Annapolis Royal, the capital of Nova Scotia. The British repulsed the attack, due largely to assistance rendered by the governor of Massachusetts, William Shirley, who saw the preservation of Nova

Scotia as vital to his colony's fishing industry. At the end of 1744 Shirley learned that Louisbourg was poorly defended. Louisbourg had been built at the end of the last war at enormous expense by Jean-Frédéric Phélypeaux, comte de Maurepas, the French naval and colonial minister from 1723 to 1749. Although it helped to stimulate the revival of the fishing industry, previously based on the island of Newfoundland, Louisbourg was poorly constructed and subject to artillery fire from neighboring hills. Its main function was to protect the annual fishing fleet from France that worked the Newfoundland and Gulf of St. Lawrence cod fisheries. These fisheries were not only enormously valuable in economic terms but also critical to the training of sailors for the French navy, which like the British navy kept few ships in service during peacetime and hence could not train its own sailors. The harsh weather and sea conditions of the fisheries made them a superb school for sailors; the fisheries were irreplaceable because they employed 10,000 to 15,000 of France's 40,000 to 60,000 trained sailors. (In mid-century the merchant marine employed more than 13,000, many of whom were in overseas trade; some 3,000 to 4,000 worked in coastal shipping or for the East India Company, while presumably many others were local fishermen.)[40]

Shirley persuaded the Massachusetts legislature to raise 3,000 volunteers to attack Louisbourg. He also wrote for assistance to the British Board of Admiralty and to Commodore Peter Warren, who commanded a British squadron at the West Indian island of Antigua. He received an enthusiastic response both from the Admiralty and from Warren, who owned land in America and was married to a New Yorker. On 13 March 1745 Warren sailed for North America with the *Superb*, 60, *Ruby*, 50, and two frigates. He rendezvoused at Canso, Nova Scotia, with troops raised by the colony of Massachusetts. They arrived on ninety transports, escorted by a frigate and a dozen smaller warships outfitted by the colony. Warren and the Massachusetts general of militia, William Pepperell, proceeded to Isle Royale. The troops landed near Louisbourg on 29 April and soon besieged the fortress. Warren was reinforced by a ship of the line and a frigate sent from England. He was able to capture the *Vigilant*, 64, which was bringing reinforcements and supplies from France. The poorly garrisoned fortress held out for a surprisingly long time before finally surrendering on 17 June. Maurepas attempted to send another relief force, but the squadron he sent contained only two ships of the line and three frigates and did not sail until after Louisbourg had surrendered.[41]

By 1746 the British navy had established clear superiority over its enemies. Partly this was due to improved leadership and strategy. At the end of 1744, the incompetent first lord of the admiralty, Daniel Finch, Earl of Winchilsea, was replaced by John Russell, Duke of Bedford. Although Bedford had an excellent mind, he was not a great administrator. He brought with him, however, a talented young follower, John Montagu, Earl of Sandwich, and a brilliant naval officer, George Anson, who recently had returned home from a four-year voyage during which his ship circumnavigated the globe and captured a Spanish galleon. Meanwhile the French navy suffered from the limited influence of Maurepas, who found little support in the Council of State for the additional funds he needed.

The new British Board of Admiralty soon approved the establishment of a permanent Western Squadron. Consisting of at least ten ships of the line, it sailed in the western approaches to the English Channel and Bay of Biscay. It thereby both protected British trade and maintained a loose blockade of the French coast.[42] The most important factor in the British superiority, however, was its increased margin of numerical superiority. Because of wear and tear, the French and Spanish navies had to retire a number of elderly ships of the line. By 1746 they were each reduced to about thirty-five in service. On 1 June 1746 the British navy had eighty-nine ships of the line in service, seven more than on 1 January 1745. It often had the assistance of about ten Dutch ships of the line.[43]

Initially the Western Squadron met an embarrassing reverse. On 22 June 1746 a great convoy of more than forty transports, storeships, and merchantmen successfully sailed from an anchorage near Rochefort under the escort of ten ships of the line. It carried 3,500 troops who hoped to protect Canada, attack Nova Scotia, and eventually recapture Louisbourg. The convoy evaded detection, and although its passage took three months, it caught the six British ships of the line at Louisbourg by surprise. During the long passage, however, the transports and their escorts were swept by typhus, typhoid fever, and scurvy. Even putting the troops ashore did not stem the epidemic, and in late October the French squadron and convoy sailed for France without attacking Louisbourg. Thousands of sailors and soldiers became ill, and hundreds died, including the expedition's commander. Only the courage and skill of the final commanding officer, Chef d'escadre (Rear Admiral) Jacques-Pierre de Taffanel, marquis de La Jonquière, held the expedition together. Most of the ships reached France safely, although two ships of the line were wrecked and another one was captured.[44]

France had one compensation. Fearing the French squadron, the British abandoned their own plans for an attack on Quebec and diverted the troops to an attack on the French East India Company port of Lorient. This expedition failed miserably, too, although this failure was more farce than tragedy.[45]

Henceforth the French navy was used almost exclusively for

convoy protection. Thanks to the Western Squadron, however, the long series of successful escapes of French convoys ended. In March 1747 the British intercepted a convoy of French East India Company warships bound for India under the escort of two French navy ships of the line and a frigate; most of the ships were forced to put back, and two ships were wrecked. In contrast, the British later in the year were able to dispatch a squadron of half a dozen ships of the line to India. Using East India Company warships, the French hitherto had held their own in India and even had captured the major British East India Company post of Madras. The reinforcements that arrived in 1748 gave the British the advantage, and they were almost able to capture Pondicherry, the chief French post in India.[46]

The Western Squadron went on to greater successes, the next of which came on 14 May 1747. Under the command of Anson himself, its fourteen ships of the line caught two convoys sailing together, one for India, the other for Canada. The escort, commanded by the gallant La Jonquière, en route to Canada to serve as governor general, included only three ships of the line; they sacrificed themselves to save the convoys, half of whose ships escaped.[47]

An even greater victory came on 25 October 1747 when Rear Admiral Edward Hawke intercepted a huge convoy bound for the French West Indies. Hawke's fourteen ships of the line captured six of the eight ships of the line protecting the convoy, although the convoy and an accompanying East India Company 60-gun ship of the line escaped.[48]

Meanwhile the French army in the Austrian Netherlands, now commanded by the brilliant Saxe, enjoyed almost uninterrupted success in 1746 and 1747. In the summer of 1747, Louis XV unsuccessfully made overtures to Britain for a mutual exchange of conquests. When France declared war on the Netherlands and invaded Dutch territory, the British-Dutch-Sardinian-Austrian alliance finally collapsed. To save the Netherlands, the Dutch and British agreed to share the cost of hiring a 30,000-man Russian army. In early 1748, however, the Dutch declared themselves unable to continue the war without British financial assistance. British taxpayers had lost faith in the war, and the British government saw no hope of preventing France from conquering the Netherlands before the Russian troops could arrive. On the other hand, Louis XV's desire for peace was reinforced by the economic misery caused by the British stranglehold on the French coast. French overseas commerce had come to a near halt. Louis was willing to give up the Austrian Netherlands and Madras in exchange for the return of Louisbourg and the establishment of Prince Philip of Spain as Duke of Parma. The British and Dutch now gave way, and on 30 April a provisional peace was signed at the neutral German city of Aix-la-Chapelle. Maria Theresa and the other participants in the war were forced to accept the terms, effectively destroying the alliance between Britain and Austria, although the Franco-Spanish alliance also was temporarily terminated.[49]

The establishment of a Prussian-Austrian balance of power in central Europe and the destruction of the Austro-British alliance were the most important accomplishments of the war for France; for the next forty years France was spared from invasion. Although Louis was mocked for surrendering the Austrian Netherlands, the very moderation of the peace treaty was an act of statesmanship. It eventually made possible an alliance with Austria that became the foundation of French diplomacy.[50]

Ironically, after nine years of war, most Britons had forgotten why the war began. The grievances between Spain and Britain of 1739 were not even mentioned in the Treaty of Aix-la-Chapelle. Philip V was dead, and his heir, the meek Ferdinand VI, had a passion not for war, conquest, and glory but for music. Soon after the war, the British sold Spain their rights to the asiento, and British-Spanish relations greatly improved. When the next French war with Britain began, France did not have the help of the Spanish navy.

4. Sea Power and the Outcome of the Seven Years' War

I

The War of the Austrian Succession, with its huge loss of life and massive expenses, was tragic not only in itself but also because it produced an unstable balance of power that soon led to a new war. Empress Maria Theresa treated the peace as only a truce, immediately plotting war against Frederick II in order to regain Silesia. She had to wait, however. For the moment most of Europe was tired of war. Indeed, in parts of Europe the peace proved to be enduring. As tension between Spain and Austria diminished, Italy entered a period of peace that lasted for almost half a century. The Netherlands entered its own period of peace, lasting more than thirty years, and the Austrian Netherlands saw no fighting until 1792. Even France and Britain were not doomed to another war. Louis XV was disillusioned with war and had become infatuated with the idea of helping to elect his distant cousin Louis-François-Joseph de Bourbon, prince de Conti, as king of Poland when the current king died. This project led to the creation of an unofficial secret diplomatic service, the "Secret du Roi" or "King's Secret." Both the official diplomatic service and the Secret du Roi were obsessed with the growing influence of Russia in eastern Europe. They saw Russia as a rival of France and a threat not only to Poland but also to Sweden and the Ottoman Empire, France's other trading partners and diplomatic friends in eastern Europe.

In order to counter Russia, the French government was interested in *improving* relations with Britain. This was particularly true of Louis-Philogène Brûlart, marquis de Puyzieulx, French foreign minister from 1747 to 1751, who was warmly regarded by the Earl of Albemarle, the British ambassador at the French court.[1] Memories of the recent war, however, made better relations difficult. George II was embittered by French support of the Stuarts, while Newcastle, secretary of state for the northern department from 1748 to 1754, was intensely suspicious of France. The war, moreover, had increased the Francophobia of the public at large.[2] The two attempts to invade England, the conquest of the Austrian Netherlands, and the support of the Stuarts marked the start of a seventy-year "cold war," exacerbated by repeated outbreaks of hostilities. The French made several attempts to improve relations, but could not overcome British mistrust.

Increasing tension in North America presented a major obstacle to better relations. To France the most important part of North America was the cod fisheries off its northeastern coast. Canada itself produced little of value except furs, which had a limited market. It was a financial drain tolerated only because it could provide food to Louisbourg and thus support the fisheries and because it could divert British attention from Europe and from the enormously valuable French West Indies. Even the fur producing part of Canada, the Upper Country (the Pays d'en haut, comprising what are now the states of the Midwest and the central provinces of Canada) was of marginal economic significance; the British Board of Trade later described Newfoundland as worth more than Canada and Louisiana combined. The Upper Country was strategically vital, however, and the fur trade provided the foundation for French alliances with the numerous Indian nations who populated the region.

France and Britain didn't bother to slow the peace discussions of 1747–48 to discuss the borders between their respective colonies in North America. Instead they appointed commissioners to discuss issues still outstanding, a standard way of dealing with secondary problems. Unfortunately the border commission did little to resolve the problems, degenerating into a sterile exchange of memoranda.[3]

In practice both countries largely delegated North American relations to their colonial governors. This proved very dangerous. The most immediate threat to peace came from Nova Scotia. Because the Treaty of Utrecht had not precisely defined Acadia, the British claimed the entire region on both sides of the Bay of Fundy while the French wished to restrict the British presence to the eastern portion of the Nova Scotia peninsula. Local authorities attempted to assert control in the traditional way, by building forts, thereby establishing a de facto dividing line. The British were left in control of what now is the Canadian province of Nova Scotia and the French in control of what now is the province of New Brunswick. The opposing forts were very close together by North American standards, and incidents occurred that led to bloodshed. The French and British governments paid enough attention, however, to defuse the situation.

The two governments failed, though, to resolve a developing crisis in what hitherto had been an area of little importance to either government, the area that today is the state of Ohio and the western half of Pennsylvania. The French long had neglected the area because of its minor importance in the fur trade of the Upper Country. Traders from Pennsylvania competed with traders from

New France to supply the various Indian nations of the area until the war of 1744–48, when the British interruption of shipping between France and Canada disrupted the supply of French trade goods. This accelerated a growing British American trade dominance. A rapid turnover of governors general in Quebec prevented the French from developing a prudent and measured response to the competition.

The French naval and colonial ministry offered little guidance to the respective governors general. In April 1749 the experienced Maurepas was relieved of his duties and exiled from Versailles by his rivals at court. The French Council of State, whose members were beholden only to the king, was more faction-ridden than the British cabinet, which had not yet arrived at the principle of collective responsibility but did need some degree of cohesion to face Parliament. Maurepas's successor, Antoine-Louis Rouillé, was a sixty-year-old career bureaucrat with little knowledge of the navy or colonies. Although his inclinations were far from warlike, Rouillé deferred to the advice of the French authorities at Quebec, who feared that the British penetration of the area would lead to the eventual severing of Canada from Louisiana; this concern was related to the long-standing fear that once British Americans crossed the Appalachian Mountains they could not be stopped before they menaced Spanish Mexico.

The main trade route from Montreal to Louisiana passed from Lake Erie along the Maumee and Wabash rivers to the Ohio River and then to the Mississippi; penetration of the upper Ohio River watershed would place the British dangerously close to this route. The traditional French policy had been that of cultivating the friendship of the Indian nations of the region through generosity and respect in order to use them to deter British American expansion.

The inexperienced new French governors general now sought a more direct military solution to the threat, after having first made a ludicrous attempt to assert French claims by burying lead tablets at strategic locations. When this failed they turned to violence. Their Indian allies destroyed the area's major British trading post, the town of Pickawillany, in 1752. The following year Governor General of New France Ange Duquesne de Menneville, marquis de Duquesne, who like his predecessors was a senior naval officer, conscripted Canadian militia to begin a string of forts linking Lake Erie with the place where the Allegheny and Monongahela rivers joined to form the Ohio River.[4]

This building of forts angered and frightened not only the Shawnees, Delawares, and other Indians of the area but also British Americans and the British government, who mistakenly saw it as the prelude to an attack on the American frontier. Lieutenant Governor Robert Dinwiddie, the acting governor of Virginia, was particularly concerned. Dinwiddie was actively involved with a group of land speculators who wished to attract settlers to the same area in which the French were building forts. When his representative, George Washington, was unsuccessful in warning off the French, Dinwiddie sent him back with a party of 150 Virginia militia. The hotheaded Washington ambushed a French Canadian patrol on 28 May 1754 and then built a makeshift fort to await the French response. When a large party of French Canadians and Indians attacked, Washington was forced to surrender, precipitating a diplomatic crisis.[5] Ironically, the person who had to respond was Rouillé. The able Puyzieulx had been forced by health reasons to resign the foreign ministry in late 1751. When his successor died in office in July 1754, Rouillé switched offices from the naval and colonial ministry to the foreign ministry.

The crisis of 1754 caught the French navy by surprise. Reduced to only thirty-three ships of the line on 1 January 1749, it had grown to fifty-seven ships of the line by 1 January 1755. Thirty-four of these ships had been launched during the previous six years, while some older ships were retired.[6] Although apparently it frightened the British, this construction program was not aggressive in nature, as the ships were built chiefly for convoy protection; the only ships carrying more than 74 guns were four new 80's. During the same six years, the British repaired a number of ships of the line, including seventeen during the years 1751–54, but launched only thirteen new ones. On 1 January 1755, however, the British navy contained more than 100 ships of the line. The Spanish navy, reduced to some twenty ships of the line at the end of the previous war, launched twenty-six during the period.[7] France was so far from expecting war that in 1752 the French navy reduced its purchases of timber and other naval materiel in order to save money.[8] When war broke out, the British navy was not only far larger than the French but also better prepared for war. Moreover, it had the expert guidance of the brilliant Anson, who became first lord of the admiralty in 1751.[9]

The British responded to Washington's surrender by sending two regiments of regulars commanded by Major General Edward Braddock to Virginia. Rouillé began negotiations to avert war, but they had little chance of success. Newcastle, now prime minister, was not anxious for war, either, but he was undercut by the interference of a war party headed by the king's favorite son, the Duke of Cumberland.[10] By the middle of March 1756, the negotiations were doomed, although Rouillé was foolish enough to let them drag on while Britain prepared for war. Meanwhile the French prepared to send 2,400 troops to Quebec and 1,200 to Louisbourg in response to the sending of Braddock's regiments. This did not really pose much of a threat to the British American colonies. Braddock's regiments alone would total 1,500 men when they were completed by recruiting in the colonies, which contained twenty times the population of Canada. Other regiments were being raised in the British North American colonies, too. On 24 March 1755, however, the inner cabinet ordered a squadron to intercept the French before they reached Louisbourg; on 27 April Vice Admiral Edward Boscawen sailed for Louisbourg with eleven ships of the line. Six days later the French squadrons for Louisbourg and Quebec sailed together from Brest; to save time, the French had temporarily converted nine ships of the line into troop transports, while their escort consisted of only four ships of the line.

The French were saved by fog off the coast of Newfoundland, which scattered their ships but kept most of them from Boscawen's grasp. On 10 June he attacked and captured the *Alcide*, 64, and one of the transports, the *Lys*, but the rest of the French fleet arrived safely at Louisbourg and Quebec. A month later General Braddock's army was virtually destroyed by Indians and marines (French-born troops with Canadian officers, who were under the control of the French naval and colonial ministry) as it approached the new French fort at the junction of the Allegheny and Monongahela. By now the British had expanded their objectives well beyond the Ohio country. The inner cabinet now planned to seize all of Canada south of the St. Lawrence River using mostly troops raised by the British American colonies. It also planned to occupy the French-held portion of Acadia.

The remaining British offensives of 1755 were only partly successful. A large force to attack Fort Niagara proceeded as far as Oswego on Lake Ontario, but was stranded there when winter set in. Another large force en route to attack Fort St. Frédéric on Lake

Champlain was attacked on the shores of nearby Lake George by a French force, including the newly arrived French regular troops. It beat back the attack and captured the French commander, but was unable to follow up the victory. The British governor of Nova Scotia captured the nearby French forts and then expelled the defenseless French-speaking civilian population of Acadia. Such cruelty threatened to become the norm; the British American frontier was swept by Indian raids once Braddock was defeated.[11]

Louis XV and his Council of State now faced massive problems, particularly the French navy's lack of preparation for war. The navy would suffer irreparable damage unless France could manage the safe return not only of the remaining eleven ships of the line at Louisbourg and Quebec but also of France's returning overseas trade, whose sailors would be needed for manning the navy's ships. Luckily it had the advice of Rouillé's replacement as naval minister, former finance minister Jean-Baptiste de Machault d'Arnouville.

Throughout the eighteenth century the British navy had far better trained ship crews and captains and, on balance, somewhat more skilled admirals. Ever since the reign of Louis XIV, however, France had the benefit of talented administrators serving as naval ministers. Generally they were highly competent, and occasionally they were brilliant. Machault was one of the most astute. He decided to send a squadron of six ships of the line to visit Lisbon and then cruise off Cape Ortegal, the northwest tip of Spain. This distracted the British navy, which feared that the squadron was the vanguard of another invasion attempt. France carefully avoided declaring war in response to Boscawen's aggression, even releasing a captured British frigate. This confounded the British inner cabinet, the informal group of Newcastle and half a dozen or so other senior officials who set policy and made strategy. By the time they ordered a general attack on French commerce, most of the overseas trade had arrived safely; even the ships from Canada returned safely except for one old ship of the line.[12]

The long-term problems facing France were even more daunting than the recent crisis had been. In spite of Machault's enthusiasm and confidence, France had virtually no chance of winning an extended predominantly naval and colonial war against Great Britain. Canada barely could feed itself and its Indian allies in the Upper Country, let alone sustain a large army of French troops. The British in contrast could draw on many thousands of British American colonial troops, while the colonies easily could feed as many troops as Britain chose to send; by the summer of 1759 British regular battalions in North America would outnumber the French by three to one (twenty-four battalions against eight). France could not send enough food to feed substantial reinforcements unless the French navy controlled the Gulf of St. Lawrence. It could not count on doing this indefinitely, because it was greatly inferior in financial resources and badly outnumbered in both sailors and ships of the line. Sixty-one British ships of the line were in service on 1 June 1755 against 21 French, 88 were in service on 1 June 1756 against 33 French, 96 were in service on 1 June 1757 against 42 French, and 104 were in service on 1 June 1758 against 25 French.[13]

II

France needed to preserve Canada not only for itself but also in order not to present in Europe an appearance of weakness that would attract predators; like all states on the European continent, France was vulnerable to attack. To preserve Canada, however, France had no choice but to find an equivalent to exchange for whatever parts of Canada Britain might take. There were three possibilities. France could try to repeat the triumphs of the previous war by attacking the Austrian Netherlands. Although some members of the Royal Council of State advocated such an attack, Louis XV's memory of the long and expensive war apparently was too fresh; moreover, the great Saxe had died in 1750 and no one could really replace him. A second possibility was seizing the British island of Minorca with its magnificent harbor, the best in the western Mediterranean. This was worth trying, but it might not be enough to force the British to make peace. The best chance of an acceptable peace was through the third possibility, the capture of George II's beloved German electorate, Hanover, whose inhabitants wanted desperately to remain neutral in case of another British-French war. Louis XV delayed making a decision until after France invaded Minorca. He also delayed negotiating a renewal of France's fifteen-year alliance with Prussia, due to expire in June 1756. Unless Prussia was willing to help France attack Hanover, the French dared not act without Austrian approval, as the Austrian Netherlands was dangerously close to the French invasion route into Germany. France needed the help of one of the two great German powers in order to avoid raising the opposition of the smaller states of the Holy Roman Empire. Obtaining the approval of Maria Theresa of Austria, however, was likely to depend on France's cooperating with an Austrian invasion of Prussian Silesia. It is hardly surprising that Louis wished to delay making the momentous choice between Austria and Prussia until after France tried to capture Minorca.

Newcastle, unsuccessful in reaching agreement with Austria for the defense of the Austrian Netherlands and under great pressure from George II to protect Hanover, now made a series of mistakes. He first arranged to hire Russian troops, as Britain and the Netherlands had done during the previous war. On 30 September his

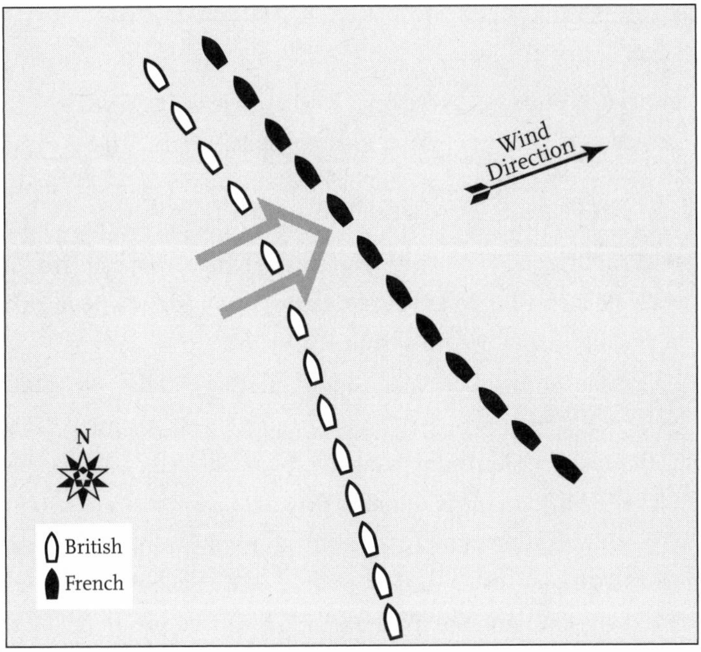

2. Minorca, 20 May 1756

ambassador in St. Petersburg signed a treaty by which Britain would pay Russia to provide 55,000 troops to defend Hanover, although it was not specified against whom. Not content with the treaty, Newcastle leaked news of it to Frederick II of Prussia, who was terrified of Russia. Newcastle suggested to him that their countries should guarantee the Holy Roman Empire against invasion. Contemptuously disregarding his existing alliance with France, Frederick agreed to this; rather than helping France capture Hanover, he agreed to help Britain defend it. Frederick also insisted that the treaty be modified so as to exclude the Austrian Netherlands, which was part of the Holy Roman Empire but not Germany. He was willing to see France attack it as long as he did not have to help. The British-Prussian agreement was signed at Westminster in January 1756.

Empress (Czarina) Elizabeth of Russia was outraged at what she regarded as a betrayal by the British, whom she had believed wished protection for Hanover from *Prussian* attack. Maria Theresa also felt betrayed because of the exclusion of the Austrian Netherlands. In April the two empresses, already allies, began preparing a joint attack on Prussia.[14] France, betrayed by Prussia, dropped plans for renewing their alliance and began serious negotiations with Austria for an alliance that would permit France to attack Hanover.

First, however, France made a final effort to end the war. While the French army assembled 70,000 troops along its Atlantic coast to threaten an invasion of England, the court collected 15,000 troops to invade Minorca. This required fifty transports and 130 supply ships, as well as an escort of a dozen ships of the line. The naval force was under the command of Roland-Michel Barin, marquis de la Galissonnière, the former acting governor general of New France whose alarmist reports had greatly influenced Rouillé. The convoy and its escort sailed from Toulon on 12 April. The troops landed on Minorca a week later. They met little resistance, as the British retreated to the great fortress of Fort St. Philip with its 600 cannon protecting the splendid harbor of Port Mahon. In the harbor were a British 58-gun ship of the line and two 50's; these managed to escape. Although the fort's garrison was only 3,000 men, the siege seemed likely to be lengthy, and help from England already was on the way.

On 6 April a squadron commanded by Admiral John Byng (son of the victor of the Battle of Cape Passaro) sailed from Portsmouth for the Mediterranean. The French had bluffed Anson and his colleagues in the inner cabinet into sending only ten ships of the line, however, and the British ships were short of crewmen. After a brief stop at Gibraltar, Byng sailed to Minorca where he found his way blocked by La Galissonnière's squadron. On 20 May Byng, reinforced by the three ships of the line that had escaped from Port Mahon, approached from windward in order to attack the French squadron.

Coordinating an attack at sea was even more difficult than coordinating an attack on land, and Byng failed to explain his plans adequately to the captains of the ships in his squadron. As his thirteen ships of the line approached La Galissonnière's waiting dozen ships of the line, the British ships at the head of the line came under heavy fire. The *Intrepid,* the sixth ship in the line, was badly damaged and dropped out of position. The ship behind her, the *Revenge,* failed to close the gap, and she and the ships behind her did not seriously engage in the battle. Although casualties in the two squadrons were approximately equal and the French squadron was forced to give way, Byng's squadron, with two ships seriously damaged, was unable to pursue; the French apparently had concentrated their fire on masts, sails, and spars to disable pursuit in case of defeat while the British had concentrated on French hulls, gun batteries, and crews. (This, however, may have been at least partly a result of the French fleet's inaccurate firing at long distance, while the approaching British waited to fire until they were alongside the French.) Byng, a chronic pessimist, declined risking another battle and retreated to Gibraltar to repair his ships, leaving Fort St. Philip under siege. On the night of 27–28 June a surprise attack breached the fort's outer defenses. The aged British commander, despairing of assistance, decided to surrender.

The French capture of Minorca did not cause the British to make peace. The English public was outraged rather than despondent at the news. To appease it, Newcastle made Byng the scapegoat for the inner cabinet's failure to send enough ships, manufactured evidence against him, and had him court-martialed. He was sentenced to death and, after the king declined to pardon him, he was executed.[15]

The Newcastle government soon suffered another setback. In April 1756 the French sent 1,000 more regulars and 1,000 recruits to Quebec aboard three ships of the line and three frigates. Aboard the squadron was a new commander for the French army contingent in Canada, Maréchal de camp (Brigadier General) Louis-Joseph, marquis de Montcalm de St. Véran. Like his predecessor, he was placed under the command of a naval officer, Lieutenant General of the Fleet Pierre de Rigaud de Vaudreuil de Cavagnol, marquis de Vaudreuil, who had replaced Duquesne as governor general of New France the previous year.

Vaudreuil had spent many years in Canada and Louisiana, and he had a matchless grasp of the best strategy for the unique conditions of North America. His strategy was to divert British forces by assisting his Indian allies to attack the frontier and to disrupt any British offensive by attacking their assembly points before they could mobilize their forces. He could do so because the American provincial regiments who served alongside British regulars were disbanded at the end of each campaigning season and had to be recruited again the following year, making mobilization very slow. Vaudreuil's strategy had been only partly successful in 1755 because the attack on the British army at Lake George had been mishandled. The attack in 1756, although risky, was more successful. Vaudreuil sent Montcalm with a mixed force of 3,000 regular troops, marines, Canadian militia, and Indians to attack Oswego. Proceeding by night in small boats to avoid the British fleet on Lake Ontario, Montcalm reached Oswego undetected and soon captured the 1,500-man garrison. He destroyed the post and then returned to Canada so his militia could attend to the harvest.[16]

This second humiliation cost Newcastle and his administration their jobs; they resigned in mid-November 1756. The titular head of the government that replaced it was William Cavendish, Duke of Devonshire, but its most dynamic member was William Pitt, the new secretary of state for the southern department. Pitt's brother-in-law, the inexperienced Richard Temple Grenville, Earl Temple, replaced Anson as first lord of the admiralty.[17]

The French could take some satisfaction in the outcome of the campaign of 1756. Although the British navy established firm control over the English Channel and Bay of Biscay and disrupted French trade, the French navy survived another campaign virtually intact. The major development of 1756, however, was the spread of war to the European continent. On 1 May France and Austria signed a treaty of defensive alliance, the Treaty of Versailles. Each party pledged to come to the aid of the other if attacked. Austria also pledged not to assist Great Britain, while France pledged not to invade the Austrian Netherlands. Immediately upon signing the treaty, the Austrian and French courts began the more complicated task of negotiating an offensive alliance that would not only permit France to attack Hanover but would also give France territorial gains in Europe to counterbalance Austria's regaining Silesia. When completed, this so-called Diplomatic Revolution saw France allied with its former enemy, Austria, while Britain was allied with its former enemy, Prussia. The French and Austrians eventually agreed that French gains would be mostly indirect. The bulk of the Austrian Netherlands was to go to Louis XV's son-in-law, Duke Philip of Parma, in exchange for the duchy of Parma and his other territories. As France and Austria negotiated, the Austrians and Russians began preparing to attack Prussia.

These plans were discovered by Frederick II of Prussia, who

decided to attack first. He launched a preemptive strike on Austria by seizing the neutral electorate of Saxony and then invading Bohemia.[18] Although the Prussians occupied Saxony, they could not capture Bohemia. This invasion gave impetus to the negotiations between France and Austria. On 1 May 1757 they concluded a second Treaty of Versailles, which, unlike its predecessor, was an offensive alliance. France entered the war against Prussia as an auxiliary of Austria and soon attacked the Prussian provinces near the Rhine before marching toward Hanover.

The new allies had a superb opportunity of winning their respective wars against Britain and Prussia. The French navy played its part by preventing Britain from conquering any new territory in Canada. The great Machault was forced into retirement on 1 February 1757 to mollify public opinion, which among other things blamed him for higher taxes. Before his retirement he set into motion one of the most complex and successful naval campaigns of the war. The French navy sent squadrons from Brest and Toulon to the Caribbean and from there to Louisbourg; later, a third squadron sailed directly from Brest to Louisbourg. These squadrons, which contained eighteen of the navy's available forty-two ships of the line, arrived unopposed at Louisbourg within weeks of each other. Without firing a shot, they were able to foil 11,000 British troops and sixteen ships of the line brought to Nova Scotia in order to attack Louisbourg. Meanwhile the British American frontier was left open to attack. Repeating his usual strategy, Vaudreuil sent Montcalm on the offensive. Montcalm captured Fort William Henry on Lake George, although the victory was marred by the killing or abduction of some of the captured British and American soldiers by Montcalm's Indian allies.[19]

George II raised an army of Hanoverians and other German

troops, the "Army of Observation," to protect Hanover. He entrusted its command to his only surviving son, the Duke of Cumberland. In 1757 a large French army defeated Cumberland and then overran Hanover. Cumberland and the French commander then signed a convention by which the Army of Observation was interned but not disarmed near the Hanoverian port of Stade.[20] The Prussians also suffered a severe defeat when an Austrian army captured Breslau, the capital of Silesia, destroying a Prussian army in the process. Three weeks earlier Frederick had crushed a French and German army at Rossbach in central Germany, but this did not counterbalance the defeat at Breslau. Just as the Prussian cause seemed doomed, everything changed. When Frederick rushed back to recapture Breslau, the Austrians unwisely left the fortified city, and Frederick attacked them. The ensuing battle of Leuthen (5 December 1757) was a total Prussian victory, followed quickly by the Austrian surrender of Breslau.[21] Cumberland's army, now commanded by Prince Ferdinand of Brunswick, a Prussian general, repudiated its agreement and in early 1758 forced the French to retreat from Hanover. The hope of saving Canada by a victory in Germany was frustrated.

The French navy suffered its own disaster. The squadrons that had joined at Louisbourg brought with them a variety of diseases. Soon the entire French fleet was swept by an epidemic even more terrible than the one that had devastated the 1746 expedition to Cape Breton Island. The highly capable fleet commander, Emmanuel-Auguste, comte de Cahideuc du Bois de la Motte, managed to get the fleet back to France without losing any ships, but the epidemic now spread to the port cities of Brest and Rochefort and the surrounding areas. Nearly half of the fleet's 12,000 officers and crewmen died, including the commander of the Toulon contingent, and there were a similar number of civilian fatalities.[22]

The French navy, short of funds, had no hope of replacing the trained sailors who had died or those captured aboard merchant ships, privateers, and warships and now in British prisons.[23] By mid-1758 only twenty-five ships of the line were still in service. The navy concentrated on saving Louisbourg to the virtual exclusion of all else; no ships of the line were outfitted to contest British control of the coastal waters of Brittany and Normandy. The British even landed large bodies of troops on the Norman and Breton coast on several occasions during 1758.[24] By enormous efforts, though, the navy did find crews for sixteen ships of the line that it attempted to send to Louisbourg virtually as fast as they could be manned. The results were disappointing, as some of them had to turn back or arrived too late. In early June a British fleet of twenty-three ships of the line appeared off Louisbourg, along with an army of 14,000 troops. The six French ships of the line in the harbor were trapped and eventually captured or destroyed, much as the Spanish squadron at Cartagena had been in 1741. The fortress did not surrender until 26 July, largely because of the caution of the British army and fleet commanders, Major General Jeffrey Amherst and Admiral Boscawen. The French prolonged their resistance just long enough that the British did not have enough time to proceed up the St. Lawrence to attack Quebec before the weather changed.[25] Another threat to the Canadian heartland was turned back when Montcalm defeated a British army of 6,300 regulars and 9,600 American provincial troops near Fort Carillon on Lake Champlain. Although outnumbered by four to one, Montcalm repulsed a series of attacks on his hastily constructed fieldworks, inflicted 2,000 casualties, and forced the British to retreat in disorder.[26]

During 1758 Prince Ferdinand of Brunswick crossed the Rhine. His invasion was repulsed, although Ferdinand won the only major battle of the year. The French maintained a foothold in Germany, although their troops remained well to the south of Hanover. Louis XV, demoralized after being stabbed by a deranged man in early 1757, had done little to animate the French cause, but at the end of 1758 he seems to have regained his nerve. He fired his defeatist foreign minister, François-Joachim de Pierre de Bernis, who had replaced Rouillé in June 1757. Bernis's successor was the French ambassador at the Austrian court, an energetic former soldier, Etienne-François, duc de Choiseul.

III

Although he opposed abandoning the war in Germany, Choiseul feared that French finances were not strong enough to fight a war of attrition against the British. He negotiated a new treaty with Austria, the third Treaty of Versailles, that reduced France's financial commitment but ended the chance of Duke Philip obtaining the Austrian Netherlands.

With the help of the army and navy ministers, Choiseul now prepared a vast plan for invading Britain. He planned to construct between 225 and 275 shallow-draft transports to carry troops and a dozen shallow-draft 22-cannon warships called prames to escort them to the landing sites. He planned to divert British attention by a landing in Scotland, after which transports and prames would cross the English Channel. His plans, which went through numerous modifications, had a terrible flaw. Any invading force would have to cross open water, where the prames could afford little protection from even a few British ships of the line. Ultimately French ships of the line would be needed, too. By the end of the summer Choiseul's colleague, Naval Minister Nicolas-René Berryer, was able to outfit 47 ships of the line (compared with some 110 British). He was able to do so, however, only by manning them largely with novice sailors. The main French fleet, 21 ships of the line at Brest, was unable to put to sea to train its sailors because the British were blockading the port tightly. Since 2 July 1757 the experienced Anson had been back at the Board of Admiralty, serving under a new government headed by Newcastle as prime minister and Pitt as secretary of state for the southern department. An unprecedented effort was made to provide the British fleet off Brest with a continual supply of fresh provisions, water, and beer, making possible a close blockade. Hawke, commanding the fleet, not only prevented the French fleet from leaving Brest but also detached ships to blockade Quiberon Bay on the south coast of Brittany where the transports for the preliminary invasion of Scotland had been assembled. Choiseul's elaborate plans seemed doomed.[27]

Elsewhere French efforts during 1759 miscarried. A promising campaign in Germany failed when Prince Ferdinand of Brunswick's army of British, Hanoverians, and other Germans won a surprising victory at Minden in northwestern Germany.[28] In the Caribbean the British failed to capture Martinique, but did land troops on the nearby island of Guadeloupe. The opportune arrival of a squadron of eight ships of the line at Martinique gave France the opportunity to save Guadeloupe. The French outwitted a larger British squadron and landed 600–800 soldiers only to discover that the island already had surrendered.[29] The French governor of Guadeloupe was afraid of reopening hostilities, and the commanding French admiral was afraid of the British navy. The troops returned to Martinique, after which the French squadron returned to Brest. When it arrived on 7 November, it provided some crewmen to help man the Brest fleet.

Another sizeable squadron, a dozen ships of the line, was outfitted at Toulon, which had escaped the terrible epidemic of 1758 except for the few ships it had sent to Louisbourg. In early August the French Mediterranean fleet sailed for the Spanish port of Cadiz.[30] During the night of 17–18 August, it passed through the Strait of Gibraltar, sailing in two columns. The British Mediterranean fleet of fifteen ships of the line immediately sailed in pursuit. The weaker column, five ships of the line and three frigates, took refuge in Cadiz and eventually returned safely to Toulon. The stronger column was not so fortunate. Two ships of the line escaped and reached Rochefort. Three others were captured, and two more were destroyed after running themselves aground near the Portuguese port of Lagos.

The French navy didn't lose warships in North America, but it could do little to save Quebec. With the British occupying Louisbourg, France decided it was hopeless to send any ships of the line to the St. Lawrence. Although it sent a large number of merchant ships to Quebec with food and supplies, it provided nothing larger than frigates to escort them. The British in contrast sent a huge fleet of twenty-two ships of the line superbly commanded by Vice Admiral Charles Saunders to escort an army of 8,500 British regulars. Defying the navigational dangers of the St. Lawrence, it delivered Major General James Wolfe's army to a safe landing point opposite the city. The French frigates there escaped upriver where Saunders's larger ships couldn't follow, but they left Saunders unopposed. On the night of 12–13 September, the small boats from his fleet ferried 4,800 British troops across the river. They mounted the cliffs near Quebec with little opposition and deployed on the Plains of Abraham facing the city. Montcalm, however, was able to bring a comparable number of troops to block their further advance. Wolfe's forces, which as yet had only two cannon with them, were in grave danger. Instead of awaiting reinforcements, however, Montcalm, who mistrusted the steadiness of the Canadian troops serving under his command, foolishly decided to attack. Although Wolfe was killed, the British repulsed the attack, mortally wounded Montcalm, and advanced on Quebec, which surrendered a few days later.[31]

The British probably would have captured Montreal, too, had not a small French squadron on Lake Champlain delayed the advance of Amherst's 11,000-man army until he built his own squadron to protect the boats carrying his troops and cannon down the lake.

The final British victory of 1759 was a battle the French did not need to fight. The fleet commander at Brest was the most respected officer in the French navy, Hubert, comte de Conflans, who held the exalted rank of marshal of France, usually reserved for army officers. Conflans had commanded the Brest fleet since 1756 without ever being able to put to sea. Abandoning the attempt to invade Britain was too much of a humiliation for him to accept. In October he received permission to sail to Quiberon. After a few weeks Hawke was forced away from his station off Brest by strong westerly winds that threatened to drive him onto a lee (downwind) shore. On 14 November Conflans sailed from Brest with twenty-one poorly manned ships of the line. On the same day Hawke sailed from his anchorage of Torbay on the south coast of England with twenty-three superbly trained ships of the line. He quickly learned that Conflans had sailed and guessed his destination. As Conflans approached Quiberon on 20 November, he sighted Hawke in pursuit. Abandoning attempts to capture the four 50-gun ships blockading Quiberon, he sought refuge within the bay. In spite of a fierce storm, Hawke sailed into the bay after him, an unparalleled feat of seamanship and courage. Two British ships of the line ran aground and were destroyed, but Conflans's fleet was crushed. Nine of his ships of the line escaped from the bay and fled to seaports to the south, although one of these ships ran aground. Seven fled up the small Vilaine River, which empties into Quiberon Bay, where they were trapped for many months, although all but one of them eventually returned to Brest. The remaining five ships of the line were captured, shipwrecked, or destroyed, including the two finest ships in the French navy, the *Formidable*, 80, and the *Soleil Royal*, 80.

Louis XV was faced not only with this series of disasters but also with partial bankruptcy and the sudden death from smallpox of his adored eldest daughter, Louise-Elisabeth. He responded with great courage. He quickly grasped that France's only hope for escaping complete disaster was to sacrifice all other considerations to the war in Germany. For the next two years the navy was so starved of funds that it leased its warships to private contractors for privateering cruises. Only fourteen ships of the line were in service on 1 June 1760, and just seventeen a year later. The navy, unable to afford to build its own ships, even purchased at a bargain price four Genoese ships of the line built of fir, vastly inferior to oak.[32]

With the navy virtually demobilized, there was no hope of preventing the fall of Montreal. The only surprise is that Amherst, with his huge superiority in men and ships, took until September 1760 to capture it. By now Pitt's objectives had expanded well beyond driving the French from Canada. He wished to deprive France of a share in the Newfoundland and St. Lawrence fisheries and ruin France as a naval power.

Ironically, it was the shift of funds from the French navy to the French army that permitted France to save its access to the fisheries on which depended the eventual rebuilding of its navy. The French army in Germany finally received a capable general, Victor-François, duc de Broglie, who proved a match for the British and German commander, Prince Ferdinand of Brunswick. Although Broglie did not advance as far as Hanover, he captured on 31 July 1760 the city of Cassel, the capital of the principality of Hesse-Cassel, which supplied many of Ferdinand's troops; the French held it until just before peace was signed. A counterattack by Ferdinand's nephew, the hereditary prince of Brunswick, threatened the great fortress of Wesel, the chief French post on the Rhine, but a surprise British-German night assault on an advancing French relief column was repulsed on 16 October 1760 at the Battle of Clostercamp. The French commander was a young general, Charles-Eugène-Gabriel de La Croix, marquis de Castries, who in 1780 would become French *naval* minister; the hero of the battle was a regimental commander, Jean-Baptiste-Donatien de Vimeur, comte de Rochambeau, who in 1780 would command the French expeditionary force sent to America. The French army minister during the latter part of the American Revolution, the marquis de Ségur, also was present at Clostercamp; the three thus formed a connection between Clostercamp and the victory at Yorktown in 1781, a victory which would not have been possible without the earlier French victory. Had the French lost Wesel and been driven from Germany, they would have had nothing to exchange for access to the fisheries and hence would have had great difficulty in finding enough sailors to mount future challenges to Britain. Part of the French preparations for joining the War of American Independence was recalling the Newfoundland fishing fleet to France in the summer of 1777.[33]

The campaign of 1761 was indecisive, even though it involved enormous financial expenses for both Britain and France. Frederick II of Prussia was losing his war against Austria and Russia, who captured two key fortresses late in the year. Just as Prussia seemed doomed, Empress Elizabeth of Russia died. Her successor, Peter III, quickly made peace with Frederick and began planning a war against

Denmark that would make Russia master of the Baltic Sea. Peter's surrender of Russia's conquests from Prussia, however, angered the Russian army and led to a 1762 palace coup after which Peter's wife, Catherine, became empress and Peter was murdered.[34]

British-French peace negotiations in the summer of 1761 failed because Pitt insisted upon a British monopoly of the fisheries, which Choiseul, who described the fisheries as his obsession, refused. The mood in Britain was changing, however. By the end of the year the British public, including the British taxpayers, had become weary of the seemingly endless war in Germany. Even support for Prussia was waning, a trend which accelerated when Russia dropped out of the war, leaving Prussians capable of defending themselves. George II died on 25 October 1760, and his young grandson and successor, George III, did not share his love for Hanover and interest in German affairs. The final push needed for a compromise peace, however, came from the entry of Spain into the war.

The peaceable Ferdinand VI died on 10 August 1759. He was succeeded by his half-brother Charles, hitherto the ruler of the Kingdom of the Two Sicilies. Charles was hostile to the British, who had humiliated him in 1742 by threatening to bombard Naples unless he withdrew his support for the Spanish army in northern Italy. Moreover, Charles now feared that once the British had crushed France, the Spanish Empire would be at their mercy; he told the French ambassador at his court that the news of the fall of Quebec turned his blood to ice. By the summer of 1761 he was prepared to come to the aid of France. Pitt wished to forestall him by attacking first in hopes of capturing the treasure fleet from the Western Hemisphere, thereby ruining Spanish finances. His colleagues in the inner cabinet were more cautious. This was particularly true of Anson, who in spite of his other accomplishments had let the

British navy decline to less than 100 active ships of the line and who feared Spain's 45 ships of the line should they be joined to France's remaining ships.[35] When Pitt was rebuffed by his colleagues, he resigned from office. Newcastle remained as prime minister, but power was beginning to shift to a colleague in the inner cabinet, George III's former tutor, John Stuart, Earl of Bute.

At the end of 1761 Spain entered the war and began planning an attack on Portugal, a traditional British ally that wished only to remain neutral in the present conflict. No military aspect of the Seven Years' War had been more misunderstood than Spain's role. Admittedly, its army and navy were miserably led. With the help of a small British expeditionary force, Portugal repulsed the Spanish attack. The British, using a brilliant plan devised by Anson, surprised Havana, trapping a fleet of ten ships of the line in the harbor. After a lengthy siege, the city itself surrendered, although British losses from disease were so heavy that without the help of sailors from the fleet in moving cannon, the siege might have failed.[36] The British even sent a small fleet and army that captured Manila, although news of the capture did not arrive until after peace had been concluded.[37] Meanwhile Choiseul had become naval minister, turning over the foreign ministry to his cousin, César-Gabriel de Choiseul-Chavigny. He wished Spain's Atlantic fleet, based in Cadiz and Ferrol, to join with French squadrons from Brest and Rochefort in order to protect an invasion of England. The Spanish fleet, however, never left port. The French navy accomplished little in 1762 beyond a raid that temporarily captured Newfoundland.

In spite of their unbroken record of failure, the Spanish did increase the burden of war on Britain, albeit indirectly. Britain had to pay for the expeditionary force sent to help defend Portugal. Trade with Spain, which was vital to the British economy, was interrupted.

This led to unemployment and public unrest, increasing the pressure on the inner cabinet to make whatever peace it could. Bute, who became prime minister on 26 May 1762, was concerned chiefly with strengthening the monarchy's role in British government. He was so anxious to rid himself of the war that when peace negotiations resumed he leaked information to Choiseul about the inner cabinet's bottom line about peace terms. He was unhappy at the arrival of news of the victory at Havana because it complicated the negotiations, which he wished completed before the British recaptured Cassel.

A preliminary agreement was reached at the royal chateau of Fontainebleau on 3 November 1762. It returned Havana to Spain in exchange for Florida and for the return of Minorca to Britain. To compensate Spain and pressure Charles III into accepting the terms, France secretly gave Spain all of Louisiana west of the Mississippi River. Except for the city of New Orleans, which also was transferred to Spain instead of going to Britain (under the convenient fiction that it was on an island between branches of the Mississippi), Britain received the portion of North America east of the Mississippi. Early in 1763 Prussia and Austria made peace on the basis of a mutual return of conquests during the war, with Prussia thereby retaining Silesia. The final British-French treaty, signed in Paris in early 1763, largely confirmed the terms of the preliminary agreement.

France lost all of New France except for two small islands off Newfoundland, but it kept access to the fisheries and the right to dry fish on part of the Newfoundland coast. Britain's conquests in the West Indies were returned, including the rich island of Martinique, which the British had captured in 1762.

The greatest long-term British gains from the war were in India. In 1757 troops of the British East India Company and a British navy squadron seized control of the rich province of Bengal, the beginning of a long process that ended in British control of all of India. During the war the French sent major land and naval forces to India. They besieged Madras, but were unsuccessful. In 1761 Pondicherry, the last French trading post in India, was captured. The peace treaty returned France's trading posts, but the French East India Company had been mortally wounded.[38]

Elsewhere the war was less decisive than it appeared. The French, as Pitt complained, had given up lands that were an economic burden to them and kept the access to the fisheries and the sugar islands on which the rebuilding of the French navy depended.[39] In the British victory lay the seeds of defeat; in the ruins of French defeat lay the seeds of future victory.

5. Winners and Losers in the War of American Independence

I

For Britain the celebration of victory in the Seven Years' War was short-lived. The British now faced a number of problems. The end of the Prussian alliance left Britain diplomatically isolated. Austria was uninterested in reviving its former British alliance. Although Russia cooperated with Britain in areas of common concern, such as Swedish politics, attempts to negotiate an alliance with the new empress, Catherine II, were unsuccessful, partly because of British unwillingness to pay her a subsidy.[1] Military triumph thus did little to improve British security, in spite of the removal of the French from the North American mainland.

The war also complicated relations with Britain's colonies in North America, whose contributions to the war effort were not well understood by the English public or even by the British government. Before the war Britain had left colonial defense to the colonies themselves, but the British government felt it was impossible to turn back the clock and did not consider withdrawing its regular troops from North America. The Indian nations of the Upper Country were outraged that the British remained in their hunting grounds in spite of having promised to leave once the French were defeated. They were further disturbed by their poor treatment by

General Amherst and by the news of the Treaty of Paris, which assigned their lands to Great Britain. They rose in rebellion, seizing a number of smaller British posts and threatening even Fort Pitt and Detroit, the two strongest forts in the Upper Country. It took a number of regular troops to stabilize the area, and the conflict, known as Pontiac's Rebellion, ended with a compromise agreement recognizing a considerable degree of Indian autonomy.[2] To pay for the troops left in America, the British tried to circumvent British American representative bodies. This led to colonial resistance, which in turn caused the British to switch some of the troops away from the frontier to areas long settled by British Americans. The presence of British troops in urban areas increased tensions and led to the so-called Boston Massacre.[3] Even the British navy was pressed into service to increase British government revenue by wiping out smuggling; this, too, led to violent incidents.[4]

British naval dominance in other parts of the Atlantic Ocean also was less than secure. A series of confrontations with France and Spain over various colonial disputes tested British resolve. The most threatening of these involved a dispute over British occupation of part of the remote Falkland Islands in the South Atlantic; Britain evaded war with Spain by a compromise in which the British government secretly promised to evacuate the islands quietly at a future date.[5] Britain sought to keep eighty ships of the line in condition to serve, but because many ships were approaching retirement age, this was expensive.[6] Britain paid the cost, but concern over the massive increase in the national debt caused by the last war largely was responsible for its disastrous policy of attempting to raise revenue from its North American colonies without their consent.[7]

For France, too, naval policy and diplomacy were weakened by financial constraints. Initially naval construction was aided by a surge of patriotism following the humiliating defeat at Quiberon Bay. Cities and corporate bodies that normally fought tax increases donated enough money to build seventeen ships of the line, although only two were launched by the end of the war.[8] Choiseul hoped that in a few years France would have eighty ships of the line and Spain sixty ships of the line in order to fight a war of revenge.[9] The king's secret diplomatic service, the Secret du Roi, began mapping landing sites along the English coast. By the end of 1766, however, the impulse for war was declining. Spanish naval reconstruction went more slowly than anticipated, and once the donated French ships of the line were launched there was no money to build more. The Russian threat to France's friends in eastern Europe, particularly Poland, had intensified so much that Choiseul left the naval ministry and returned to the foreign ministry, thereby swapping places with his cousin Choiseul-Chavigny, now the duc de Praslin. Most important, Louis XV gradually lost interest in a foreign war; he even dismissed Choiseul as foreign minister during the Falkland Islands crisis because he feared Choiseul was ready to support Spain in going to war. Until he died of smallpox in May 1774, Louis concentrated on strengthening the monarchy's position within France. From 1766 through 1774 the navy launched only eleven ships of the line; in mid-1774 it had sixty ships of the line available for service, only thirteen more than at the end of the last war. Britain, which had launched as many ships as France and Spain combined during the last decade, had 106.[10]

King Louis XV was succeeded by his nineteen-year-old grandson, who became Louis XVI. Like his grandfather at the same age, the new king was intelligent and well-intentioned, but indecisive and severely lacking in self-confidence. His grandfather had matured in the job, growing wiser and stronger as he aged, largely because of his underlying flexibility and moderation. Louis XVI did not develop in the same way. Although decent and honorable, he was dogmatic and emotionally undemonstrative, lacking his grandfather's warmth and charm. Worse still, he was a poor judge of character and unable to tell good advice from bad. As a great diplomatic historian noted, he was a devout Christian and a good man, but no king.[11]

Initially it seemed that the new king would continue his predecessor's peaceful foreign policy. A great war in eastern Europe had just ended with Poland losing substantial territory to Prussia, Russia, and Austria. With Russia exhausted by the long war and Catherine II and the other despoilers of Poland satiated with their gains, there seemed little likelihood of a general war in the near future.[12] Britain was preoccupied with breaking the resistance of its American colonies to taxation by Parliament, a resistance that had led to the Boston Tea Party of December 1773. The new king's inclinations were far less martial than his grandfather's had been as a young man. He professed more interest in the well-being of his subjects than in military glory. Unfortunately, though, he idealized his late father, a pious nonentity, and was ashamed of his grandfather because of his scandalous personal life; the old king had even selected a commoner, Mme du Barry, as his final mistress. Thus the new king did not take advantage of the hard-won wisdom of his grandfather, who in spite of his marital failings was an exceptionally loving father and grandfather with much to teach. Once he became king, Louis XVI quickly recalled the Parlements, the law courts that his grandfather had replaced with a more tractable judicial system, and dismissed his grandfather's ministers.

He selected as his unofficial first minister the comte de Maurepas, the former naval minister who had spent the last twenty-five years in exile from the court. Although intelligent, Maurepas was too jealous of any potential rivals to serve the new king disinterestedly. Worse still, unlike Fleury, who had guided the inexperienced young Louis XV, Maurepas does not seem to have had a policy of his own. Not surprisingly, Maurepas helped steer the new king away from any foreign minister who might challenge his influence. The king, too, did not want an aggressive foreign minister, so he does not seem to have seriously considered Choiseul or the comte de Broglie, the former head of the Secret du Roi. Instead he chose a veteran diplomat known for his caution, Charles Gravier, comte de Vergennes, the former French minister in Constantinople and Stockholm.

On the surface Vergennes seems an unlikely person to have led France into a new war with Britain. Not only was he a specialist on eastern Europe, but he looked fondly (or would come to do so) on the days of the Franco-British alliance.[13] Vergennes, however, was not what he seemed. He had been a leading member of the Secret du Roi, which had been devoted to countering Russian expansion, and he saw Britain as a supporter of Russia.[14] Britain not only had recently helped refit a Russian fleet en route to the Mediterranean to fight the Turks but also had prevented France's outfitting a fleet of its own to support the Swedes when they, too, were in danger from Russia.[15] With Russia temporarily immobilized, France had a chance to weaken Britain and hence Russia; once Britain was weakened it might even come to accept French leadership on the continent. Vergennes did not question the standard belief that Britain would be seriously weakened if it lost its monopoly of American trade.[16]

II

The American rebellion, which began in April 1775, gave Vergennes his chance. Britain responded to the news of Lexington and Concord by the use of force, both military and naval, to restore its American colonies to obedience, but it tried to do so while spending as little money as possible. It failed to provide enough ships to blockade the American coast and to cut off the rebels' supply of munitions from Europe and the Caribbean.[17] In late 1775 Vergennes sent a secret agent from the West Indies to ascertain the needs of the American revolutionaries. This agent met in Philadelphia in December with Benjamin Franklin and other members of the American Continental Congress, who informed him that they would welcome the chance to trade with France and to obtain French arms. When Vergennes learned this, he proposed to Louis XVI's Council of State that France try to prolong the American conflict. To overcome the king's scruples, Vergennes portrayed his proposal as a way of buying time to protect the French West Indies from a British attack. Vergennes's real motive, however, seems to have been that of buying time for France to prepare to enter the conflict directly should the Americans not win independence on their own.

The naïve young king gave his consent to Vergennes's plan. To help shield the French government from British retribution, Vergennes established a trading company to purchase surplus French army muskets and other munitions at cost and then to exchange them for American tobacco. The government loaned it 1 million livres (equivalent in contemporary terms to at least $5 million) for start-up costs. To head the company Vergennes chose the playwright and adventurer Pierre-Augustin Caron de Beaumarchais, whom he had previously used to pay off the disgruntled former head of the Secret du Roi in England who was threatening to reveal its operations. Beaumarchais named the new company Roderigue Hortalez & Co. It did not prosper, as the British navy made it very difficult to send tobacco to Europe, but the munitions it sent, particularly gunpowder and muskets, were invaluable to the poorly equipped American Continental army.[18]

When Vergennes persuaded the king to aid the Americans, he also persuaded him to arm a few ships of the line as a precaution. Again he seems to have been deceiving the king into approving the opening stages of what became a full-scale rearmament plan. Vergennes found a very willing ally in the French naval minister, Antoine-Raymond-Gualbert-Gabriel de Sartine, the former chief administrator of the city of Paris, who during Louis XV's reign had been appointed to the Secret du Roi to protect its secrecy. Like Vergennes, Sartine was willing to concede to Maurepas primacy in the Council of State, which advised the king on all major questions of war and diplomacy, in exchange for control over the day-to-day operations of his department. Sartine also was wise enough to find a knowledgeable chief assistant, Charles-Pierre Claret de Fleurieu, a future naval minister himself. With Fleurieu's help Sartine became one of the greatest naval ministers of the eighteenth century, rivaled only by Machault.

For the only time between 1688 and 1815, the French navy had two full years before the start of a war to build and repair its ships and to fill its dockyards with timber, masts, and other naval materiel. It also tried to compensate for the British navy's advantage in experience by conducting training cruises and evaluating its officers. Given time to prepare, the French navy would enjoy greater success in the coming war than in any other during the period. In late 1774 only twenty-four of its sixty ships of the line were ready for use, but when war with Britain began in late June 1778, it placed fifty-two ships of the line in service.[19]

The British navy, already committed to blockading the American coast and to supporting the operations of the large British army in North America, now had to worry about a French attack.[20] The British government, anxious to crush the American rebellion before France could become involved, was reluctant to respond to French provocation; it protested clandestine French arms shipments but threatened war only when France failed to take effective action to prevent American privateers from using French ports. This forced France to expel a squadron of American privateers in the summer of 1777, as the French naval rearmament program was not yet complete. By now three American diplomats headed by the shrewd Franklin were in Paris in search of a commercial treaty; they accepted the French decision and waited for the French to change their policy.

Vergennes by now was almost ready to go beyond clandestine assistance to America. By the autumn of 1777 the rearmament program had sufficiently progressed that Vergennes began pressuring Spain to join in a war against Britain. Spain, unlike France, saw the American Revolution as a dangerous example to its own colonies. Although willing to help prolong the war, it had little inclination to participate in it unless substantial incentives were offered. This did not change when news of the American victory at Saratoga arrived in December. Vergennes, already committed to war, now had a weapon to use against Louis XVI's scruples and Charles III of Spain's reluctance. He argued that America was likely to make a compromise peace with Britain and then to join Britain in attacking the French and Spanish West Indies. The logic of the argument was dubious at best—why should the Americans abandon their claims to independence at the moment of their greatest victory? The argument worked, however, with the gullible Louis XVI. The Americans obtained a French military alliance in exchange for a commercial treaty, an essential point for France; the signing of a commercial treaty with the rebels certainly would be regarded by Britain as an act of war, and France would need the cooperation of the Continental Army if France and the United States were to avoid being defeated one at a time. Once it was clear that Spain would not join the treaties, the negotiations with the American representatives in Paris were concluded quickly, as the Americans did not object to a prohibition on either party making a separate peace. Both the Franco-American alliance treaty and a Franco-American commercial treaty were signed on 6 February 1778.

France now was free to prepare openly for war. Although the British knew of the treaties, they did not declare war, even after the French in March publicly announced the existence of the commercial treaty. They thereby left France the choice of where and when to begin hostilities. In April a squadron of a dozen ships of the line commanded by Vice Admiral Charles-Henri, comte d'Estaing, sailed from Toulon, the same number of ships as La Galissonnière's squadron of twenty-two years earlier. This time the French squadron was bound for New York, the central British position in North America, which was defended by a squadron smaller than d'Estaing's. The British first lord of the admiralty, John Montague, Earl of Sandwich, was afraid, as Anson had been in 1756, that the French squadron was bound for Brest in order to support an invasion of England. Prodded by the cabinet, he fitted out a squadron to rescue New York but waited to be certain that d'Estaing was bound for America before sending it. D'Estaing thus had a head start of several weeks and received a bonus when the British squadron pursuing him was scattered by a storm. A pattern, moreover, was established, that of Britain's trying to establish naval superiority both in Europe and in America. The most astute modern British naval historian of the period argues that the squadron in New York should have been left to its own resources, as it largely was anyway, and all efforts instead should have been made to reinforce the Western Squadron and blockade the French coast.[21] Such a strategy likely would have been successful eventually, but so too might have the opposite strategy, that of disregarding the danger of invasion and defeating the enemy abroad. Sandwich and the British cabinet did not have the courage to adopt wholeheartedly either strategy, and by trying to maintain superior numbers in every theater of war they allowed the enemy to keep the initiative. The power of public opinion was partly to blame by making it more difficult to adopt any risky strategy.

Now that war was certain, France's immediate concern was to maneuver Britain into firing the first shot in European waters before d'Estaing reached America. If successful, France could call for assistance under its defensive alliance with Austria, while Britain would have difficulty in calling for assistance from the Netherlands under *their* defensive treaty. France did not expect Austrian assistance, but wished to have an excuse not to become involved in a budding war in Germany between Austria and Prussia. Vergennes kept up the alliance, but consistently used it to thwart Austrian ambitions, a subtlety lost on the French public. Britain was foolish enough to fall into the French trap. On 18 June the British Western Squadron had a confrontation with three French frigates, capturing two of them and badly damaging a third, the *Belle-Poule*, which became a symbol of French courage. It is unclear who fired the first shot, but circumstances made it appear that Britain was the aggressor as it had been in 1755.

Sending d'Estaing to America where he might be trapped by superior forces was an act of exceptional courage, perhaps rashness, but this gamble was based on need. Because the British took so long to mobilize their fleet due to their dependence on pressing sailors from incoming merchant ships, the French enjoyed near parity for the first campaign of the war; on 1 July 1778 they had fifty-two ships of the line in service, while the British had only sixty-six in service. Not since the 1690s had the French come so close to equality.[22] This near parity could not last. By the following year the British navy would be fully manned and the French hopelessly outnumbered unless they could procure the help of the Spanish navy. The French Council of State placed on d'Estaing its hopes of winning the war in a single campaign. Vice Admiral Richard Howe had only eight ships of 50 or more cannon, but he anchored them off Sandy Hook to the south of New York harbor where d'Estaing's larger ships dared not approach for fear of running aground. D'Estaing instead sailed to attack the 5,000-man British garrison at Newport, but again was foiled by Howe (who had been reinforced by four ships of the line) and by a storm. D'Estaing then sailed to Boston to repair his ships, having accomplished nothing.

Off the French coast, however, the French navy was more successful. Refusing to let the British have free rein in French waters, Sartine, Vergennes, and the Council of State sent all thirty-two ships of the line at Brest to fight the twenty-nine ships of the line of the British home fleet, which on average had more cannon than the French ships. Having no ships in reserve at Brest, the French were taking a breathtaking risk. On 27 June 1778 the two fleets fought to a draw off Isle d'Ushant at the tip of Brittany. Both fleets suffered significant casualties but lost no ships. The British commander, Admiral Augustus Keppel, and his chief subordinate, Vice Admiral Hugh Palliser, blamed each other for the lack of a victory, much as Mathews and Lestock had done after the Battle of Toulon in 1744. The British navy was divided by the dispute, while the French navy took courage from its ability to fight the British on even terms.

With the entrance of France into the conflict, the War for American Independence became a worldwide conflict like the Seven Years' War. The British quickly seized Pondicherry in India, which had taken them four years to capture in the previous war. Detaching troops from America, they also were able to capture the strategically important island of St. Lucia in the West Indies and repel a French counterattack led by d'Estaing, who brought his squadron from Boston to the Caribbean. Although the French did not lose a single ship of the line in 1778, their attempt to win the war in a single campaign had failed totally. They could count on no more than sixty ships of the line in 1779 to fight ninety British. Only the Spanish Navy, with its nearly sixty of the line, could help; the tiny Continental navy of the United States had nothing larger than a frigate and was of negligible importance.[23] The British government easily could have purchased continued Spanish neutrality by returning Gibraltar to the Spaniards. Contemptuous of the Spanish navy and fearing English public opinion, it made the fatal mistake of not doing so. In late 1778 Spain broke off discussions with Britain and turned to France. Vergennes begged the king to pay any price that Spain demanded. The price was high. France had to agree not only to continue the war until Spain obtained Gibraltar but also to participate in a joint invasion of England; Spain wanted to end the war in a single campaign before its huge but ill-defended colonial empire came under British attack. Louis XVI consented, and by the 12 April 1779 Convention of Aranjuez, Spain and France became allies. It should be noted that although the United States and Spain were both allied with France, they were not technically allies of each other. However, it would have been virtually impossible for the United States to establish its independence without the help Spain gave to the allied cause.[24]

The invasion attempt of 1779 was a far more massive naval operation than the successful Dutch invasion of 1688 or the prior French attempts of the eighteenth century. Its objectives, however, were far more limited. Neither France nor Spain wished to replace George III; indeed Vergennes worried about reducing Britain's place in the balance of power, as sooner or later he might have to call for its help in restraining Russia. Instead the Bourbons (France and Spain) wished to provoke a financial panic in London that would force Britain to make a compromise peace. Thus their campaign plans bore little resemblance to the invasion plans of 1744–45 or 1759 or even to the plans drawn up by the Secret du Roi. The French and Spaniards planned to land 20,000 troops on the Isle of Wight, where they could menace the great naval port of Portsmouth but would not have to alarm Europe by marching on London. To escort the troops, the allies assembled a fleet worthy of comparison with Tourville's great fleets of the 1690s, thirty-six Spanish and thirty French ships of the line. Even so great a fleet, however, was prone to the same obstacles that had foiled earlier invasion attempts—contrary winds, delays in assembling, and the spread of disease aboard crowded ships. Although the British had fewer than forty ships of the line and did not attack the allied fleet, the invasion attempt fell victim to delays and sickness. The transports did not sail, and their escort had to take refuge in Brest.[25]

After the failed attempt, France forced a reluctant Spain to change strategy by threatening to make it share the costs of another invasion. Although the threat of invasion continued to concern the British, the Spaniards shifted their focus to blockading Gibraltar while the French shifted forces to the West Indies. The British were outnumbered by the combined forces of France and Spain: sixty-three French and fifty-eight Spanish ships compared with ninety British on 1 July 1779; sixty-nine French and forty-eight Spanish against ninety-five British on 1 July 1780. The British found means of compensating for being outnumbered. In August 1778, an experienced but hitherto unremarkable captain named Charles Middleton was appointed comptroller of the navy, a key administrative position on the Navy Board involving supervision of the dockyards. Middleton quickly proved himself the most brilliant British naval administrator since Pepys. He pushed through a program to sheath the hulls of the navy's warships with copper plates so as to prevent the growth of marine organisms that slowed ships' speed. The copper plates also protected the hulls from the ravages of the Teredo navalis, a shipworm that devoured wood. Making use of Britain's plentiful domestic supply of copper, he sheathed all of Britain's ships between early 1779 and the end of 1781, even though it cost £1,500 (about 35,000 livres) to sheath each 74-gun ship. Because of insufficient research, the work was so flawed that it had to be redone after the war, but in the short run it was a great success. Short of money, rolled copper plates, and copper nails, France and Spain were slow to follow, giving British ships a significant advantage in speed as well as saving time in maintenance. British warships also gained an advantage in power, thanks to Middleton's other great innovation, the use of carronades, truncated cannon with a large bore that could fire very heavy cannonballs for close-in fighting. Nelson later would making a point of carrying aboard his ships carronades firing a 68-pound ball. The British also developed the gunlock, a mechanism for firing a cannon by pulling a short rope instead of using a slow burning match.[26]

The British, however, made poor use of their superior ships. By failing to concentrate their efforts in one theater of operations, the British found themselves outnumbered in all theaters. They began feeling the results of this almost as soon as the Spaniards entered the war. In the summer and autumn of 1779 Admiral d'Estaing captured the valuable Caribbean island of Grenada, fought off a British squadron, and then, returning to North America, attacked the isolated British garrison of Savannah. His attempt failed, but the British were so frightened that they evacuated the exposed garrison of Newport. D'Estaing thus accomplished from a distance what he had failed to do the year before. This indirect victory was very important because it would provide the French navy with a base near New York.

The riskiest part of the new French strategy was that it depended on the Spanish navy to help divert British forces. At the end of 1779 the British sent a large supply convoy, escorted by twenty-one ships of the line commanded by Rear Admiral Sir George Rodney, to replenish the blockaded fortress of Gibraltar. On 16 January 1780 Rodney's squadron surprised a squadron of eleven Spanish ships of the line blockading Gibraltar and captured or destroyed six of them. After replenishing Gibraltar, Rodney split his fleet, taking part of it to the West Indies and sending the rest back to England.

Rodney's victory almost knocked Spain out of the war, which would have doomed the French navy to eventual defeat and the United States to eventual financial and military collapse. It took a month for Charles III to decide to continue fighting. In late February 1780 he told the French he would send 8,000 to 10,000 troops and twelve to fourteen ships of the line to the West Indies. On the other hand, he rejected French plans for a joint cruise in British waters, electing to keep most of the Spanish fleet off Gibraltar. The French in turn decided to send 4,500 troops and seventeen ships of the line to Martinique. They also sent 5,500 troops and seven ships of the line to Newport, as George Washington finally had written to tell the marquis de Lafayette that a French expeditionary corps would be welcome in America; Lafayette passed the message to Vergennes.

The convoy for Martinique sailed in February 1780, the Spanish convoy in late April, and the convoy for Newport in early May. Britain now had its best opportunity to win the war; the capture of the Spanish convoy doubtless would have been decisive and the capture of either of the French convoys a major triumph. All three of the convoys arrived safely, however, the Spanish one first putting into Guadeloupe to evade Rodney's fleet. Thereafter Rodney fought three battles against the newly arrived French squadron, but none were decisive. Afterwards, the French squadron returned directly to Europe without stopping in North America. Sartine also sent a squadron of sixteen ships of the line to Cadiz to bolster the Spaniards. In August a combined fleet of thirty-three French and Spanish ships of the line captured off the Azores almost an entire British merchant convoy of sixty-seven ships from the Caribbean. On the other hand, the war in America seemed to be turning in favor of the British, who opened a new front by capturing the important port of Charleston, South Carolina.

Although the 1780 campaign was encouraging for France and Spain, the Bourbons had not yet won a decisive victory. The war was becoming one of attrition in which the British, able to borrow money at a lower interest rate, had a considerable advantage. Since the start of the naval rearmament program, France had spent more than 500 million livres on its navy and colonies. The king did not wish to anger the public by raising taxes as Louis XV had done during the previous war. Up to now he had borrowed sufficient money, thanks to the acumen and salesmanship of his finance minister, Jacques Necker. By late 1780, however, Necker turned against the war because of its expense. He largely was responsible for forcing Sartine from office in October 1780, because of Sartine's unauthorized spending on the war, although Sartine also was used as a scapegoat to placate the Spaniards and French public opinion. Necker then attempted to force his way onto the Council of State and to arrange a compromise peace. He failed and was driven from office, partly because of the opposition of Vergennes and Maurepas and partly because he was a Protestant. Although Vergennes and Maurepas were rid of one rival, they had to accept another, Sartine's successor as naval minister, the marquis de Castries, the general who had won the battle of Clostercamp twenty years earlier. The French monarchy's financial problems persisted for the rest of the war. By late 1782, Castries was begging Necker's successor for advances so he could pay his bills, while Vergennes admitted that France's financial means were exhausted.[27]

Already in the spring of 1781 Vergennes warned his ambassadors that France might be forced to abandon its commitment to the territorial integrity of the United States, although it would do so only in the last extremity. By now American currency was virtually worthless, and the American Continental Congress had become almost totally dependent on French financial assistance. Even American agriculture, deprived of outlets for its surpluses, was on the verge of collapse.[28] If the British army in North America and the British navy could continue to apply pressure, Britain might yet win the long war of attrition.

Unwisely, however, the British had initiated hostilities on 20 December 1780 against another enemy, the Dutch, fearing that otherwise the Dutch would join the League of Armed Neutrality, a coalition of neutral states with maritime interests organized by Catherine II of Russia. The British misjudged the situation of the

French dockyards, which generally were adequately supplied with timber, masts, hemp, and various other naval stores brought by neutral ships or sent along inland canals from the Netherlands to the Loire River. The British thereby needlessly added another enemy when the balance of forces already was against them; on 1 April 1781, ninety-four British ships of the line were opposed by seventy French, fifty-four Spanish, and fourteen Dutch.[29] By adding the North Sea as another theater of operations, the British put more pressure on their navy, which also repeatedly had to divert forces to replenish Gibraltar and Minorca. Even the half dozen ships sent to the North Sea in the early summer of 1781 were not insignificant when the fate of the war hinged on the number of ships each side could send to North America. The balance of forces was as even and the outcome as uncertain as during the 1940 aerial Battle of Britain.

In March 1781 a huge convoy of 156 merchant ships and transports escorted by twenty-six ships of the line and eight smaller warships sailed from Brest. It was not intercepted; a larger British fleet was off Ireland preparing for another replenishment mission to Gibraltar instead of watching Brest.

The merchant ships, transports, and warships had three separate destinations. Once clear of European waters, five of the ships of the line left the others and sailed for India with part of the convoy. After an indecisive battle with a British squadron encountered in the Cape Verde Islands, they landed troops to protect the Dutch colony at the Cape of Good Hope, forestalling a British attack. They then proceeded to the French Mascarene Islands (now Mauritius and Réunion) in the Indian Ocean where they joined six ships of the line already on station. Commanded by the brilliant and aggressive Chef d'escadre Pierre-André Suffren de Saint-Tropez, the

French squadron sailed for India on 7 December 1781. It fought five naval battles over the next year and a half, recaptured the Dutch port of Trincomalee (in what is now Sri Lanka) from the British, and covered the landing of a French expeditionary force in India. Its exploits largely went to waste. Like the British capture of Manila in the previous war, news of most of Suffren's exploits reached Europe only after peace already had been signed, although the peace treaty did restore Pondicherry and the other French trading posts captured by the British at the outbreak of war. Never again would the French send an expeditionary force to India. Suffren often is compared to the great English admiral Horatio Nelson; although he lacked Nelson's rapport with his captains, Suffren possessed a similar energy and like Nelson repeatedly took the offensive in battle.[30]

One ship of the line sailing from Brest in 1781 escorted a vital supply convoy to North America, eventually joining the French squadron at Newport. The remaining twenty ships of the line leaving Brest were commanded by Lieutenant General of the Fleet François-Joseph-Paul, comte de Grasse. They sailed to Martinique, captured Tobago, and then escorted a large European-bound convoy to St. Domingue, arriving in late July.

The British fleet in the West Indies still was commanded by Rodney. As soon as he learned of the British declaration of war against the Netherlands, he captured the island of St. Eustatius in the Dutch West Indies. St. Eustatius was the major smuggling post in the Caribbean, and it provided Rodney's fleet with £3 million (equivalent to 70 million French livres) worth of booty. This distraction helped de Grasse arrive safely at Martinique, and when Rodney sent the booty to England, most of it was captured by a French squadron commanded by Chef d'escadre Toussaint-Guillaume, comte Picquet de La Motte (better known as La Motte-Picquet), one of the boldest admirals in French history.

Naval Minister Castries had met at Brest with de Grasse just before he sailed. While traveling from Versailles to Brest, Castries by good fortune had encountered Lieutenant Colonel John Laurens, a young staff officer in Washington's army, who had come to France in search of money and military supplies.[31] Laurens's account of the woes of the Continental army doubtless was passed on to de Grasse, who proved very receptive to the calls for help from North America that later reached him in St. Domingue. Both General Rochambeau, commanding the French expeditionary corps at Newport, and the French minister in Philadelphia reported that the main British southern army was now in Virginia and suggested de Grasse sail promptly to Chesapeake Bay. Because of prior French commitments, Spain could have vetoed de Grasse's leaving the Caribbean. Luckily for the Americans, that decision was in the hands of the Spanish governor of Louisiana, Bernardo de Gálvez, who not only was one of the finest generals of the war but also a good friend to the United States. He had sent munitions up the Mississippi to the Americans and recently, with the help of a Spanish and French squadron, had captured the important British post of Pensacola. His representative at St. Domingue, Francisco Saavedra de Sangronis, agreed to de Grasse's sailing to the Chesapeake provided he returned to the Caribbean in November.[32] The people of Havana raised 1 million piastres (5 million livres) in a single day for paying Rochambeau's troops; de Grasse picked up the money en route to North America.

De Grasse brought twenty-eight ships of the line to Chesapeake Bay, leaving behind only one to escort the homeward bound convoy. He could do so because merchants did not have the same influence

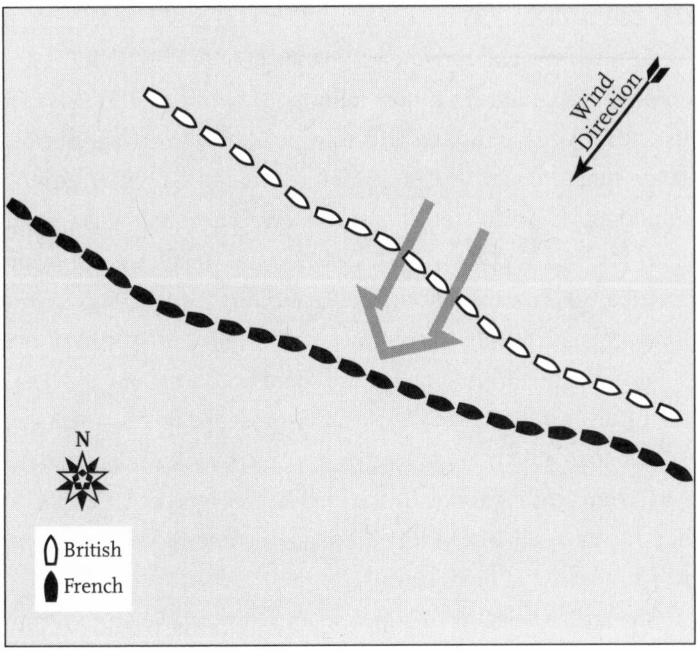

3. The Chesapeake, 5 September 1781

in France as they did in England. In contrast, Rodney, who returned to England, sent only fourteen of his twenty ships of the line to New York. They were under the command of his subordinate, Commodore Samuel Hood. Once arrived, Hood placed himself under the command of Commodore Thomas Graves, the station commander at New York. Graves sailed for Chesapeake Bay with twenty ships of the line, including one of 50 guns, to rescue Lieutenant General Charles Cornwallis, whose 6,000 troops were trapped at Yorktown by 16,000 French and American regulars and militia. As Graves approached the entrance to Chesapeake Bay on 5 September 1781, de Grasse sailed out to meet him with twenty-four ships of the line. Rather than attacking immediately, Graves waited until de Grasse formed his line. The subsequent battle was a tactical draw.

The British van and center engaged the French closely, but Hood, commanding the rear, rigidly followed Graves's signal to remain in line of battle, although Graves wished him to engage at close range, too. Although de Grasse captured no ships, he won the most important victory in French naval history. Graves and Hood had to return to New York for repairs. The Newport squadron meanwhile reached Chesapeake Bay with siege artillery for Washington and Rochambeau. While Graves was in New York, he received two ships of the line from Jamaica and three from England, too small a reinforcement to turn the tide; the presence of a Spanish and French fleet off the south coast of England had intimidated Sandwich from sending more. By the time Graves returned, Cornwallis had surrendered. The victory came just in time, as the allied army was almost out of food.[33]

The British defeat at Yorktown doomed the government of Prime Minister North, who resigned on 20 March 1782. It did not mean the war was over. The House of Commons voted to end offensive operations against the American colonies, but the new government of Charles Watson-Wentworth, Marquess of Rockingham, was committed to gaining from France and Spain recompense for their loss. By now the allied margin of superiority had grown, as seventy-three French, fifty-four Spanish, and nineteen Dutch ships of the line opposed ninety-five British.[34] The allied position had its weaknesses, however. One was the lack of enthusiasm in the United States for continuing the war to help its ally France, let alone Spain, whose invaluable help was not recognized; without continued American pressure on the British garrisons of New York, Charleston, and Savannah, the British would be able to shift at least some of these troops to the West Indies. Charles James Fox, the new secretary of state for foreign affairs, was prepared to buy peace with an immediate recognition of American independence, but Benjamin Franklin was too canny to accept the offer. He chose to work with the new secretary of state for home and colonial affairs, William Petty, Earl of Shelburne, in hopes of obtaining not only eventual recognition but also a generous territorial settlement. Another weakness was France's continuing financial problems. Vergennes, moreover, was very concerned about the danger of a general war in eastern Europe arising from a dispute between Russia and the Ottoman Empire over control of the Crimean peninsula. The most immediate problem, however, was the declining effectiveness of the French navy.

With British recognition of American independence now seemingly inevitable, France's major concern was satisfying the demands of Spain. Spanish and French troops captured Minorca in early 1782, but the British garrison of Gibraltar continued to survive the Spanish blockade. The only British possession worthy of exchange for Gibraltar was the rich sugar island of Jamaica. The months following Yorktown were a race to reinforce the Caribbean, the British to protect Jamaica, the French to acquire a naval force sufficient with Spanish help to protect a 20,000-man army to invade it. The French lost the race, largely because Castries tried simultaneously to prepare a major naval force for India. Only on 10 December 1781 did the West Indian convoy sail from Brest. By then the British were ready for it. A British squadron commanded by one of the navy's most talented officers, Rear Admiral Richard Kempenfelt, intercepted it off Isle d'Ushant, evaded its escort, and captured twenty merchant ships. A few weeks later the convoy encountered a severe Atlantic storm and still more ships put back. De Grasse, back in the Caribbean, received only two new ships of the line instead of six and only a small part of the supplies he needed. A new convoy and three more ships of the line did not reach de Grasse until 20 March 1782. In the interim Rodney returned to the Caribbean, bringing with him a sizeable reinforcement from England. When de Grasse sailed from Martinique on 8 April to rendezvous with a Spanish fleet at St. Domingue, he was outnumbered, thirty-seven ships of the line to thirty-six.

The quality of the French navy had declined as the number of its ships increased. It had too few officers to meet the demand, partly because of resistance from its aristocratic officer corps to expanding the use of auxiliary officers, who mostly were not of noble birth. Also it had difficulty in raising the unprecedented number of crewmen it needed.[35] De Grasse lost several ships in collisions caused by poor seamanship and had to detach other ships to escort the troop convoy accompanying him. On 12 April he fought Rodney off the Saintes, a group of small islands south of Guadeloupe. Rodney's fleet outnumbered his, thirty-six ships of the line to thirty. As the fleets passed closely in opposite directions, twenty British ships of the line passed through the French line of battle, probably by accident because of a shift of the wind, and the battle became a melee.[36] De Grasse's flagship and four other French ships of the line were captured. The remainder of the French fleet, now downwind of the British, escaped, but two French ships of the line that had not participated in the battle were taken a few days later. The rest of the French fleet proceeded to St. Domingue, but the invasion of Jamaica had to be postponed. The best ships of the French fleet now went to Boston for repair.

The French public responded to the news of the Saintes as it had to the news of Quiberon by pledging money to build replacements for the captured ships. They would not be ready in time to help the navy, which continued to suffer losses. During the first four years of

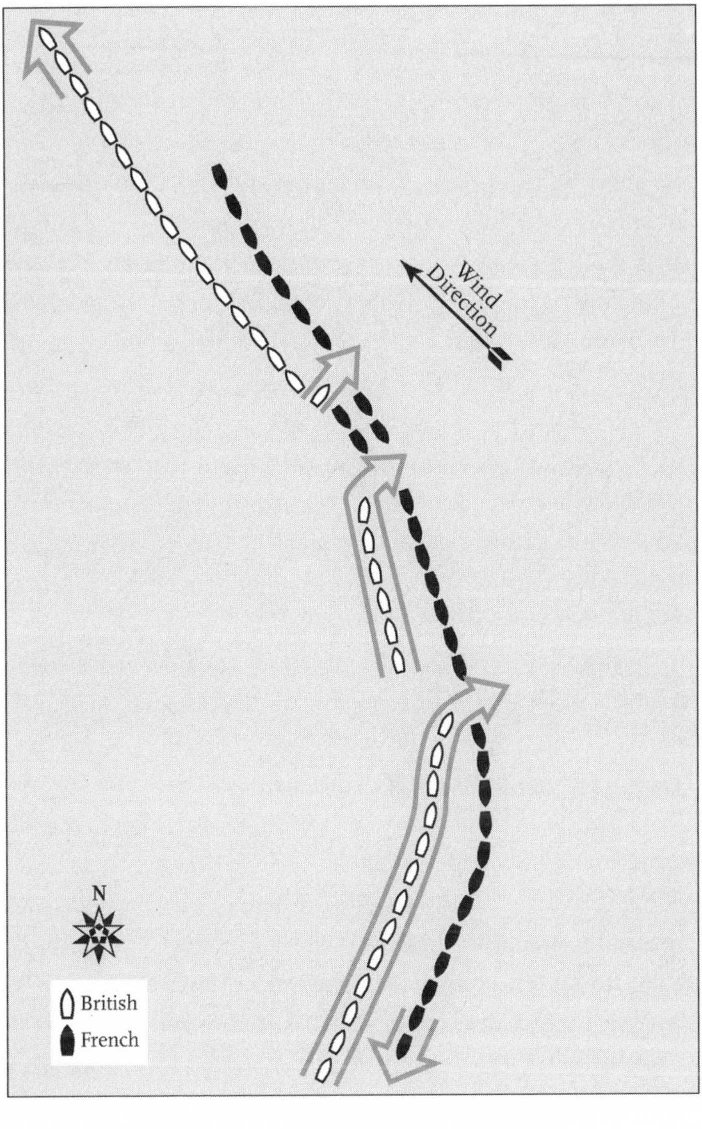

4. The Saintes, 12 April 1782

the war, the navy had lost only four ships of the line, three of them by accidents, whereas during 1782 it lost fifteen of the line from various causes.[37] The losses were significant in themselves, but were even more worrisome as a sign of the navy's declining effectiveness. In contrast the British raised their fleet to nearly 100 ships of the line by taking sailors off colliers, hitherto left untouched because of the importance of coal (which had to be brought by sea) to the British economy. Moreover, the British repulsed a direct Spanish attack on Gibraltar in September, inflicting heavy casualties, and then successfully sent a convoy to replenish the fortress. As the year came to an end, a huge fleet of French and Spanish warships prepared to take troops to the West Indies for another attempt to capture Jamaica, but the French Council of State was so pessimistic that d'Estaing, the fleet commander, was given secret orders to delay his departure as long as possible.

The fate of the French and Spanish navies now depended on the diplomats. Rockingham died on 1 July. His successor was Shelburne, who took control over all the negotiations. He quickly caved in to Franklin's demands, offering all the territory between the Appalachians and the Mississippi to the United States if it would make a separate peace. Soon thereafter he persuaded Vergennes to begin serious discussions by hinting that Britain would cooperate with France to restrain the Russians in the worsening Crimean crisis. By late November, a complicated series of territorial exchanges was arranged whereby Spain would obtain Gibraltar and France would obtain the peace it so desperately needed. On 30 November 1782, however, Franklin and three other American negotiators in Paris agreed to a separate peace on the conditions offered by Shelburne. In theory the agreement was conditional upon France making peace, too, but in the United States the agreement was first reported in the newspapers as meaning the end of the war. It destroyed the proposed agreement among Britain, France, and Spain. The British public would not tolerate the loss of Gibraltar as well as the loss of all of North America between Canada and Florida. Peace was saved by the courage of Pedro Pablo Abarca de Bolea, conde de Aranda, the Spanish ambassador at the French court, where the British negotiations with France and Spain were being held. On his own initiative he agreed to accept Minorca and Florida in lieu of Gibraltar. France had to settle for minor gains, chiefly Tobago, as well as the return of her trading posts in India and the island of St. Lucia. Although Britain lost all its colonies in North America south of Canada, its only other major loss was Minorca. It even gained a Dutch post in India as a result of the agreement forced on the Dutch by the other participants in the negotiations.[38] Although Britain's losses were a severe psychological blow, the damage to its economy and even to its diplomatic reputation in Europe proved surprisingly easy to repair. France, which on the surface appeared to be a victor because of the opening of American trade to all of Europe, did not fare as well.

6. Change and Continuity during the French Revolution

I

Shelburne's government, upon which Vergennes had placed such hope, did not long survive the peace. Although the House of Commons grudgingly accepted the terms it had negotiated, it forced Shelburne and his colleagues to resign. They were succeeded by a coalition government whose most powerful members were Lord North and the strongly anti-Bourbon Charles James Fox. Vergennes's hopes of weakening Britain also failed, as Britain quickly regained the major share of American trade. Vergennes now devoted his skills to preserving the map of Europe and to preventing another war. He persuaded the Turks to accept the loss of the Crimea to Russia as the price of avoiding war. Thereafter, with little help from Britain, he foiled Austrian plans to obtain Bavaria or to open the River Scheldt to shipping and thereby establish the Austrian Netherlands as a shipping center. Castries, his rival in the Council of State and an ardent colonialist, was eager for a war with Britain. Vergennes, anxious to defuse tensions with the British, was successful in negotiating a commercial treaty with Britain in 1786, but the treaty had mixed results economically and brought France no diplomatic benefits.[1]

Meanwhile Louis XVI faced a severe financial crisis. During

the American conflict, France for once did not have to pay for both a naval war and a land war in Europe. Even so, the war was enormously expensive for France as well as for Britain. French naval expenses, although less than Britain's, were more than 1 billion livres. Both the British and French governments, having fought three gigantic wars in the last half century, had accumulated enormous debts. The French had spent perhaps 3.5 billion livres and the British some £245 million (equivalent to about 5.75 billion livres) on these wars.[2] The British, however, paid only 3 to 4 percent interest to service their debt while France paid twice as much. The British also benefited from the wise administration of William Pitt the Younger, son of the secretary of state during the Seven Years' War, who became prime minister in 1784. Pitt set aside funds in the budget to service and retire the debt, while still spending generously on the navy. In contrast, Louis XVI had the bad judgment to adopt a program devised by his new finance minister, Charles-Alexandre de Calonne, to maintain the government's credit, that of pursuing a massive public works program in order to reassure its creditors.[3]

The French navy enjoyed some of the benefits, spending almost 30 million livres on an artificial harbor at Cherbourg and, like Britain and Spain, engaging in a substantial shipbuilding program, which continued even as the financial crisis worsened. During the ten years after the end of the war, France launched thirty-eight ships of the line, while Great Britain launched 44 and Spain 23. Not surprisingly, the result of French deficit spending was disaster. The government grew increasingly unable to meet interest payments on its debt, which by 1787 reached 5 million livres, more than twice what it had been in 1764.[4]

The French government's financial paralysis rendered it impotent in foreign affairs, as was revealed in 1787, when France was unable to protect its ally the Netherlands from invasion by a Prussian army. As a result the powers of the anti-French stadholder William V of Orange were restored, and the Netherlands, Prussia, and Great Britain became allies, ending Britain's diplomatic isolation. During the same year Austria and Russia went to war with the Ottoman Empire, which soon received help from Sweden. Although France's network of client states in eastern Europe was imperiled, France was unable to do anything to help and even halfheartedly considered joining in dismembering the Ottoman Empire; ultimately the Turks escaped with relatively minor losses, due largely to Austria's withdrawal from the war.[5]

Finally Louis XVI reluctantly agreed to summon the Estates-General, a nationwide assembly which had not met since 1614.[6] He took no steps, however, to manage the elections to the three estates of which it was to be composed, the first estate consisting of the clergy, the second of the nobility, and the third of the commoners, that is, those Frenchmen, however wealthy, who had not inherited or purchased titles of nobility. The king did not really settle the question of whether the Estates-General would function by majority rule or would require a consensus of all three estates. He permitted the third estate to elect some 600 members, while the other two elected about 300 apiece, but in effect he required decisions to be approved by all three estates. This attempt to split the difference between irreconcilable positions caused confusion. Soon after the three estates convened at the royal chateau of Versailles on 5 May 1789, they found themselves paralyzed by the ambiguity as to how decisions would be reached. The third estate and its supporters among the other two estates formed a majority of the delegates, but they had no way of imposing their will.

In mid-June the third estate proclaimed itself the National Assembly and vowed not to leave Versailles until the king recognized its legitimacy. Louis XVI summoned some 20,000 troops, who surrounded Paris, which was near Versailles and was the leading center of support for the third estate. It is likely he hoped to intimidate the Estates-General into accepting his proposal for a compromise that would leave the first two estates with veto power over matters concerning their privileges (or, if this failed, to rule without it). The people of Paris, however, began seizing weapons to defend the city. The garrison of the Bastille, a fortress and prison in which gunpowder and arms were kept, resisted. On 14 July 1789 about 100 people were killed before it was captured. The king now backed down and withdrew the troops from Paris. The National Assembly, which renamed itself the Constituent Assembly, began making laws and drafting a constitution.

Later that year the king and his family were forced to leave Versailles and take up residence in the Tuileries, a royal palace in Paris adjoining the Louvre. The king and queen did not accept this strange condition in which they were still treated as royalty but given only limited freedom of movement. In June 1791 the royal family attempted to flee to the French border with the Austrian Netherlands, where they hoped they could rally their supporters and restore the power of the monarchy. They even brought into their plot Marie-Antoinette's brother, Emperor Leopold II, who was both the Holy Roman Emperor and the archduke of Austria. Louis XIV and his mother had fled Paris in 1649 and later returned in success. Louis XVI, however, did not have a Mazarin to guide him. The royal family was apprehended near the border and brought back to Paris, where Louis and his wife were treated with even more suspicion than previously.[7]

Shortly thereafter the Constituent Assembly completed a constitution by which France became a limited monarchy like Great Britain, although with a unicameral legislature. Over the previous two years, it also had remodeled France's social, legal, religious, and financial institutions, which had not greatly changed since the reign of Louis XIV. Although the changes were creative and bold, they failed to resolve the underlying financial, social, and political problems that had caused the Revolution and had left France helpless to conduct foreign affairs and to protect French interests.

The Constituent Assembly created many enemies by attempting to establish the government's financial solvency. It instituted new taxes in 1790, but was unable to collect them. It also nationalized and sold the extensive lands owned by the Catholic Church in order to provide backing for a new type of government bond, the *assignat*. This soon became a form of currency and lost its value, much as had the currency of the United States a decade earlier. As the Assembly now had to assume the Church's role in providing social services, it nationalized the Catholic Church itself as an organ of the state. This led to a dispute with the Catholic hierarchy, caused a split within the clergy, alienated a substantial share of the French public, and destroyed any possibility that a king as religious and traditional as Louis XVI would accept a partnership with the Assembly.

Under great popular pressure, the Constituent Assembly also abolished the seigneurial or "feudal" dues that formed part of the income of the French nobility, causing many of them to actively oppose the Revolution.[8] Some noblemen attempted to foment counterrevolution, while others formed armed camps just across France's borders. These émigrés were led by the king's brothers, the comte d'Artois and the comte de Provence. The king and queen were unfairly suspected of directing the actions of the king's brothers;

although they shared the brothers' hatred of the Revolution, they were aghast at their imprudence.

The king pretended to acquiesce in the decisions of the Constituent Assembly while secretly regarding it as illegitimate. His attempted flight from Paris cost him most of the goodwill of the French people, but the Constituent Assembly was not prepared to look too deeply into his motives. After completing its work, it dissolved itself, and a permanent body, the Legislative Assembly, was elected.

II

Initially, other European rulers welcomed the Revolution because it crippled the French army and navy and left France a nullity in international affairs. Most of the army's officer corps and virtually all of the navy's officer corps were noblemen, and as the Revolution became increasingly radical, many emigrated. The problem, particularly in the navy, was as much professional as social. Distrusted by the crews of their ships, many officers chose flight over the humiliation of being unable to inspire or compel obedience. The problem was compounded by the breakdown of central authority over local municipalities. The problem was particularly acute in Toulon, the second most important naval port in France, where local authorities challenged the navy's control over the dockyard. Eventually this even led to the murder of the naval commandant by a mob.[9]

Not surprisingly the monarchy had great difficulty in finding and keeping naval ministers, since they too were unable to effectively exercise their authority. The veteran Castries had spent the postwar period planning a war of revenge against Britain that Vergennes did not support. Castries resigned during the Dutch crisis of 1787 to protest French passivity and the monarchy's attempts to limit the naval budget. His successor, César-Henri de La Luzerne, a colonial administrator and brother of the second French minister to the United States, served until October 1790, when he was replaced by Charles-Pierre Claret, comte de Fleurieu, the brilliant collaborator of Sartine during the American war. Fleurieu served only six months before being denounced by his subordinates. During the remaining fourteen months of the monarchy there were four other short-term naval ministers: Antoine-Jean-Marie Thévenard, the capable former port commandant of Lorient, Antoine-François, comte de Bertrand de Molleville, a former government official, Jean, baron de Lacoste, a former commissioner in Martinique, and François-Joseph de Gratet, vicomte du Bouchage, a former artillery officer.[10]

With the army and navy crippled by internal division, lack of support from the central government, and inadequate financing, it is not surprising that France continued to be humiliated by other nations. In 1790 Spain and Britain became involved in a dispute resembling the Falkland Islands crisis of twenty years earlier, this time the seizure of several British ships in Nootka Sound, a body of water to the north of Spanish California. Again Spain was forced to back down because France was unable to help. While British and Spanish fleets of more than thirty ships of the line each were at sea (as well as ten Dutch ships of the line in support of the British), France was unable to find crews to outfit a fleet of fifteen ships of the line. Bereft of French assistance, the Spaniards had to give in to the British.[11]

The newly elected Legislative Assembly convened on 1 October 1791. Although most delegates were moderate by inclination, they were inexperienced, because former members of the Constituent Assembly had not been eligible for election. They also faced a situation not conducive to moderation. Religious and political dissidents both within France and just outside its borders threatened to overthrow the assembly by force. France was still ruled by a king whom few trusted. Emperor Leopold II made the situation worse by issuing a joint declaration with Frederick William II of Prussia inviting the other powers of Europe to restore Louis XVI's powers. Actually the declaration was a face-saving gesture with no prospect of immediate action; Leopold was more concerned with ending his war with the Turks and with overcoming political dissension in the Austrian Netherlands than he was with the fate of a sister whom he had not seen for twenty-five years. He also considered the émigrés an annoyance and did not wish for war with France. Unfortunately, by attempting to intimidate the Legislative Assembly, he instead assisted the demagogues within the Assembly. Many of them belonged to a faction usually called the Girondins because some of its leaders came from the department of the Gironde, centered around Bordeaux. They also were called the Brissotins because their chief spokesman was a former writer named Jacques-Pierre Brissot.[12]

Some legitimate diplomatic issues had been raised by French conduct, particularly the Constituent Assembly's violation of international law in annexing the papal enclaves of Avignon and the Comtat Venaissin, which lay within France and were themselves in a virtual state of civil war. Nonetheless war might have been averted were it not for the Girondins, who hoped that war would force the king's hostility toward the Legislative Assembly into the open. Leopold played into their hands by responding to threats with threats of his own. War was declared on 20 April 1792, soon after Leopold's unexpected death, possibly from pneumonia. He was succeeded by his son Francis, who was violently hostile to the French Revolution.[13]

Even had the Girondins been less rash, it would have been a challenge to avoid war, particularly after the death of the cautious and peaceable Leopold. France appeared weak and hence was vulnerable; it was safe only as long as the attention of Austria, Prussia, and Russia was fixed on the even more vulnerable Poland and Ottoman Empire. War proved riskier than the Girondins anticipated, largely because France was unable to restrict it to fighting only Austria. They were all too successful, however, in destabilizing the French monarchy. Not only did Louis XVI secretly hope for an Austrian victory, but his wife smuggled French war plans to her brother. Louis's position became weaker and weaker, but in the process the Revolution also came under terrible threat. Contrary to the Girondins' expectations, Prussia, the traditional enemy of Austria, joined the fight against France. In fact the Prussians provided more than half of the 80,000 Austrian, Prussian, and émigré troops that invaded eastern France in mid-August 1792 and threatened to destroy Paris if the French royal family was harmed. Meanwhile 30,000 Austrians and émigrés operating from the Austrian Netherlands besieged Lille.

The invasion of France doomed Louis XVI and Marie-Antoinette. On 10 August 1792 an armed body of radicals seized the Tuileries and arrested the royal family. The Legislative Assembly called elections for a new executive and legislative body, the National Convention, which on 22 September declared France a republic. The army that had invaded France failed to rescue the royal family. Its commander was Duke Ferdinand of Brunswick, who thirty-two years earlier had lost the Battle of Clostercamp to Castries (now a leader of the émigrés). Having become cautious in his old age and with his army plagued by logistical difficulties, Ferdinand advanced so slowly toward Paris that the French army was able to gather enough troops to stop him. On 20 September Ferdinand's army was unable to dislodge the French from their defensive position at Valmy, 100 miles east of Paris. Ferdinand soon had to retreat, leaving the small Austrian army in the Austrian Netherlands so isolated that in November a far larger French army defeated it. The French then quickly overran the virtually undefended Austrian Netherlands. Imprudently the Convention, led by the Girondins, now threatened the neighboring Dutch Netherlands and declared the Scheldt River open to shipping, even though its mouth was in Dutch territory.

Until now the British government had observed a strict neutrality. Quickly it changed its policy. The Dutch were British allies, and the Austrian Netherlands was a potential launching place for a French invasion of England. Within barely two months British relations with France deteriorated into war. The Convention executed Louis XVI on 21 January 1793. Eleven days later France declared war on both Great Britain and the United Provinces of the Netherlands.[14] Soon a number of other states joined the coalition of France's enemies, including Spain, whose navy included seventy-six ships of the line.

III

Thus far the French navy had shared in little of the new republic's military glory. Until the outbreak of the Austrian war, its chief responsibility had been convoying reinforcements to the French West Indies where white planters rebelled against the Constituent Assembly's 15 May 1791 decision to enfranchise *gens de couleur* (mulattos) born of free parents. (This rebellion was followed in St. Domingue by separate uprisings of mulattos and slaves.) The outbreak of war in Europe gave the navy new responsibilities. In September 1792 the Kingdom of Sardinia joined the alliance of

Austria and Prussia. The French navy supported operations not only against the island of Sardinia but also against Piedmont, one of the two portions of the kingdom on the Italian mainland; the other portion of the kingdom, Savoy, which was on the French side of the Alps, welcomed the French army.

On 24 September the French captured Nice with the help of five ships of the line from Toulon commanded by Rear Admiral Laurent-Jean-François Truguet. Soon ten ships of the line from Brest and Rochefort arrived as reinforcements. Truguet had enough ships not only to support military operations along the Italian Riviera but also to send a squadron under Captain Louis-René-Madeleine Le Vassor, comte de La Touche-Tréville, to Naples. La Touche-Tréville threatened to bombard the city if it opposed France, much as Commodore William Martin had threatened Naples in 1742. This intimidation was successful for the moment, as none of the other states of Italy came to the assistance of Sardinia. A French attempt to invade the island of Sardinia in January 1793, however, revealed the deficiencies of both the French army and the French navy. The untrained invading troops were defeated, and the French navy lost two ships of the line to accidents. Another French ship of the line serving in the Caribbean surrendered itself to Spain rather than serve the French republic.[15] When Great Britain, the Netherlands, and Spain joined France's enemies, the French navy faced insurmountable difficulties.

The most immediate problem faced by the French navy in 1793 was a shortage of officers. This remained a serious problem throughout the ensuing war. In contrast, the newly promoted officers of the French army, even at the highest level, eventually proved superior to those of the Old Régime (prerevolutionary) army. The army of 1789 was clogged with officers whose high rank was based solely on birth or seniority, but it also had a large supply of experienced nonaristocratic junior officers and noncommissioned officers. The Revolution cleared away the deadwood, albeit often brutally, leaving a path for the young and talented.[16] It appeared the same thing might happen in the French navy. On 15 March 1792 the navy conducted a survey to see how many naval officers were still willing to serve. The results were more positive among junior officers, whose career paths had been blocked by the fact that the navy was a gerontocracy. (Promotion usually had been by seniority in order to prevent officers from claiming a right to promotion because of superior birth, that is, of higher or more ancient noble title.) While the responses of admirals were overwhelmingly negative, 65 of the 180 captains responding, 362 of the 800 lieutenants, and 175 of the 200 ensigns indicated their availability.[17] The subsequent overthrow of the monarchy and execution of Louis XVI, however, drove away most of the favorably disposed officers.

The French navy did not recover from their loss. Unlike the army, it had few officers who were not of noble birth. This largely was an eighteenth-century development. Louis XIV's navy initially had many nonaristocratic officers, although few rose above the rank of captain. In his successors' navy, however, limited opportunities were open to "blues" (auxiliary officers were called this because the breeches of their uniforms were blue instead of red), who were mostly former merchant ship and privateer captains, including a few of noble birth. In 1782, for example, noble officers petitioned against increasing the number of auxiliary officers aboard warships, in spite of the chronic shortage of junior officers. Thus during the French Revolution the navy had to make do with a very mixed group of captains, which included a few nobles such as the gifted La Touche-Tréville, some former "blue" officers, some former privateer captains, and some merchant ship captains whose experience did not include joint maneuvering with other captains.[18]

Even with the best of officers, however, the navy would have stood little chance against the large and well-manned British navy. It faced many other obstacles including shortages of supplies, funds, and trained sailors. On paper the French navy on 1 February 1793 contained seventy-two ships of the line, including eight that soon were ordered to be reduced to large frigates. The British had 125 ships of the line of 64 to 100 cannon, plus 17 ships of 50 cannon. The French navy could put in service only about 40 ships of the line during the opening campaign against Britain, as for several years it had neglected repairs to its ships and the purchase of wood, copper, and other supplies for its dockyards. Cannon were in particularly short supply, as were copper nails. Although the British navy began 1793 with only thirty-three ships of the line (including seven 50's) in service, by the end of the year it had at least 88 (including seven 50's) in commission.[19]

Half of the French ships served in the Atlantic. The British could easily have destroyed them given the inexperience of their officers and crews, but Admiral Richard Howe took five months to outfit the main British fleet and then failed to intercept the fleet of Vice Admiral Justin-Bonaventure Morard de Galles, which in the summer of 1793 cruised off the south coast of Brittany.[20] Much of Brittany and the region to its south, particularly the area around the department of the Vendee, were in rebellion against the Convention because of its religious policies and its conscription for the army. The British were hopelessly slow in establishing contact with the rebels, while the untrained rebel armies failed to capture a port through which the British could send troops or supplies.

Pitt, Home Secretary Henry Dundas, and Foreign Secretary

William Grenville, the three men chiefly responsible for British strategy, sent most of the British, Hanoverian, and Hessian troops at their disposal in 1793 to the Austrian Netherlands. They even diverted some troops intended for an expedition against the French West Indies that was Dundas's chief priority. The troops in the Austrian Netherlands were commanded by the king's favorite son, the Duke of York, much as George II's favorite son, the Duke of Cumberland, had commanded the Hanoverian Army of Observation in 1757, an ominous parallel.[21] By mid-August 1793 his 6,000 British and 22,000 German troops, along with 15,000 Dutch and 90,000 Austrian troops, had recaptured the Austrian Netherlands and had made major progress in breaking through the chain of fortresses protecting the Paris region. A Prussian army and another Austrian army threatened the northeast portion of French defenses near the Rhine, Italian and Austrian troops threatened southeastern France, and Spanish troops advanced in the Pyrenees. France's enemies, however, still saw the French Revolution as an opportunity to be exploited rather than as a threat to be eliminated; they were more concerned with grabbing territory than with overthrowing the Convention, which faced almost as great a threat from domestic rivals as from foreign invaders. In addition to the full-scale revolt in the Vendee region and Brittany, several major cities, such as Caen, Lyons, Bordeaux, Marseilles, and later Toulon, refused to obey the orders of the Convention. This so-called Federalist revolt coincided with a shift of power in the Convention on 2 June 1793, when a faction known as the Montagnards (or "The Mountain," based on the lofty location of their seats in the Convention) expelled Brissot and the other Girondins and adopted much of the economic and political program of the radicals who dominated Paris.

Like the Continental Congress during the American Revolution, the Convention conducted much of its work in committees. By the late autumn of 1793, the Montagnard-dominated Convention had delegated responsibility for directing the war to the twelve members of the Committee of Public Safety. This was an extremely heterogeneous group ranging from the moderate and humane Robert Lindet to the sociopathic Jean-Nicolas Billaud-Varenne and Jean-Marie Collot d'Herbois. Among its members was a brilliant army engineer, Lazare Carnot, who largely took charge of expanding the army and organizing the production of war materiel. Eventually, a radical former lawyer named Maximilien Robespierre became the most influential member of both the Committee of Public Safety and the Convention.[22]

The Committee of Public Safety found itself in the position of Frederick II of Prussia during the Seven Years' War, who also had to deal with enemies pressing him from virtually every direction. France was saved in 1793 as Prussia had been in 1757 by firm control over its generals (the guillotine being even more frightening than the wrath of Frederick the Great, although not by much), by interior lines, and by the mutual suspicion and lack of cooperation among its enemies. The Austrians and Prussians of 1793 were even more suspicious of each other than the Austrians and Russians had been thirty-five years earlier. The British pursued their own agenda, departing from the main Austrian force in mid-August to attack Dunkirk. When the Prussians halted their offensive in eastern France in order to prepare for an invasion of Poland, the French were able to save Dunkirk and then to bring the Austrian offensive in northwestern France to a halt. French armies recaptured the Vendee area and crushed the Federalist revolt; in the region of the Vendee alone probably more than 200,000 people were killed, many of them after being captured or arrested.[23]

After capturing Marseilles on 25 August 1793, an army loyal to the Convention began advancing on Toulon, which had joined the Federalist revolt. Off the port of Toulon was the British Mediterranean fleet of twenty-one ships of the line commanded by Vice Admiral Samuel Hood, the same officer who had played an important part in the 1781 and 1782 campaigns in North America and the Caribbean. The city officials of Toulon feared they would be killed if the city was captured by the approaching French army. They invited Hood's Mediterranean fleet into the roadstead; during the negotiations Hood was joined by a fleet of seventeen Spanish ships of the line. The French fleet of seventeen ships of the line, paralyzed by indecision, did not resist. (Another ten French ships of the line were in port without crews.) Hood disarmed the French fleet and took possession of it and of the city in trust for Louis XVI's imprisoned young son. He was unable, however, to adequately defend the city, which was surrounded by hills, thereby necessitating lengthy defense lines and a large army to man them. A considerable detachment of Spanish soldiers was used to help defend the city, but they were unenthusiastic about helping the British, particularly since Hood refused to give Spain any of the captured French ships. Some troops from Naples and Sardinia also served, but few British reinforcements arrived because of the competing demands of the Austrian Netherlands and the Caribbean upon the British army and the limited number of troop transports. The Austrians failed to send help until it was too late. On 19 December the French recaptured the city. The British destroyed wood for construction and other naval supplies. They burned nine ships of the line and took away another four, but ten escaped the flames, mostly because of Spanish reluctance to carry out their share of the destruction. An additional four ships of the line already had been sent by Hood to

Brest, Rochefort, and Lorient with prisoners; some 7,500 inhabitants of Toulon escaped with the fleeing British.[24]

The Committee of Public Safety responded to the naval setbacks of 1793 with the same energy it brought to the creation of an enlarged and reinvigorated French army. It sent commissioners to the various ports to stimulate naval construction and repair. The most important of these was André Jeanbon Saint-André, a former officer in the merchant marine and now a member of the Committee of Public Safety. He was not an expert on naval matters, and he made some serious mistakes, particularly on 30 January 1794 when he dismantled the corps of naval artillerymen; for the next twenty years most French warships would fire their cannon slowly and inaccurately. On the other hand he had enormous energy and integrity and considerable common sense, particularly in the choice of admirals and ship captains for the French fleet. The former commander, Morard de Galles, was well motivated but ineffective; his crews had rebelled, forcing the fleet to return to Brest. Army commanders were sent to the guillotine for less, but Jeanbon Saint-andré at least recognized his loyalty, and his life was spared. He was replaced as fleet commander, though, by the sternest disciplinarian in the fleet, Louis-Thomas Villaret de Joyeuse, a former comte. Like Morard de Galles, Villaret de Joyeuse had commanded a ship in the squadron of the demanding Suffren; Jeanbon Saint-André was wise enough to value his experience and ability in spite of his noble birth.

By enormous efforts Jeanbon Saint-andré replaced the losses of 1793. By the middle of May 1794, some fifty ships of the line were in service or about to enter service, including seven at Toulon, whereas the British had eighty-six of the line and six 50-gun ships in service, including seventeen ships of the line in the Mediterranean

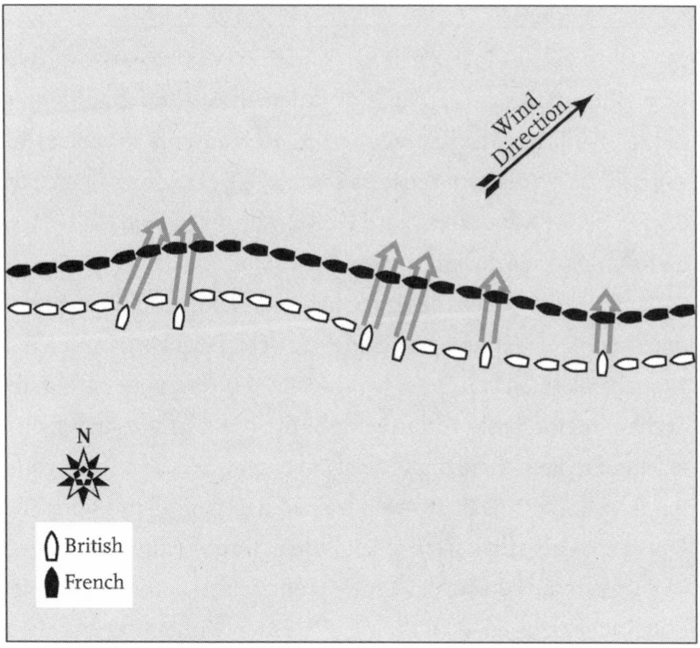

5. The Glorious First of June, 1 June 1794

or at Gibraltar. The officers and crews of the French fleet, however, generally were untrained, and many of the ships were not in good repair.[25]

There was no time for training. At the end of 1793 two ships of the line under a capable commander, Rear Admiral Pierre-Jean Vanstabel, had been sent to Chesapeake Bay to escort ships carrying grain purchased for France, much as the great French sailor Jean Bart had been sent in 1693 to Norway to bring a grain convoy to a famine-stricken France. On 10 April 1794 Vanstabel began his return to France with a huge convoy of more than 100 merchant ships. Somehow they had to be brought safely through the British blockade. Abandoning plans to invade the British Channel Islands, the French navy made saving the convoy its chief priority. On 16

May 1794 Villaret-Joyeuse sailed from Brest with twenty-five ships of the line. After several days of skirmishing, he fought a great battle on 1 June. Having received reinforcements to replace his initial losses, Villaret-Joyeuse had twenty-six of the line against the twenty-five of Admiral Richard Howe, who, like Hood, had played a prominent role during the American war.

Howe's tactics were designed to take advantage of the inexperience and poor gunnery of the French fleet. Attacking from windward, he planned to have all his ships pass through the gaps in the French line of battle and then fight from leeward or downwind, leaving the French no opportunity of escape. He, of course, could not have done so against a well-trained fleet sailing in a tight line. Only six of his ships were able to break through the French line. The British captured or sank nine French ships of the line, but the remainder escaped, including half a dozen without serious damage. The aged Howe, physically exhausted and satisfied with his victory, failed to pursue the survivors.

A few days later, Vanstabel and his great convoy reached Brest safely. It is unclear how much grain reached Paris, but its psychological effects were important. The arrival of the grain from America as well as French victories in the Austrian Netherlands promised the alleviation of the grain shortage and hence undercut the financial basis of hoarding. The convoy's arrival and the courage shown by Villaret-Joyeuse's sailors made the Battle of the First of June almost as glorious for the French as it was for the British.[26]

IV

The great naval battle coincided with turning points in the fortunes of war elsewhere. Until recently the campaign of 1794 had gone well for Britain. The British invaded Corsica, captured the port of

Bastia, and in June began the siege of Calvi on the west coast, the last French strongpoint. A force of 6,000 troops and five ships of the line captured Martinique in March. The British then seized Guadeloupe and the rest of the French West Indies except for a portion of St. Domingue. The war in the Austrian Netherlands was still in doubt, but agreement had been reached to subsidize a Prussian contingent to join the Austrians, Dutch, British, and Britain's hired German troops.

On 2 June 1794 the tide turned in the West Indies. On that day some 1,000 French troops landed at Pointe-à-Pitre, Guadeloupe. They came from Rochefort on a tiny fleet of two frigates, a corvette, and six transports. Their arrival caught the British by surprise, and when a counterattack failed, the British were forced to evacuate Grande-Terre, the less mountainous eastern half of the island.[27] Most of the French troops soon perished from tropical diseases, but their commander, Victor Hugues, informed the slaves of Guadeloupe that the Convention had abolished slavery (by unanimous vote on 4 February 1794) and armed them. Not only did his troops recapture all of Guadeloupe but, after the arrival of 2,000 reinforcements aboard a convoy of fifteen ships in January 1795, they took the neighboring island of St. Lucia and invaded the islands of St. Vincent and Grenada. The British had to send nearly 20,000 men to the Caribbean in 1796. They recaptured St. Lucia, St. Vincent, and Grenada, but more than half the British troops died from disease.

The British, furthermore, were not strong enough to attack Guadeloupe, which remained a major privateering center for the remainder of the war.[28] Hugues, the French commander, was cruel and greedy, but those who portray the British as heroes and the French as villains can do so only by ignoring the fact that the French, however self-interested were their motives, fought to abolish slavery while the British, in spite of Prime Minister Pitt's personal feelings, fought to reestablish it. British conduct in Europe was also less than exemplary. In spite of their reservations, they aided the attempts of Prussia, Austria, Spain, Sardinia, and the émigrés to re-impose on France the seigneurial system, under which great social, political, and economic privileges were conferred on those fortunate enough to be of noble birth.

On the northern border of France, the efforts of France's enemies seemed close to success in early 1794, but here as well the tide soon turned, largely because of continuing conflicts among France's enemies. Prussia and Russia had partitioned Poland in 1793, taking even more Polish land than in the earlier partition of 1772. A Polish uprising in 1794 again caused Prussia to divert troops from the attack on France. The British and Austrian advance was checked at the 17–18 May Battle of Tourcoing. Emperor Francis II had been accompanying the Austrian army. He now departed, along with the Austrian chief of staff, fearing that Prussia and Russia would further partition Poland without Austria gaining a share. On 26 June the advancing French army defeated the Austrians at the Battle of Fleurus. The beaten Austrian army, uncooperative Dutch army, and demoralized British army began a retreat that did not end until France had conquered both the Austrian Netherlands and the United Provinces of the Netherlands. In 1795 the British expeditionary corps was evacuated from the continent via Bremen, and Hanover dropped out of the war. Not until 1799 would a major British army return to the continent.

Even the British navy's performance in 1794 was not all it should have been. Howe, in poor health, failed to follow up his 1 June victory by blockading Brest closely. His fleet remained in port for almost all of the second half of the year. Although Howe was not permitted to resign his command, his second-in-command, Sir Alexander Hood, Lord Bridport, became de facto commander of the Channel fleet. Although Bridport was the brother of the great Samuel Hood, he was little more energetic than Howe. The main change was to the central direction of the navy. First Lord of the Admiralty John Pitt, Lord Chatham, William Pitt's older brother, was a lightweight who had lost the respect of the navy and his fellow cabinet ministers. At the end of 1794, he was given another cabinet post and replaced by Lord George John Spencer, who was intelligent and well-meaning but inexperienced in naval matters. His authority was challenged by the navy's best admiral, Samuel Hood, and by the most competent naval officer on the Board of Admiralty, Admiral Charles Middleton. Spencer won, but both Hood and Middleton were lost to the navy, although the gifted Middleton returned in 1805 as first lord of the admiralty.[29]

The French navy was too damaged by the battle of 1 June to take real advantage of its rival's problems. Its protection of the grain convoy and role in the recovery of Guadeloupe were its last enduring accomplishments. After June 1794 it met with repeated defeats and humiliations. By fighting the British navy before being adequately prepared, the French navy began a vicious circle that lasted until 1815. Repeatedly it was assigned missions beyond the capabilities of its inadequately repaired and undermanned ships. With each failure the situation worsened, as the navy faced insurmountable difficulties in finding crews, materiel, and money. Unlike the army, it could not exist on the plunder gained during successful foreign campaigns, even though it did gain some supplies and money by capturing merchant ships.

This pattern was shown following the 1 June 1794 battle. On 5

June 1794 Rear Admiral Pierre Martin, the new commander of the Mediterranean fleet, sailed from Toulon with four ships of the line for a cruise along the coast. Samuel Hood almost intercepted him with thirteen ships of the line, but Martin found a protected anchorage near Nice where he could not be attacked. He was blockaded until November, when he returned safely to Toulon.

In December the Convention attempted to send a reinforcement of six ships of the line from Brest to Toulon, using thirty ships of the line of Villaret-Joyeuse's fleet to escort them. The Convention ignored the poor condition of the fleet, which was still not fully repaired from its June battle, its lack of trained sailors, and the dangers of naval operations in the Atlantic during December. On his first attempt to sail, 24 December 1794, Villaret-Joyeuse saw one of his largest ships, the *Républicain* (*ex-Royal Louis*), 110, shipwrecked. A week later he was able to sail. Before he returned in early February 1795, he lost three more ships of the line, although he captured more than 100 prizes. The departure of the squadron for Toulon was postponed; it finally sailed on 22 February and arrived safely on 4 April. The British, it should be noted, also disregarded the dangers of winter sailing; convoys for the West Indies suffered severe damage from storms in November 1794 and again in November and December 1795.

Before the reinforcements arrived from the Atlantic, Martin sailed from Toulon with his fifteen ships of the line to take troops to Corsica. He captured a British ship of the line, but near Genoa he encountered the British Mediterranean fleet of fourteen ships of the line. Fortunately for him, Samuel Hood, who was on leave in England, had been replaced by the cautious Vice Admiral William Hotham, who satisfied himself with driving Martin back to the French coast, capturing two ships of the line. After being reinforced by the ships from Brest, Martin sailed again on 7 June 1795, this time with seventeen ships of the line. He again encountered Hotham, now with twenty-three ships of the line, and was chased back to Toulon, losing another ship of the line.

By now Villaret-Joyeuse was back in action. Sailing on 12 June 1795 with nine ships of the line to rescue three ships of the line being blockaded near the island of Belle-Isle, he encountered a squadron of five British ships of the line commanded by Vice Admiral William Cornwallis, who was able to fight off the French and escape. A week later Villaret-Joyeuse failed to capture a British squadron escorting a landing force of French Royalists toward the French coast. He then encountered fourteen British ships of the line under Bridport coming to the rescue of the threatened troop convoy. They chased him into Lorient after capturing three French ships of the line. The Royalists landed on a peninsula on the eastern side of Quiberon Bay, where they eventually were trapped and destroyed by a gifted young French general, Lazare Hoche. The British-sponsored invasion was ill-conceived, its commanders were incompetent, and the attempt deepened French hatred of the British and lessened the chance of any compromise peace.[30]

Because of the shortage of crews, it took a year for the French squadron at Lorient to return to Brest, using the same sailors to man several small squadrons sequentially, much as the squadron trapped in the Vilaine River had returned to Brest thirty-five years earlier. After his defeat, Villaret-Joyeuse offered his resignation, but the Convention refused it. Nevertheless the disasters of the last year caused it to rethink its strategy. The French navy had seventy-five ships of the line at the beginning of the war with Austria. By the end of the summer of 1795, it had lost or converted to other uses thirty-seven, as well as losing three of the dozen it had launched in the interim. In contrast, the British navy lost only three ships of the line between early 1793 and August 1795, although it disposed of or converted another twenty. Even though the British navy launched or captured only a dozen ships of the line during the period, it still had some 130 on its books. Only thirty of the remaining French ships of the line were still in service, whereas the British had 105 ships of the line and seventeen ships of 50–56 guns in service at the end of 1795.[31] All that saved the French navy from virtual annihilation was the cautiousness of admirals like Bridport and Hotham. Without sailors, supplies, or money, it could not hope to defeat the British in battle.

In the interim the political situation in France had changed. The dominance of Robespierre and his allies in the Convention and Committee of Public Safety had produced a wave of executions. In his paranoia Robespierre came to equate his political rivals with enemies of France. Fearful for their lives, moderates in the Convention initiated their own coup during Thermidor, one of the months in the Revolutionary calendar. On 28 July 1794 Robespierre and his closest allies were guillotined. With the Convention safely in their hands, the moderates ended Robespierre's "Terror," greatly reducing the use of the guillotine. The Convention also drafted a new constitution, which came into effect on 27 October 1795, at which time the Convention was dissolved. It was replaced by a two-chamber elected legislature, the Council of Five Hundred and the Council of Elders, and a rotating chief executive of five members called the Directory.[32] The Constitution of 1791 had prohibited members of the Constituent Assembly from standing for election; the new constitution required that in the first election two-thirds of the members of new councils be chosen from among members of the Convention. This virtually guaranteed the continuation, at least initially, of the Convention's social, military, and diplomatic policies.

V

During their three-year existence, the Convention and the Committee of Public Safety had dictated naval policy to three naval ministers: the mathematician Gaspard Monge (August 1792–April 1793), the former privateer captain Jean Dalbarade (April 1793–July 1795), and the port official Jean-Claude, comte de Redon de Beaupréau (July–October 1795; however, he no longer used his title of comte). These men had been mere figureheads. Henceforth naval ministers, although subordinate to the Directory, possessed some authority over French ports and fleets. The Directory's first naval minister was Vice Admiral Truguet, who had performed poorly as commander of the Mediterranean fleet in 1792 and early 1793, but who was tactful and polished.

As had happened frequently in past wars, the Directory demobilized the navy, except for a few small squadrons, mostly used to raid British commerce. The largest of these, a half dozen ships of the line commanded by Rear Admiral Joseph de Richery, sailed from Toulon for North America just before the Directory took office. Soon after entering the Atlantic, it captured almost an entire 30-ship convoy, which it took to Cadiz, where it was blockaded by the British. A smaller squadron sailed from Toulon to the eastern Mediterranean, where it, too, took numerous prizes. This was making the best of a bad situation, although in general the war on British trade had only a minor impact.[33]

The navy also continued to support France's West Indian colonies, successfully sending two small squadrons to St. Domingue and one to the Indian Ocean in 1796. Although its reduced role had little glamour, it at least shielded the navy from further humiliation.

Meanwhile the great coalition that had opposed France disintegrated. At the end of 1794 the Netherlands was captured by the French army, and soon it became a French puppet state, the Batavian Republic. Frederick William II of Prussia, whose only interest was the aggrandizement of his state, signed an interim peace with France in April 1795 and soon turned all of northern Germany into a Prussian-dominated neutral zone. In response Austria signed a formal military alliance with Great Britain in May. During the same month, however, the Batavian Republic agreed to an offensive and defensive alliance with France. This added the North Sea as an area of concern to the British. The Dutch navy contained twenty-eight ships of the line, although most of them were small and not all of them were usable; the Dutch agreed to furnish a dozen of them to France. In the short run, though, Britain profited from the Dutch switch of alliances. With the exiled stadholder's approval, it occupied (although not without opposition) the Cape of Good Hope, Ceylon, and other Dutch colonies in the Caribbean and the Far East.[34]

The disintegration of the anti-French coalition continued. In July 1795, Spain made a peace treaty with France by which the French gained Santo Domingo, the eastern portion of the island on which St. Domingue was located. The ongoing British attempt to capture St. Domingue itself gradually failed. After the French abolition of slavery, most of the rebellious former slaves professed loyalty to France. Their brilliant leader, François-Dominique-Toussaint Louverture, was shrewd enough, however, to hedge his bets, permitting the British to evacuate their forces in 1798 and promising not to attack Jamaica.[35]

In late 1795 Catherine II of Russia agreed to provide troops to fight the French, but she delayed sending them. Thus the French army had little more than the Austrian army and the Sardinian army with which to deal. During 1796 France advanced into Germany and invaded Italy. The attack on the Austrians in Germany failed (as had a French offensive in Germany in 1795), but in Italy the French enjoyed great success under their new army commander, Napoleon Bonaparte. He quickly drove the Sardinians out of the war and captured Milan, the center of Austrian power in Italy. By April 1797, he had occupied almost all of northern Italy and advanced to within seventy-five miles of Vienna. He then offered the Austrians territory taken from Venice in exchange for acceptance of the republics he had established in Italy and of French acquisition of the Austrian Netherlands. He and the Austrians signed a suspension of arms, which the Directory did not dare to repudiate, even though it would have preferred France to make its gains along the Rhine instead of in Italy. Napoleon anticipated that France would acquire the west bank of the Rhine when the final peace was signed. Soon after the Austro-French armistice, Napoleon signed an agreement with Venice giving the French three ships of the line; eventually France acquired seven more Venetian ships of the line, although these ships carried only 64 guns and were of marginal utility.[36]

By now the French navy had acquired more substantial assistance. The total domination of the British navy aroused the fears of Spain as it had in 1761. In August 1796, Spain signed an offensive alliance with France. This caused the French to switch naval strategy again. On paper the Spanish navy was far stronger than the French. It now contained the recently rebuilt *Santísima Trindad* of 136 cannon, as well as ten 112-gun ships and sixty-four smaller ships of the line. Short of money and sailors, the Spanish navy planned to man forty-six of these.[37]

Spain's impending entry into the war caused the British to evacuate Corsica in October 1796 and to withdraw their Mediterranean fleet to Gibraltar and then to Lisbon; the cabinet feared the Mediterranean fleet would be unable to withstand the forty or so ships of the line of the Spanish and French Mediterranean fleets. The combination of the Spanish, French, and Dutch navies threatened a return to the days of 1781, when the British navy was outnumbered by the same three navies. The British still maintained a small overall margin of numerical superiority, however. There was little immediate danger of their enemies sending to sea more than ninety ships of the line (about forty-five Spanish, thirty French, and fifteen Dutch), whereas on 1 September 1796 the British had in service 104 ships of the line and another fourteen of 50–56 cannon. The British intermittently received the help of Russian squadrons in the North Sea and the Mediterranean[38] as well as the help of the small navies of the Kingdom of the Two Sicilies and Portugal; unfortunately for the British, the new Russian emperor, Paul I, recalled his squadrons when he assumed the throne upon the death of his mother, Catherine, in November 1796. The main British problem, however, was that because of their navy's other commitments, they did not have superiority in numbers in European waters and hence could not closely blockade Brest; on 1 September 1796 the British navy had twenty-four ships of the line in the Mediterranean, 10 ships of the line and two 50's at the Cape of Good Hope and in the East Indies, eight ships of the line and three 54's at Jamaica, eleven ships of the line and a 54 in the Leeward Islands (the British West Indies and nearby conquests), two ships of the line and two 50's in Newfoundland and Nova Scotia, and a ship of the line and a 50 en route to the Cape of Good Hope.[39]

The situation was not as dire as it appeared, though. The ships of the French, Spanish, and Dutch navies were ill-prepared and poorly manned. The French government largely had ceased to collect taxes, inflation was out of control, and the navy, unlike the army, had no captured territory to pillage. In facing a coalition of opponents, the British navy now enjoyed the same advantage the French army had enjoyed since 1792. Coordinating the activities of the widely separated French, Spanish, and Dutch navies proved as difficult as coordinating the armies of Britain, the Netherlands, Prussia, Austria, Sardinia, and Spain had been for France's enemies.

In late 1796 Truguet and the Directory, disregarding the dire condition of the navy, ordered the fleet at Brest to outfit as many ships as possible so as to invade Ireland with nearly 15,000 troops commanded by General Hoche. Villaret-Joyeuse, pessimistic about the operation, was replaced by Morard de Galles. The French fleet, which included seventeen ships of the line, sailed in mid-December for Bantry Bay (site of the 1689 French victory), even though a reinforcement of five of the line from Toulon had not yet arrived. Not surprisingly, it met terrible weather off the Irish coast and returned to port without landing its troops. Even had they been landed, they would have faced great obstacles, as they were virtually without artillery, had almost no food or money, and had not coordinated their plans with anti-British organizations ashore. The British navy played little role in the campaign, as Bridport's fleet stayed at anchor until the French had turned back. Amazingly only two French ships of the line were shipwrecked, but the Brest fleet was not able to conduct another cruise until 1799. Thus the French were unable to take advantage of the widespread mutinies over inadequate pay that swept the British fleets in the English Channel and North Sea during the spring and summer of 1797.[40]

The main Spanish fleet of twenty-three ships of the line was defeated on 14 February 1797 off Cape St. Vincent on the southern coast of Portugal by Vice Admiral John Jervis's fifteen ships of the line of the British Mediterranean fleet. The Spaniards, caught by surprise while escorting a convoy, were not in a line of battle; Jervis was delighted when Commodore Horatio Nelson's *Captain*, 74, left the British line of battle in order to arrive sooner at the disorganized enemy. Also distinguishing themselves were Captains Saumarez, Collingwood, and Troubridge, all future admirals. Although the Spaniards lost only four ships of the line in the melee, the Spanish navy was badly demoralized.[41] The British Mediterranean fleet blockaded the survivors of the battle in Cadiz, while escaping the mutinies that paralyzed the British fleets in home waters. It did not yet reenter the Mediterranean, however.

Jervis's victory was counterbalanced by Austria's withdrawal from the war. Having lost their last major ally, the British were willing to discuss peace, if only in the hope of causing dissension among the French. Two of the five members of the Directory—Carnot, who by now had become an opponent of the Jacobins, and the veteran diplomat François de Barthélemy—were ready to restore France's conquests beyond its "natural frontier" of the Rhine, if Britain restored the colonial possessions it had taken from France, Spain, and the Netherlands. The British, however, insisted on retaining the Cape of Good Hope, captured from the Dutch, and Trinidad, captured from the Spaniards early in 1797. Barthélemy was prepared to compromise, but diplomacy was intertwined with French domestic politics. Monarchists and moderates now dominated the two chambers of the legislature and were anxious to make peace. Their opponents, however, included the three other directors, as well as the leading generals of the French army. The British, who provided financial assistance to the moderates and monarchists, awaited the results.

Britain's hopes were in vain. On 4 September 1797 (18 Fructidor of the revolutionary year V) an army-supported coup purged the directory of Carnot and Barthélemy. It also removed royalist sympathizers and moderates from the legislature and local governments. Naval Minister Truguet already had been replaced by Rear Admiral Georges-René Pléville Le Pelley, one of the French peace negotiators, who was regarded as a loyal republican. The remaining directors named two new members to the Directory, ended negotiations with the British, and established what effectively was a near dictatorship, although one considerably less bloody than that of the Committee of Public Safety. Although executions did not cease, often its opponents were sentenced to the "dry guillotine," which meant exile to Guinea on the north coast of South America, where many died from ill treatment and tropical diseases. (A few of the exiles, including Barthélemy, managed with British assistance to escape.)[42] The directors, however, ultimately depended on the goodwill of the leading generals of the French army, particularly Napoleon Bonaparte, who had sent Charles-Pierre-François Augereau, one of the generals serving under him, to assist the coup of Fructidor. Napoleon's chief rival in the French army, General Hoche, died from an unknown cause soon after the coup.

Napoleon now moved quickly to make a final peace with the Austrians before the Directory could forestall him. On 18 October 1797 he and an Austrian representative signed the Peace of Campo Formio. Austria now gained the city of Venice, while most of northern Italy went to a French puppet state. Austria promised to support France's claims along the Rhine, although the final decision would be made by the Holy Roman Empire. The peace confirmed the French acquisition from Venice of the Ionian Islands on the eastern side of the entrance to the Adriatic Sea. These islands, however, menaced the Balkans, an area which technically was part of the Ottoman Empire but which was regarded by Paul I as part of Russia's sphere of influence; this made war with Russia likely. The peace, furthermore, would last only as long as France could intimidate Austria. Not only did the Austrians break their promises to support the French at the meeting of the Holy Roman Empire; eventually they murdered two of the French delegates and wounded the third.[43]

The French war against Britain continued. In 1797 the French government proclaimed its intention to invade England or Ireland but did little to prepare landing ships or an escorting fleet. The only ships to leave port were fifteen Dutch ships of the line that undertook a short cruise in the North Sea, hoping to demonstrate their commitment to the French alliance without having to fight the British. Before they could return to port, however, they were intercepted by fourteen British ships of the line and two 50's commanded by the fearless Admiral Adam Duncan, who promptly attacked without waiting to form a line of battle. The resultant Battle of Camperdown (12 October 1797) cost the Dutch nine ships of the line.[44]

VI

After the signing of the peace treaty with Austria, the French stepped up their plans to invade England, naming Napoleon as the army commander. When Napoleon inspected the ports that would be used for embarking troops, he discovered that the operation could not be undertaken in the immediate future for want of ships and men. On 4 March 1798 he proposed to the Directory using the attack on England as a feint and instead attacking Egypt, thereby menacing British communications with India. His proposal quickly was accepted. Rear Admiral François-Paul Brueys d'Aigailliers, commanding the fleet at Toulon, was promoted to vice admiral and ordered to outfit as many ships of the line as he could to escort the troops. Naval Minister Pléville Le Pelley was replaced by the energetic Vice Admiral Eustache Bruix. Although the Brest fleet had only fifteen ships of the line ready for sea, it provided a diversion that forced the British to keep ships near home. It outfitted three separate squadrons to assist a great rebellion sweeping Ireland. The first squadron, three frigates and 1,200 troops, reached Ireland safely in August, but the other two squadrons (one consisting of a ship of the line and seven frigates, the other of three frigates) were unsuccessful. The French landing force was hopelessly outnumbered and eventually captured. The French captives, unlike the Irish, were treated decently as prisoners of war; the British repressed the Irish rebellion with almost as much brutality as the Russians used to subdue the Polish uprising of a few years earlier.[45]

The Irish expeditions were a missed opportunity for France, but they did little harm to the navy, because its commitment of forces was so minor. The attack on Egypt was a major effort, and its results were disastrous for the French navy and for French diplomacy. The Egyptian operation had numerous flaws: grandiose expectations, an excessive belief in the value of superior technology, a lack of understanding of Islamic fervor, and an insufficient commitment of force to ensure success, particularly that of adequate naval force.[46]

Napoleon saw the navy as little more than a servant of the army, useful for convoying landing parties. His escort of thirteen ships of the line was unnecessarily large if the British stayed out of the Mediterranean and too small if they returned. Moreover, like the ships of the ill-fated Irish expedition, the ships were in terrible repair and short of crewmen.

On 24 May, four days after the fleet and transports sailed from

Toulon, a reinforcement of ten ships of the line arrived from England for the British fleet blockading Cadiz; Pitt, Grenville, Dundas, and Spencer had disregarded the advice of the admirals serving on the Board of Admiralty, who feared weakening the home fleet. Jervis, now the Earl of St. Vincent, already had sent Rear Admiral Horatio Nelson with three ships of the line to watch Toulon. He now sent ten of his best ships of the line and a 50-gun ship to join Nelson.

Only by extreme good fortune did the French avoid being intercepted by Nelson's squadron. After capturing Malta while en route to Egypt, Brueys's fleet reached Alexandria on 1 July 1798. On the previous day Nelson, who had beaten him to Alexandria, sailed away, believing he had misjudged Brueys's destination. After the 35,000 French troops had landed, Brueys, who was unwilling to enter the cramped port of Alexandria, remained in the exposed anchorage of Aboukir Bay some twenty miles northeast of the city. Doubtless he took the risk because of Napoleon's reluctance to have him return to Toulon or take refuge at the island of Corfu off the entrance to the Adriatic. With a tightly spaced line and support from shore batteries, an anchored fleet can be formidable. Howe and Hood had made brilliant use of such positions during the American war. Brueys, however, anchored his fleet too far from the shore, depriving himself of support from shore batteries. When Nelson discovered his mistake and returned to Alexandria on 1 July, he caught the French by surprise. Many French crewmen were ashore, and the French ships were not cleared for battle. Part of Nelson's squadron sailed between the French line and the shore, permitting the British to attack in turn the undermanned French ships from both sides simultaneously. Only two French ships of the line escaped; two others were destroyed and the remaining nine captured. One of those destroyed was Brueys's flagship, the *Orient*, 120, which was

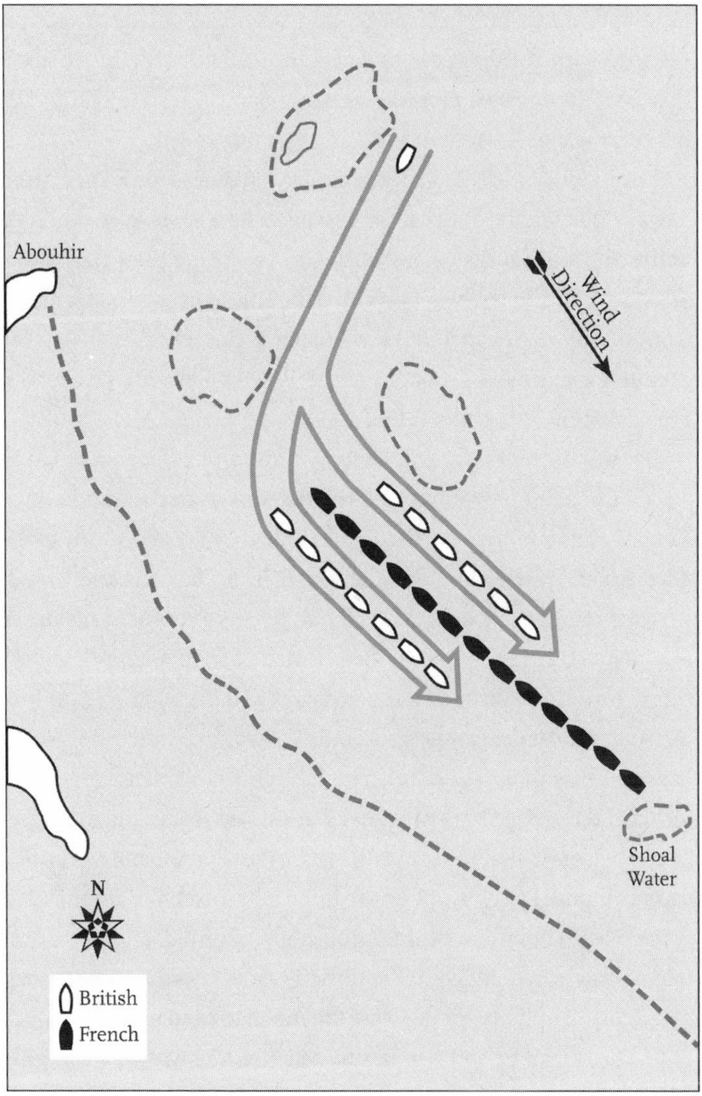

6. Aboukir, 1 August 1798

set afire with combustible material by a British ship in violation of accepted practices of naval warfare. Napoleon soon completed his conquest of Egypt, but his army was trapped.[47]

The Battle of the Nile had terrible consequences for France. It led to war with both the Turks and Russians, who were both so outraged at the French that they were willing to overcome their traditional animosity; the Turks even permitted the Russians to send warships from the Black Sea through the Bosporus and Dardanelles to the Mediterranean. The Kingdom of the Two Sicilies entered the war, too, attacking French-held Rome.

By the summer of 1799 a second coalition had been formed in which the chief powers were Great Britain, Austria, and Russia. Prussia almost joined, but then pulled back. Only the disunity of the allies saved France from being invaded. The Russians and British invaded the Netherlands, while the Russians and Austrians drove the French from Italy and captured much of Switzerland. The Austrians, however, fearing that the Russians and British would capture the Austrian Netherlands without them, withdrew their portion of the key army in Switzerland. The French were able to defeat the outnumbered Russian army near Zurich and regain the initiative. They also defeated the attack on the Netherlands, although the British captured nine Dutch ships of the line at the Texel, the chief Dutch naval base. The inherent difficulties of combined land and naval operations, when added to the difficulties of coordinating British and Russian military forces, were too much to overcome; moreover, North Sea weather and Guillaume-Marie-Anne Brune, the highly capable French commander, were formidable opponents.

In 1800 Austria bore the brunt of the fighting, which mostly occurred in Italy, because Russia dropped out of the war. Emperor Paul I had joined the coalition in order to preserve the balance of power and initially was not interested in Russian expansion. Instead he wished to force France to make a moderate peace that would restore the former rulers of the territories it had captured. He now saw Austria as not only unfaithful to its alliances but also aggressive and expansionist. He also turned against Britain, partly because it did not break with Austria and partly because of the way the British navy interfered with neutral shipping; he expelled both the British minister to the Russian court and the British chargé d'affaires.[48]

After the Battle of the Nile, the main focus of the French navy was supporting the French army in Egypt, Malta, and Corfu, the largest of the seven major Ionian islands. The biggest effort was made in 1799, when a fleet of twenty-five ships of the line commanded personally by Naval Minister Bruix sailed from Brest, deceiving the British who expected him to sail for Ireland and eluding the inept Bridport. Admiral Sir George Keith Elphinstone, Baron Keith, who was cruising off Cadiz with fifteen ships of the line, was too weak to prevent him from entering the Mediterranean, but Bruix's ships were in such bad condition that he sailed to Toulon instead of attacking the scattered units of the British Mediterranean fleet. All he managed was a short cruise off the Italian coast before returning to Brest. Given the poor condition of his ships, he was fortunate that he had no contact with the British navy. He arrived at Brest on 8 August 1799, after his three-and-a-half-month cruise, to find that the Directory had replaced him as naval minister with a bureaucrat, Marc-Antoine Bourdon de Vatry. He brought with him eighteen Spanish ships of the line that had joined him at Cartagena.[49] By combining the two fleets, he left the British with fewer ports to blockade. After Bridport was replaced by Admiral St. Vincent in April 1800, Brest was subjected to the tightest blockade since the Seven Years' War.

Two weeks after Bruix arrived in Brest, a squadron of two frigates and two smaller ships commanded by Captain Honoré-Joseph-Antoine Ganteaume sailed from Egypt for France, carrying Napoleon and a few of his officers. Soon after arriving, Napoleon overthrew the Directory and established himself as the most powerful of the three consuls who became rulers of France. Early in 1800 a plebiscite approved a new constitution that regularized the new regime. Napoleon now took personal charge of what proved to be the decisive theater of war, again driving the Austrians from northern Italy. On 15 June 1800, the day after Napoleon won the Battle of Marengo, the Austrians agreed to an armistice covering Italy, and a month later they signed an armistice in Germany. After a brief resumption of hostilities, the Austrians signed the 9 February 1801 Treaty of Luneville. They now recognized French control of the west bank of the Rhine and conceded much of northern Italy to a French client state, the Italian Republic.

The British in turn captured Minorca from Spain in 1798 and Malta from France in 1800, while the Russians and Turks captured the Ionian Islands. The French army in Egypt tried to capture Syria but was forced to return to Egypt after failing to capture the strategically vital port of Acre. France made another attempt to relieve the army in Egypt in 1801. A squadron of seven ships of the line under Ganteaume, now a rear admiral, reached Toulon from Brest in February 1801, with 5,000 soldiers, in spite of the terrible condition of his ships. The following month the British landed an army of 15,000 in Aboukir Bay, fearing that if the French were left in uncontested control of Egypt, they would seek to retain it when they made peace with Britain; this would menace the parts of India held by the British. The French force in Egypt already had diverted British forces in the Indian Ocean from attacking such attractive targets as Dutch Java and the French Mascarene Islands.[50] Four of Ganteaume's ships of the line subsequently reached Alexandria, but they were unable to land their troops and so returned to Toulon.

Three of Ganteaume's ships now were sent to Cadiz to help form a new squadron to intercept British convoys for Egypt. They expected to join six ships of the line that Spain was transferring to France, five Spanish ships of the line, and five French ships of the line expected from Rochefort (but which did not sail). After the squadron from Toulon moored at Algeciras (near Gibraltar), it beat off an attack by six British ships of the line and captured one of them. Reinforced by five Spanish and one French of the line, it sailed on 12 July for Cadiz. That night a pursing British squadron captured a French ship of the line while in the confusion of battle two Spanish 112's, one of which was aflame, collided, and both soon exploded. The rest of the squadron reached Cadiz. This was the last major French or Spanish naval action of the war.[51]

By the end of 1801 the British forced the French army in Egypt to capitulate, the first British victory following a string of embarrassing failed combined land-sea operations—in the north of Holland in 1799, and at the Quiberon peninsula, Ferrol, and Cadiz in 1800. As during the War of American Independence, the British never decided on a clear war strategy. Dundas sought to win the war by colonial conquests, while Grenville's chief hope was finding allies on the European continent. Pitt attempted to follow both strategies simultaneously, but Britain lacked the necessary resources for success.[52]

In early 1801 Britain had become involved in another war while continuing to fight France. Distrusting Paul I, British failed to honor a verbal agreement that the Russians would share in the occupation of recently captured Malta. Paul, who was grand master of the Knights of Malta, the titular sovereign of the island, treated this as a personal affront. In December 1800, he signed a Treaty of Armed Neutrality with Sweden, Denmark, and Prussia, patterned roughly after the agreement of 1780. He prepared to raise a force of thirty ships of the line, half of them Russian, to deny the British access to the Baltic. Britain was dependent on supplies of naval materiel and grain from the Baltic, particularly since the harvests of 1799 and 1800 were so poor that there was a threat of famine. The British treated the formation of the League of Armed Neutrality as equivalent to a declaration of war and ignored hints from Paul that he was prepared to compromise about Malta. In March 1801 Britain sent to the Baltic a fleet of eighteen ships of the line, a 54-gun ship, and a 50-gun ship. The fleet was commanded by Vice Admiral Hyde Parker, with Vice Admiral Nelson as second in command. Before it could attack the Russians, it had to open a passage into the Baltic. It did so by destroying an anchored Danish fleet on 2 April 1801. The ships doing the bulk of the fighting were nine British ships of the line commanded by Nelson and seven mostly superannuated Danish ships of the line. After the British overcame the resistance of the Danish fleet, they threatened to destroy Copenhagen. The Danes agreed to an armistice, removing any danger to the British fleet from the remainder of the Danish navy.

The British did not need thereafter to attack the Russian or Swedish fleets. Paul I was assassinated on the night of 23–24 March 1801, much as his father, Peter, had been in 1761; before leaving Russia, the British ambassador may have provided funds to those who plotted the assassination. His successor, Alexander I, took only three months to make peace with Britain and abandon the League of Armed Neutrality.[53]

The elimination of this threat to British naval supplies was counterbalanced by the loss of the Austrian alliance. By now Pitt was no longer prime minister. He resigned in early 1801 after a disagreement over permitting Irish Catholics to enjoy public office. Pitt viewed this as a manner of honor, being part of the political understanding by which Ireland joined Great Britain to form the United Kingdom. Pitt's greatest biographer believes Pitt's action may also have been motivated in part by a desire to ease peace discussions with France, Pitt having lost faith in the British public's willingness to continue supporting a losing war and heavy taxes. Pitt was succeeded by his close friend Henry Addington, the able and popular speaker of the House of Commons.[54]

Addington's government signed a preliminary agreement with France on 1 October 1801. The French made peace just before the British learned of the surrender of Alexandria, the last French post in Egypt, much as peace had been reached in 1762 just before news arrived of the British capture of Cassel. Further negotiations largely confirmed the peace terms, and a final treaty was signed at Amiens on 27 March 1802. Even Pitt applauded the peace, although the terms were highly unfavorable to Great Britain. Britain accepted the cessions made by Austria at the Treaty of Luneville. It settled for minor gains abroad to counterbalance the huge French gains on the European continent. It received only Ceylon and Trinidad, while it promised to return its other conquests, including returning Malta to its former owner, the Knights of Malta. In exchange France promised to evacuate southern Italy. Although many Britons expected the settlement to last, Napoleon was not as optimistic. He realized that only exhaustion had led Austrian and Britain to accept France's massive gains. Although he hoped peace would last a few years, he believed that only intimidation would keep Austria from seeking revenge and knew that a new war on the Continent would involve Britain.[55] After the four previous wars, France had sought better relations with Britain; this peace was little better than a truce. Far sooner than either country wished, the underlying mistrust between them would bring a new war.

7. The Role of the Navies in the Napoleonic War

I

By the time hostilities were suspended in November 1801, the French navy was reduced to four ships of 110 to 118 cannon, four of 80, and thirty-seven of 74 (including four recently acquired from Spain).[1] This fleet was dwarfed by the British fleet of twenty-three ships of 90 guns or more, nine of 80–84, sixty-seven of 74, twenty-four of 64, and twelve of 50–56. One hundred and fifteen of these British ships were in service.[2] Most of the French ships were in need of repair, but they were given no rest. Napoleon immediately began a new military operation, that of reestablishing control over St. Domingue with its enormous trade in sugar, which was important to the French economy. Toussaint Louverture and his followers, fearing the re-imposition of slavery, resisted. Although their great leader was captured and taken to France, where he died in captivity, the French attack failed despite the encouragement the French had received from the new Jefferson administration in Washington. When the French evacuated their former colony at the end of 1803, they left behind more than 50,000 dead, mostly from disease.[3] Some thirty-three French and Spanish ships of the line and 80,000 soldiers had been used in the operation. Although only one of these, the *Desaix*, 74, was destroyed, service in tropical waters damaged others and disease ravaged their crews.[4] France lost St. Domingue (renamed Haiti by the victors), formerly the richest colony in the world, and in the process Napoleon's plans to restore a French presence in North America were foiled. In October 1800 he had obtained from Spain the promise of Louisiana plus six ships of the line in exchange for establishing Tuscany as a kingdom for Prince Louis of Parma, who was Charles IV's son-in-law; this was confirmed by the 21 March 1801 Treaty of Aranjuez, by which Parma itself became part of France. The hostilities in St. Domingue postponed France's taking control of Louisiana. When a new war with Britain seemed likely, Napoleon sold Louisiana to the United States partly to keep it out of British hands and partly because he was desperate for money.

France, however, did regain control over Martinique, where slavery had not been abolished, and re-imposed slavery on Guadeloupe. The reintroduction of slavery not only was a moral abomination but also deprived France of a potential weapon against Britain. Had Napoleon confirmed the abolition of slavery, Britain's West Indian colonies would have been vulnerable to another slave uprising, which could have had serious consequences for British diplomacy and war strategy. Napoleon, who had recognized the military potential of cooperating with Toussaint Louverture and his 25,000 troops, later admitted that it had been folly to attempt to reconquer St. Domingue rather than recognize its independence and send it assistance.[5]

Although Napoleon may have been influenced by his wife Josephine, who had been born as a privileged white colonist in Martinique, the restoration of slavery chiefly appears to have been part of Napoleon's efforts to strengthen the French economy and bolster the legitimacy of his rule. To win support he also reestablished peace with the Catholic Church, while obtaining papal consent to his appointing bishops. He permitted the return of émigrés and gave them appointments in the French armed forces. He began the codification of French law, although its provisions in such matters as divorce were less liberal than those of the Revolution. In 1802, he became first consul for life, which was ratified by a plebiscite; he then proclaimed a new constitution that concentrated power in his hands. Two years later he became emperor, an apt title given the similarity of his powers to those of a Roman emperor. Nonetheless Napoleon's rule lacked the traditions of the former Bourbon rulers of France. He felt himself dependent on a successful foreign policy to retain his popularity, believed the alternative to success was the risk of invasion and civil war, and feared weakening France's control over its satellite republics along its northern and eastern borders even though Austria was too exhausted at the moment to renew war.

During the months after the Treaty of Amiens, Napoleon moved aggressively to cement France's control over the states along its borders. Although this did not violate the Peace of Amiens, the British grew alarmed. They also were alarmed by France's protectionist trade policies, its actions in St. Domingue, and perhaps most of all by its hints that it might again invade Egypt. What precipitated war, however, was the strategically vital island of Malta, which the British had promised to return to the Knights of Malta. The British regretted their promise, and fearing the French would capture the island again, they refused to comply with the terms of the Treaty of Amiens. Napoleon considered this a provocation that he could not accept without showing weakness. In May 1803, barely a year after the signing of the formal peace, a new war began. Napoleon had not expected a lengthy peace, but he did not wish war to begin before he was ready. Unfortunately he and the British government each had attempted the dangerous tactic of using threats to force the other to back down, such as French bluster about a new attack on Egypt. Given the mutual suspicions of the two countries, this virtually guaranteed war.[6]

This premature war caught both the French navy and the British navy unready. The French had inadequate time to rebuild their navy, particularly given the wear and tear caused by the St. Domingue operation. Although the French navy still had a dozen ships in construction from the previous war and had begun half a dozen more since its end, it had launched only one ship of the line since war's end and acquired two from Spain as the final installment of their 1800 agreement. Moreover, its existing ships still needed repair. The worst were the *Terrible*, 110, and ten 74's, which were judged beyond repair; only twenty-three ships of the line were at sea or in condition to serve, including thirteen still in the West Indies. Furthermore the dockyards had not yet been replenished. Napoleon admitted in 1802 that the French navy needed more than ten years to match the British.[7]

Fortunately for France, the Addington government initially had taken the Peace of Amiens seriously and had demobilized the British fleet. Worse still, its new first lord of the admiralty, Earl St. Vincent, promptly began an ill-timed economy campaign that disrupted the work of the shipyards. During the period between hostilities, the British navy launched only two 74's and two 50's, while only ten ships were on the building slips when war resumed. Not surprisingly, it took the British even more time than usual to mobilize their fleet. Only seventy-six ships of the line and ten ships of 50–56 guns were in service on 1 January 1804, and only about a dozen ships of the line and 50's were added over the course of the year.[8]

Napoleon and his naval minister, the naval architect Pierre-Alexandre-Laurent Forfait, immediately began planning to invade England. In March 1801 the Consulate had ordered the construction of a flotilla of landing craft and of shallow draft prames to escort them, although little work was completed before the end of the war; only one of the 110-foot prames (carrying 12 cannon) was launched in 1801, for example. Similar delays had plagued the attempts of Choiseul to build 22-gun 130-foot-long prames for his invasion attempt of 1759; twelve were launched, but not until after the invasion attempt had been abandoned.[9]

Napoleon now began a new and much more massive effort to build a flotilla of landing craft; between September 1803 and September 1804, more than 25 percent of the French budget was spent on the navy, including some 15 million francs donated by various municipalities for shipbuilding as had been done following the defeats of Quiberon and the Saintes. By mid-1805 the navy had launched nineteen prames, more than 300 *chaloupe cannonières* (approximately 80 feet long and carrying 4 or 5 cannon), and numerous other vessels. An army of more than 100,000 men was assembled along the Straits of Dover and trained to board its landing ships quickly.[10] Without an escorting fleet of numerous ships of the line, however, the invasion flotilla could not sail. The British navy blockaded the twenty ships of the line available in Brest, five at Ferrol returning from the Caribbean, and half a dozen or so at Rochefort. For this duty the British made use of forty-five to fifty ships of the line, of which at least thirty were always at sea.

The French lacked the strength to break the blockade unless the British were lured off station or the dozen ships of the Toulon fleet could elude the British and reach Brest. Both were slim possibilities, particularly since command of the British fleet off Brest was given to Admiral William Cornwallis, an experienced commander respected by both St. Vincent and Nelson.[11] The squadrons of Toulon and Rochefort were not able to sail until the beginning of 1805. By then Napoleon had placed the navy under an experienced naval officer, Rear Admiral Denis Decrès, who served as naval minister until the end of 1814. Napoleon continued to direct naval strategy, but without appreciating its inherent difficulties. Unlike Napoleon's armies, the French navy could not disregard wind and weather, and it was never able to train the crews of its ships adequately.

The British political situation had changed. On 10 May 1804 Pitt, who had become disillusioned with the Addington government, returned to office. His political position was far weaker than during his previous administration; even his cousin Grenville had become a political opponent. His friend Dundas, now Viscount Melville, however, was willing to serve in his cabinet. Pitt named him to replace the misguided St. Vincent as first lord of the admiralty. Melville, a fine administrator, served for only eleven months before resigning because of his involvement in a financial scandal. He was replaced by his friend and relation, the exceptionally experienced and able Charles Middleton, who was raised to the peerage as Baron Barham.

Upon resuming office Pitt quickly turned his attention to creating a new coalition to oppose Napoleon on the European continent, eventually enlisting Russia and Austria but not Prussia. It was not until 1805, however, that war on the continent resumed. In the interim Britain added to its own enemies. Although Spain was trying to remain neutral, Pitt assumed she was preparing to join France. In a similar circumstance in 1761, Pitt's father had argued unsuccessfully for seizing a Spanish treasure fleet expected from the Western Hemisphere. The younger Pitt met no opposition within his cabinet when he proposed doing the same thing. On 5 October 1804 a squadron of British frigates intercepted four Spanish frigates carrying treasure. It captured three, while the fourth exploded with heavy loss of life. The court of Charles IV of Spain was outraged. Spain joined the war as a French ally.[12]

Such ruthlessness was a mark of the times. In one way the British were even more ruthless than the French; even under the Terror, the Convention rejected the idea of assassinating William Pitt, whereas the British government was involved in attempts to assassinate Napoleon. The Britain of Pitt and the France of Napoleon were heirs to the brutal legacy of Cromwell's England, Louis XIV's France, Frederick the Great's Prussia, and Catherine the Great's Russia. Napoleon's subsequent savage repression of Spain did not differ greatly except in scale from the Russian treatment of Poland or the British treatment of Ireland. None could really compare with the horrors of the twentieth century, the closest approximation being the unrestrained cruelty and racism of the war in St. Domingue. Although Napoleon was arrogant and duplicitous, some of his policies were progressive, like his support of religious toleration. For all his faults, he was more similar to Louis XIV than to madmen like Robespierre or Hitler.[13]

Spain's joining the war was opportune for the French navy. Prior to late 1804, France received naval assistance only from the Batavian Republic. After the loss of ships at Camperdown and the Texel, however, the Dutch had only about fifteen ships of the line and could arm fewer than ten of them. The Spanish navy, even after its disasters, still had on paper some fifty ships of the line. In January 1805 the crown promised to arm thirty-two of them by the end of March, although barely half were ready by then. France had about forty-five in service in March 1805. The Dutch, French, and

Spanish fleets were divided between the Texel, Brest, Rochefort, Ferrol, Cadiz, Cartagena, and Toulon. Although the British navy had only eighty-three ships of the line and ten 50's in service on 1 March 1805, most of them were serving in or near home waters or in the Mediterranean; eight ships of the line and two 50's were in the East Indies, three of the line were at Jamaica, one of the line was in the Leeward Islands, and a 50 was at Nova Scotia. Melville had laid the foundation for repairing and expanding the fleet during his tenure. By the end of the summer, 100 of the line were in service.[14]

Napoleon devised plan after plan to unite the fleets of France and its allies; the historian N. A. M. Rodger counts eight such plans.[15] The plan that finally was used selected Martinique as a rendezvous point for various squadrons in Spanish and French ports. Not surprisingly, it failed. Five ships of the line from Rochefort reached Martinique in February 1805 and sailed for France at the end of March, which was about the time the eleven ships of the line of the Toulon squadron finally left port under the command of Vice Admiral Pierre-Charles-Silvestre de Villeneuve, a survivor of the Battle of the Nile, who had been appointed after the death of its former commander, the gifted La Touche-Tréville. After gathering six Spanish and one French ship of the line from Cadiz en route, Villeneuve reached Martinique on 16 May. Although he was joined by another two French ships of the line, he accomplished almost nothing. The veteran Villaret-Joyeuse was in command of the French islands. Had he been sent orders to take command of Villeneuve's fleet, it might have escaped its subsequent disaster. This likely would have meant, however, that he would have had to turn over his own command to Villeneuve in exchange. This would have displeased the local French planters, because Villaret-Joyeuse was a fervent supporter of slavery.

Nelson soon arrived at Barbados from the Mediterranean with ten of the line. Villeneuve, recognizing the inferior quality of his ships and crews, quickly returned to Europe; meanwhile the twenty ships of the line at Brest were too intimidated by Cornwallis's magnificent fleet to sail. Villeneuve's returning twenty ships of the line were able to fend off Vice Admiral Sir Robert Calder's British squadron of fifteen ships of the line near the Spanish coast, but lost two Spanish ships of the line. After a brief stop at Vigo, where he left one French and two Spanish ships of the line damaged in the recent battle, he reached Ferrol on 2 August. Although he added nine Spanish and five French ships of the line from Ferrol to his fleet, it numbered only twenty-nine ships of the line, too few to challenge the British fleet off the French coast, particularly since his ships were in terrible condition and his crews still needed training. He did sail briefly toward the English Channel, but quickly lost heart and went instead to join the Spanish fleet at Cadiz. This doomed the invasion of England that Napoleon had been planning for two years.

Napoleon now took the army that had been intended for embarkation and used it instead to attack a Russian and Austrian army gathering in central Europe at the instigation of Alexander I. Receiving reports that the British and Russians were planning a joint operation in the central Mediterranean, Napoleon ordered Villeneuve to sail to Naples, where he should disembark the few thousand troops he had aboard. (Some 14,000 Russian and 6,000 British troops did go to Naples at the end of November 1805, but accomplished little before they departed.)[16]

Villeneuve also was ordered to attack the British blockading squadron if he outnumbered them. Napoleon then sent another admiral to replace Villeneuve, urging him to be prudent. He failed

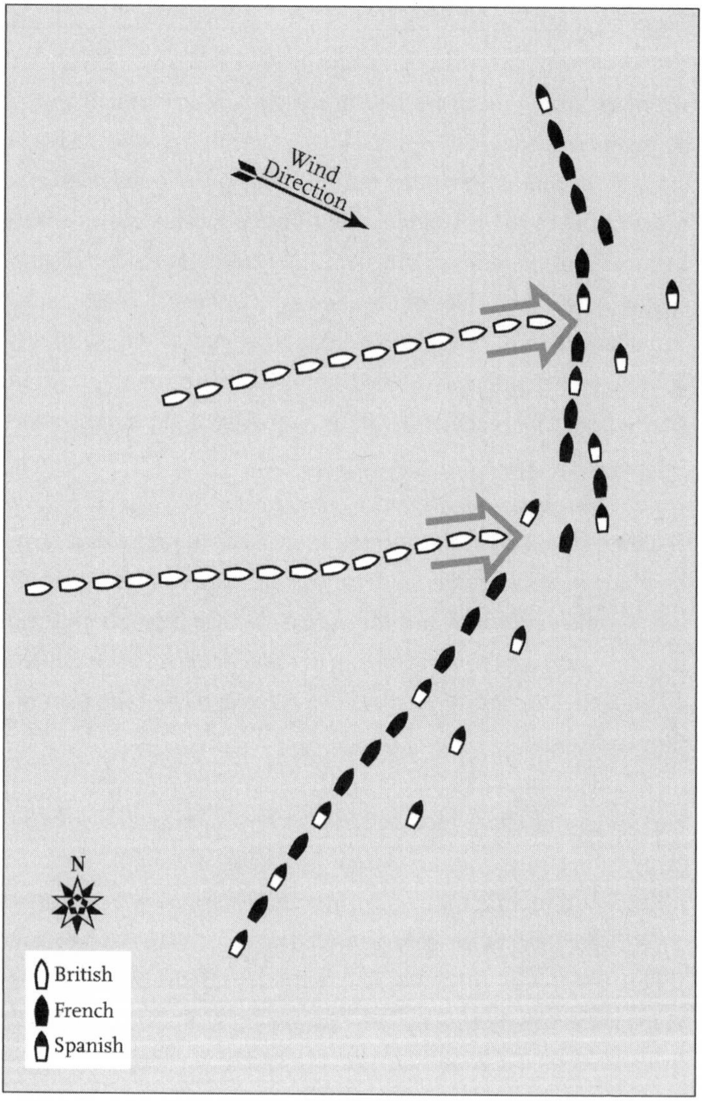

7. Trafalgar, 21 October 1805

to countermand Villeneuve's orders, though, and the news of his impending demotion seems to have been more shame than Villeneuve could bear. It became a matter of honor to carry out his orders in full before his replacement arrived. Villeneuve took his undermanned fleet of eighteen French and fifteen Spanish ships of the line to sea on 20 October 1805 to challenge the twenty-seven British ships of the line off nearby Cape Trafalgar. The results of the following day's battle were so foreordained that Nelson deliberately sought what virtually every admiral from 1650 to 1945 sought to avoid: approaching an enemy line of battle in a column perpendicular to the enemy's line or, in the expression used more recently, letting the enemy "cross the T." In Nelson's case there were *two* columns, one of twelve ships of the line he commanded personally, the other of fifteen ships of the line commanded by his close friend Vice Admiral Cuthbert Collingwood. The leading ships of both columns, the *Victory* and *Royal Sovereign*, should have been crippled before they reached the enemy line, but French and Spanish gunnery was so poor that both flagships penetrated the enemy line, followed by most of their respective columns. It is possible that a more orthodox parallel approach to the enemy would have been more successful, as only about half the ships on either side participated in heavy fighting. In the battle Nelson was killed, but no British ships of the line were lost, whereas eight French and nine Spanish ships of the line were captured and a ninth French ship of the line was destroyed. After the battle one French and one Spanish ship of the line were recaptured and returned to Cadiz, but another French ship of the line and two more Spanish ships of the line ran aground and were wrecked. Moreover, a terrible storm destroyed most of the prizes captured in the battle, although no British ships were lost, largely because of the superb seamanship of Collingwood.

Another four French ships of the line that had survived the battle were captured two weeks later while returning to France. The five remaining French ships of the line were trapped at Cadiz until 1808, when they were forced to surrender to Spain.[17]

II

Trafalgar marked the virtual end of the Spanish sailing navy. No ships of the line were launched in Spain between 1798 and 1853, and the existing ships' crews and officers were too demoralized to be effective; after Trafalgar, only some twenty ships of the line remained in service.[18]

The French navy was reduced at the end of 1805 to three usable 118-gun ships, three 80's, twenty-five or so 74's, and one 60, but it was somewhat more resilient. On 13 December 1805 five ships of the line were sent to the West Indies, where they were captured in early February. Another six went on a long cruise that took them from the South Atlantic to the Caribbean to Chesapeake Bay, where one ship was destroyed by the British and a damaged ship was sold.[19] Thereafter Napoleon and Decrès used the navy to support military operations and menace British bases, primarily in the Mediterranean. In 1809 an attempt was made to send supplies to the West Indies, which led to a squadron of eleven ships of the line being trapped in the roadstead off Rochefort, where the British destroyed four of them.

In late 1806, having forced Austria and Prussia to make peace, Napoleon issued the Berlin Decrees, which in response to the British blockade of France attempted to undermine the British economy by closing its European markets. Britain suffered a serious temporary drop in its reserves of specie (gold and silver) as well as short-term declines of exports and manufacturing, but the effects of this and subsequent decrees were mitigated by new markets and by the resistance of European consumers, who were happy to defy the French and purchase smuggled British goods. British countermeasures to restrict trade with France also were of limited effectiveness, partly because of the protection from foreign competition that France gave its manufacturers. French productivity improved, wages increased, and French life expectancy was higher than before the Revolution, even though France suffered nearly a million deaths during the wars of 1803–15.[20]

Nonetheless the trade war was a disaster for France. The need to close more markets to British goods helped lead Napoleon into wars in Portugal in 1807, Spain in 1808, and Russia in 1812. These wars did enormous damage to the French army, the bulwark of an empire increasingly based on force.

Napoleon hoped to create a new navy of 100 or 110 ships of the line capable of challenging the British. To do so he acquired ships from his satellite states and constructed others at various dockyards like Antwerp, Venice, and Trieste. This may have had some influence on the American decision to go to war with Britain in 1812 by adding to American confidence that Britain could not defend Canada.[21] But the French building program had no real chance of success without sailors to man the new ships. By the beginning of 1813, after which the French had to disarm its ships to use the crews ashore, the French navy had grown to seventy-four ships of the line—seven of 110–18 cannon, two of 90, sixteen of 80, forty-four of 74, and five of 64. Only fifty-six of these were seaworthy, however.

At the same time, the British had five ships of 110 to 120 cannon, eighteen of 98–100, seven of 80–84, one hundred and ten of 74–76, six of 64, and four of 50–56, plus the help of fifteen

Russian ships of the line. Although Napoleon's finances were more regular than those during the French Revolution, the French navy continued to be outspent by the British; during the years 1807–13 the annual French naval budget averaged 130,230,000 francs, while Parliament voted an average of £19,675,000 (roughly equivalent to 354,000,000 francs) per year.[22]

As during the French Revolution, the British government had a great deal of difficulty in finding the best use for its army, but the British navy was strong and efficient.[23] This continued even after the death of Pitt and retirement of Barham in early 1806, although subsequent first lords of the admiralty were not outstanding and the shortage of sailors was so critical that the British resorted to taking sailors off American merchant ships, eventually helping to cause a war with the United States. Nevertheless, the British navy successfully protected British trade, which provided the underpinnings of the British economy, the British state, and the British war effort. It supported combined operations not only in Europe but also in Africa, the Indian Ocean, the Caribbean, North America, and South America. Some of these, such as the 1806 and 1807 attacks on Buenos Aires and the 1807 attack on Egypt, ultimately were unsuccessful, but eventually nearly all of the overseas empires of France and its Dutch satellite were captured.[24] The British even had enough resources in reserve to fight a war against the United States from 1812 to 1815, when they repulsed attacks on Canada, blockaded American ports, and attacked Washington, Baltimore, and New Orleans.[25] The accomplishments of the British navy were not as much the product of battle as they were the result of superb organization and administration, the culmination of developments going back to Pepys almost a century and a half earlier. British admirals, officers, and sailors deserve much credit, but also important were, for example, the thousands of employees of the Victualing Board who baked the navy's biscuit, brewed its beer, prepared its salted meat, and made the casks to store food and drink.[26]

Among the most crucial British naval operations were those in the Baltic and in the Mediterranean. The Russians and French made peace in 1807, again creating the danger of Russian domination of the Baltic, particularly since the Russians secretly promised to join the war against Britain and resurrected a coalition to protect neutral shipping rights, as in 1780 and 1801. The Danes again were caught in the middle, threatened by Russia and France by land and Britain by sea. They had little choice but to regard the former danger as more dire, since the British could not guarantee the safety of all of Denmark. Having threatened to burn Copenhagen in 1801, the British returned in 1807 and did so, causing numerous civilian casualties and turning Denmark into the most faithful of France's allies. They also seized almost the entire Danish fleet, carrying off fifteen ships of the line.[27] Sweden became implicated in the attack, which led to a Swedish war with Russia and Denmark during which a British fleet in the Baltic supported the Swedes. Two British ships of the line fought a Russian squadron, destroyed a Russian ship of the line, and forced eight other Russian ships of the line to take refuge in port. The Russians, however, captured Finland from Sweden; the Swedes then deposed their king, made peace with Russia, and joined the war against Britain.[28]

The Russians remained at least a nominal French ally until the French attack on Russia in 1812, but they offered minimal assistance to the French navy, as Alexander I had little real desire to help Napoleon. A Russian fleet of nine ships of the line in the Mediterranean, for example, took refuge from the British in the Tagus River of Portugal; after the French army in Portugal surrendered, it was interned in Britain.[29] Relations between France and Russia soon deteriorated. Alexander did not help Napoleon during his 1809 war with Austria, and in late 1810 he withdrew his cooperation from the French "blockade" of the United Kingdom. He considered attacking France, but decided to wait until France attacked Russia first, which it did in 1812.

In sharp contrast to Britain's brutal Danish policy was the subtlety of its subsequent policy toward Sweden. After helping the Swedish navy against the Russian navy in 1808–9, Britain found herself nominally at war with Sweden from 1810 to 1812. The Swedes, however, did not want war with Britain. The wise and prudent Vice Admiral Sir James Saumarez, commanding the British Baltic fleet, took steps to prevent actual hostilities.[30] When Napoleon invaded Russia in 1812, the British switched their attention to assisting the Russians, and the Swedes began negotiations to join the coalition against Napoleon.

Perhaps the British navy's most important theater of operations was the Mediterranean, where Collingwood commanded the British fleet from Nelson's death until just before his own in 1810. The scale of Collingwood's responsibilities was enormous, as the cabinet wisely left him great leeway. Fearless, selfless, a peerless ship handler, a superb strategist, a master of diplomacy like Norris, Wager, and Saumarez, and a man of complete integrity, Collingwood had few equals in the age of sail. His fleet protected the great British base of Malta as well as the island of Sicily, whose defense largely became a British responsibility. He assisted Russia during its 1806–12 war against the Ottoman Empire until Russia became a French ally, after which he helped keep the Russians in check. Most of all he helped prevent the French from exploiting their position in the Ionian Islands to dismember the Ottoman Empire or to turn it into a French satellite and thereby imperil the British position in India. One of his most serious crises came in early 1808 when a squadron of five ships of the line escaped Rochefort, entered the Mediterranean, and joined forces off Toulon with another five of the line. Rather than attacking Sicily, however, they contented themselves with convoying supplies to the French garrison at Corfu before returning to Toulon.[31]

With the French invasion of Portugal and Spain in 1807–8, the Iberian peninsula became a major theater of operations for the British army, which landed 33,000 soldiers in Portugal in August 1808. After French forces in Portugal negotiated their own safe departure, the British sent an army into French-occupied Spain. It was nearly trapped by a large French army brought into Spain by Napoleon himself. It managed, however, to reach Vigo and Corunna, where its 26,000 remaining soldiers were evacuated by the British navy. The following year the British entered Spain again, but were forced to retreat. They also attempted to destroy the great French shipbuilding facilities at Antwerp, using thirty-nine ships of the line and 40,000 troops. The British army suffered terrible losses from disease, and it, too, had to be evacuated.[32]

After 1809 the British subordinated all their other efforts to the war in Portugal and Spain. The Mediterranean fleet and detachments from the main fleet near the English Channel played important roles in hindering French resupply efforts and in supporting the Duke of Wellington's military operations. The need for troops for the Russian campaign caused the French to evacuate much of their army from Spain. The stalemate with Wellington's forces ended, and the French were driven from Spain in 1813. Early the following year Wellington's army entered southern France.[33] The main credit for defeating Napoleon, however, belongs to the Russian,

Austrian, and Prussian army that captured Paris in March 1814 and forced Napoleon to abdicate.[34] The British army played a vital role in defeating Napoleon, however, when he briefly seized power in 1815. The French role in Europe was diminished, but the main accomplishments of the French Revolution—religious liberty, social equality, and constitutional government—survived to some degree. Subsequent attempts to restore the dominance of the Bourbon monarchy, the aristocracy, and the Catholic Church failed. Except for limited hostilities in 1940–42, the French and British navies did not fight each other again. Although they competed in colonizing Africa, Asia, and the Pacific, their rivalry was not serious enough to lead to war. When war occurred in Europe in 1854, 1914, and 1939, the French and British navies fought as allies.

8. The Ingredients of Supremacy in the Age of Sail

Napoleon's defeat in 1814–15 brought to an end seventy years of frequent hostilities interspersed with short periods of peace. The war against Napoleon represents a major departure from earlier wars. The British people finally were willing to fight a war to its conclusion whatever the cost; the wealthy were even willing to pay an income tax. This war approached being the kind of total war that demonstrates the strength of representative governments. That strength has its moral and psychological components, but one of its most important dimensions is economic. Admittedly, qualitative factors like leadership and skill were then, as now, critical during wartime; British crews were better trained and healthier, while British admirals and captains generally were more skilled than their French counterparts. The British, too, were quicker to adopt new technology, perhaps because the French were more enamored with theoretical science. Perhaps most important in the ultimate British victory, however, was the way popular support made possible the financing of a European coalition against Napoleon.

Quantitative factors were just as important in the other wars between Britain and France during the age of sail. By the beginning of the eighteenth century, England with its superior governmental finances surpassed France in the number of sailors it could muster, the amount of naval materiel like masts, timber, and naval stores in its dockyards, and the number of ships at its disposal, particularly the number of ships of the line. These factors influenced behavior. During the one subsequent war in which the French navy was not badly outnumbered, that of 1778–83, French admirals like Suffren and La Motte-Picquet acted with the audacity generally associated with British admirals, while British admirals became more cautious (or to look at it from another angle, French admirals began acting like French generals). The most important quantitative factor of all was money, whether it was raised by taxes or was borrowed. Money was indispensable in order to pay sailors, fill the dockyards with supplies, and build and repair ships. As Henry Dundas described it, war was a contestation of purse.[1] The British consistently won that contest.

Most naval historians have treated the series of wars between 1688 and 1815 as proof of Britain's greater skill at war and its superior political and social system.[2] At least implicitly, Britain's ultimate victory in war has been treated as proof of its moral superiority. There is some truth to these assumptions. As even the comte de Vergennes admitted, Britain's system of government permitted it to raise money more easily than did France.[3] Having a share in government, wealthy Britons were more willing than wealthy Frenchmen to pay taxes and to settle for low interest rates when subscribing to government loans. Between 1715 and 1730, Britons paid twice as much per capita in taxes as Frenchmen did, and during the French Revolution they paid three times as much. Because France had three times the population of Great Britain, the French government's net income before 1789 was higher: for example, between 1750 and 1755 it was about 260 million livres per year compared with an average British income equivalent to about 170 million livres. The British had more to spend on the army and navy, however, because much of the French royal income was spent on pensions, public works, and administration. Even more significantly, the British government's reputation for credit trustworthiness gave it easy access to low-interest credit.

There were drawbacks, though, to the British system of government that gave a share of political power to the wealthy and some influence to merchants and nontitled landowners. Prior to the Napoleonic War, the wars of this period were ones of attrition fought for limited objectives. This kind of conflict is disliked by taxpayers, who tend to have limited patience. Britons paid higher taxes than did Frenchmen, but they expected results for the money; furthermore, British lobbyists had greater influence than did their French equivalents, such as the chambers of commerce of the great French port cities. Until the great war with Napoleon, the British taxpayer blinked before the kings of France (or the first consul of the republic) did. Thus none of the wars before the Napoleonic War established permanent naval superiority; the British had to reassert it repeatedly in the following conflict. Indeed before 1815 even such apparent victories as that claimed by Britain in 1763 or by France in 1783 brought benefits that mostly proved illusory and were not worth their costs.

Until 1789 the French and British economies were of relatively equal size, even though France had three times the population. The following twenty-five years were a disaster for French colonial trade, ruining great ports like Bordeaux, even though the French army and portions of the French economy prospered from French conquests in Europe. Until then the amount of French and British foreign trade was fairly similar, although the British public often feared that France would surpass Britain. By the Napoleonic War,

Britain was on its way to victory in its long economic rivalry with France—British trade now was far greater than France's, and with the Industrial Revolution well under way the British economy was able to support Britain's becoming the paymaster of Europe against Napoleon.[4]

The more centralized French system of government did provide an important benefit for its navy. The French frequently drew on proven administrators, like ex-finance ministers, generals, or lieutenants general of police for Paris, to head the naval ministry. These men tended to be tough and skilled; the best, like Machault and Sartine, had the nerves of a riverboat gambler. Former admirals like Massiac, Truguet, Pléville Le Pelley, Bruix, and Decrès on balance were less successful. In the British system the first lords of the admiralty had not only to represent the navy in the inner cabinet but also to justify its actions to Parliament. Thus many first lords were politicians such as Winchelsea, Temple, Sandwich, and Chatham, with a politician's innate caution. High-ranking naval officers such as Admirals Russell, George Byng, Hawke, Saunders, Keppel, Howe, and St. Vincent frequently served as first lords of the admiralty, too. The most successful were those with previous experience on the Navy Board or Board of Admiralty, such as Wager, Anson, and Barham. On balance, the British navy was strongest at the bottom, with its incomparable sailors and shipboard officers, while the French was strongest at the top, with its often excellent naval ministers.

When it came to naval warfare, the clearest British advantage was the level of financial support it received. Britons were not reluctant to spend money on the navy, which protected not only British soil from invasion but also British commerce, generally regarded as the source of its power and prosperity. In France the army was more popular and prestigious than the navy. Geography was even more important than public opinion. The British, protected by the English Channel and their navy, did not need a huge army to defend themselves, whereas France generally did; when the British faced higher army expenses than did France because of the war in America (1775–83), the French navy came relatively close to parity in size and income to the British. This is shown by the average annual French and British naval expenditures for the American war compared with the two previous wars:[5]

Years	*Average French Appropriations*	*Average British Appropriations*
1744–48	32,170,000 livres	£3,035,000 (71,300,000 livres)
1756–62	36,670,000 livres	£4,730,000 (111,160,000 livres)
1778–82	138,435,000 livres	£6,720,000 (157,900,000 livres)

Funding differences led to differences in manning; during the War for American Independence, not only did desertions decline but France was able to recruit sailors from abroad. In 1757, the French navy's year of peak effectiveness during the Seven Years' War, it could muster about 35,000 crewmen compared with more than 60,000 British, while in 1782 it could muster some 90,000 compared with 95,000 British.[6]

France often compensated for its inferior resources by accepting the help of its allies such as Spain and the Netherlands. Unfortunately for France, this usually came after the French navy had already been weakened; again the exception is the War for American Independence, during which Spanish and Dutch help permitted France enough margin of superiority to maintain the initiative, at least until 1782. Moreover, until Napoleon's victories came to an end, the French could use victories on land in the various wars to counterbalance, at least partially, British victories at sea or outside of Europe. The French, indeed, sometimes used their navy to assist their army in its victories, such as at Minorca in 1756 and at Yorktown in 1781, although its attempts to cover invasions of England, Scotland, or Ireland proved unsuccessful. Britain was more successful at combined operations abroad, such as Louisbourg in 1758 and Quebec in 1759, than it was in Europe. The French strategy was well adapted to France's usually limited naval resources, while Britain's strategy usually made good use of Britain's naval superiority.

With the exception of the War for American Independence, most of France's victories were on the European continent or in the Mediterranean and hence were of great concern to British statesmen. Britain and France were chiefly concerned with their security, and neither could ignore the Austrian Netherlands or Germany; moreover, after 1714 Hanover became a security concern for Britain for dynastic reasons. Ironically, the period of greatest security for both countries came when they were allies.

It has been common to call the entire period from 1688 to 1815 the "Second Hundred Years War," successor to the fourteenth- and fifteenth-century dynastic conflict between the rulers of England and France.[7] This implies that conflict between France and Britain was inevitable, either because the two were colonial rivals or because they were ideological or religious enemies. Both are oversimplifications.

Colonial rivalry in itself was not sufficient to cause the wars between Britain and France. Unlike the Anglo-Dutch wars of the seventeenth century or the War of Jenkins's Ear, Franco-British wars chiefly were about national security. Even the wars of 1755 and 1778, which appear to be colonial conflicts, were closely connected to French fears about European rivals such as Russia and to British perceptions that economic dominance, naval power, and security were interconnected. During the century after Waterloo, the United Kingdom and France remained at peace with each other in spite of colonial rivalry in Africa and elsewhere, largely because the Low Counties (the Netherlands and Belgium) were not linked with a major European power and hence were not a threat to either France or the United Kingdom. British naval dominance was so complete that France could be intimidated from challenging it, since French borders and hence security were not at stake. The British and French finally became allies in 1904, and when the Germans invaded Belgium and France in 1914, they overcame their mutual distrust to fight in common.[8]

Religion and ideology certainly were important factors during the first Anglo-French war, that of 1688–97, particularly in England. Louis XIV's support of the deposed Catholic king of England, James II, was perceived as a threat to Parliament and Protestantism, especially since Louis recently had revoked the rights of French Protestants. For France, on the other hand, the war against England was subordinate to the war against France's traditional enemy, the Habsburgs of Austria, who were fellow Catholics. The War of the Spanish Succession, too, was chiefly a struggle between the French House of Bourbon and the Austrian House of Habsburg for control of the Spanish throne. Between 1715 and 1792, ideology played virtually no role in Franco-British rivalry, and religion played only a minor role. For reasons of state, France disregarded religious differences in order to maintain cordial relations with the Islamic Ottoman Empire. It even provided support to the American Revolution, disregarding its antimonarchical and anticolonial character.

For most of the period, Britain and France had much in common in their foreign policy. Both were conservative and traditionalist, wanting to preserve the map of Europe largely intact (except for Louis XV's folly in attacking Austria in 1741, which he came to regret). Both usually were protectors of the small states of Germany—France to protect her own security by using them as a buffer, Britain to preserve the security of Hanover. Both were content to see the Austrian Netherlands in the hands of a power that barely could protect the area, let alone use it to threaten them. Both benefited from their alliance of 1716–31, made possible when the area became Austrian. The real enemies of both were expansionist states like Russia, which threatened the status quo.

There were other similarities between Britain and France. Both had mixed governments, in which the king regarded foreign policy as his prerogative but needed to placate public opinion and win consent to taxes. Too unpopular a policy or minister could not be sustained in either country; French naval ministers Machault and Sartine had to be sacrificed in spite of how well and faithfully they had served. In both France and Britain there were enormous advantages to holding a noble title, but wealth was the ultimate source of power; even though some seats in the British House of Commons were popularly elected, Britain basically was an oligarchy. Even in France, wealth could purchase nobility, and the whole system of feudal privilege was becoming an anachronistic system of financial exploitation, which finally shared in the collapse of a monarchy unable to sustain the costs of war and debt. France and Britain with their advanced political, social, and economic systems, however, had more in common with each other than either had with true absolutisms like Prussia and Russia.[9]

Even during the war of 1792–1801, ideology was less important than greed in the foreign policies of France's enemies, and France itself soon subordinated idealism to expansionism. Britain was willing to tolerate even the overthrow of the French monarchy until that expansionism posed a security threat to Britain, the moment when France first occupied the Austrian Netherlands. In 1801, however, the British were so exhausted by war that they accepted a peace that left part of the coast of the North Sea in French hands. This, however, was too unnatural a situation for peace to be stable.

The war of 1803–15 differed from previous wars in its scope rather than in its nature. Napoleon tried to introduce French principles such as civil equality into the countries he conquered, but he was more of a realist than an ideologue; he once wrote to Frederick William III of Prussia, "The foreign policy of all states is based on their geography."[10] His victories, however, disrupted the balance of power so seriously that almost all of Europe eventually came together to destroy his empire. For a change British and French differences were irreconcilable. Once Napoleon was replaced by Louis XVIII, a younger brother of the late Louis XVI, and the Low Countries again paid no threat to either the United Kingdom or France, their wars finally came to an end.

The age of sail probably would have been less interesting for historians had Britain and France remained allies after the 1720s and continued to force the other states of Europe to respect the existing borders of Europe. The people of not only Britain and France but also the other parts of Europe, however, likely would have been spared several wars. Let us leave the final word to the comte de Vergennes, who came to regret having led France into the War of American Independence:

"There is nothing I would not do to change its [Great Britain's] jealous policy, which is our misfortune and its own, and which is founded on an illusion. For 150 years we have ruined each other to enrich Europe, to strengthen powers from which we should have had nothing to fear or to create new ones. As a result we decline while others increase, and we will finish by having them equal to us, whereas otherwise it would have taken ten centuries."[11]

Notes and Suggested Further Reading

1. The Ship of the Line Begins Its Reign

1. These measurements are for sailing ships of the line and are the length of the gun deck; steam-powered wooden ships of the line were as long as 260 feet. There are a number of excellent books in English about the ship of the line. The best survey of European sailing navies and warships is Jan Glete, *Navies and Nations: Warships, Navies, and State Building in Europe and America, 1500–1860*, 2 vols. (Stockholm: Almqvist & Wiksell International, 1993). For a brief introduction to sailing warships, see Robert Gardiner, ed., *The Line of Battle: The Sailing Warship, 1650–1840* (London: Conway Maritime Press, 1992). More detailed and beautifully illustrated are Brian Lavery, *The Ship of the Line*, 2 vols. (Annapolis: Naval Institute Press, 1983–84); Jean Boudriot, *The Seventy-four Gun Ship: A Practical Treatise on the Art of Naval Architecture*, 4 vols., trans. David H. Roberts (Annapolis: Naval Institute Press, 1986–88); and Rif Winfield, *The 50-Gun Ship* (London: Caxton Editions, 1997). Extremely useful, even though nominally restricted to a narrow period, is Brian Lavery, *Nelson's Navy: The Ships, Men, and Organization, 1793–1815* (London: Conway Maritime Press; Annapolis: Naval Institute Press, 1989); shorter introductory books are David Davies, *Nelson's Navy: English Fighting Ships, 1793–1815* (Mechanicsburg PA: Stackpole Books, 1996); and Bernard Ireland, *Naval Warfare in the Age of Sail: War at Sea, 1756–1815* (New York: W. W. Norton, 2000). For those who read French, there are Patrick Villiers, *La Marine de Louis XVI*, a volume of text and a box of ship plans (Grenoble: J. P. Debbane, 1985), as well as a number of other books by Boudriot including *Les Vaisseaux*

de 50 et 64 canons: Etude historique, 1650–1780 (Paris: ANCRE, 1994) and *Les Vaisseaux de 74 à 120 canons: Etude historique* (Paris: ANCRE, 1995). The best introductions to how the British and French navies functioned are N. A. M. Rodger, *The Command of the Ocean: A Naval History of Britain, 1649–1815* (London: Allen Lane, 2004); John Ehrman, *The Navy in the War of William III, 1689–1697: Its State and Direction* (Cambridge: Cambridge University Press, 1953); Daniel A. Baugh, *British Naval Administration in the Age of Walpole* (Princeton: Princeton University Press, 1965); and James Pritchard, *Louis XV's Navy, 1748–1762: A Study of Organization and Administration* (Montreal and Kingston: McGill-Queen's University Press, 1987). For the *Santísima Trinidad*, see John D. Harbron, "The Spanish Ship of the Line," *Scientific American* 251 (1979): 116–29; and Peter Goodwin, *The Ships of Trafalgar: The British, French, and Spanish Fleets, October 1805* (London: Conway Maritime Press; Annapolis: Naval Institute Press, 2005), 209–12.

2. See Peter Padfield, *Tide of Empires: Decisive Naval Campaigns in the Rise of the West*, 2 vols. (London: Routledge and Kegan Paul, 1979–82), 1:46–53; John F. Guilmartin Jr., "The Earliest Shipboard Gunpowder Ordnance: An Analysis of Its Technical Parameters and Tactical Capabilities," *Journal of Military History* 71 (2007): 651, and N. A. M. Rodger, "The Development of Broadside Gunnery, 1450–1650," in Jan Glete, ed., *Naval History, 1500–1680* (Burlington VT: Ashgate, 2005), 239–62, esp. 253. The Portuguese presence in the Indian Ocean is discussed in Jan Glete, *Warfare at Sea, 1500–1650: Maritime Conflicts and the Transformation of Europe* (London: Routledge, 2000), 76–92; this work is a naval history of unsurpassed originality, sophistication, and breadth of coverage. Glete's other writings include *War and the State in Early Modern Europe: Spain, the Dutch Republic, and Sweden as Fiscal-Military States, 1500–1660* (New York: Routledge, 2002), and "Naval Power, 1450–1650: The Formative Age," in Geoff Mortimer, ed., *Early Modern Military History, 1450–1815* (Basingstoke, UK: Palgrave Macmillan, 2004), 81–100.

3. Glete, *Navies and Nations*, 1:128, 130, 134, 156, 163, 167; Rodger, "Development of Broadside Gunnery"; J. J. A. Wijn, "Maarten Harpentszoon Tromp: Father of Naval Tactics (1578–1653)," in Jack Sweetman, ed., *The*

Great Admirals: Command at Sea, 1589–1945 (Annapolis: Naval Institute Press, 1997), 36–57; Carla Rahn Phillips, *Six Galleons for the King of Spain: Imperial Defense in the Early Seventeenth Century* (Baltimore: Johns Hopkins University Press, 1986), 214–22.

4. For English ship development, see Lavery, *Ship of the Line*, 1:10–15, 16–24, 158–59; N. A. M. Rodger, *Command of the Ocean*, 216–25, and *The Safeguard of the Sea: A Naval History of Britain, vol. 1, 660–1649* (London: HarperCollins, 1997), 386–89, 481–82. J. J. Colledge and Ben Warlow, comps., *Ships of the Royal Navy: The Complete Record of All Fighting Ships of the Royal Navy from the Fifteenth Century to the Present* (London: Chatham, 2006), is informative but difficult to use for studying changes over time because it is arranged alphabetically. Spain's continuing reliance on galleons is detailed in Carla Rahn Phillips, *Six Galleons* and *The Treasure of the* San José: *Death at Sea in the War of the Spanish Succession* (Baltimore: Johns Hopkins University Press, 2007). For the development of the frigate, see R. A. Stradling, *The Armada of Flanders: Spanish Maritime Policy and European War, 1568–1668* (Cambridge: Cambridge University Press, 1992), 164–73. Note that during these years, England also launched a 56-gun ship and a 48-gun ship that were not of the *Speaker* class.

5. Lavery, *Ship of the Line*, 1:21, 116–17; Paul M. Kennedy, *The Rise and Fall of British Naval Mastery* (Basingstoke, UK: Macmillan, 1983), 47–50; J. R. Jones, *The Anglo-Dutch Wars of the Seventeenth Century* (London: Longman, 1996), 41. Jones's study is a superb combination of naval, diplomatic, and political history. Roger Hainsworth and Christine Churches, *The Anglo-Dutch Wars, 1652–1674* (Phoenix Mill, UK: Sutton, 1998), is more conventional; see also R. C. Anderson, "The First Dutch War in the Mediterranean," *Mariner's Mirror* 49 (1963): 241–65, and M. A. J. Palmer, "The 'Military Revolution' Afloat: The Era of Anglo-Dutch Wars and the Transition to Modern Warfare at Sea," in Glete, *Naval History*, 286–311. Those interested in the social history of the English navy should consult Bernard Capp, *Cromwell's Navy: The Fleet and the English Revolution, 1648–1660* (Oxford: Clarendon Press, 1989). The best overall history of the English navy before 1815 is to be found in the two incomparable books of N. A. M. Rodger, *Safeguard of the Sea* and *Command of the Ocean*; Rodger is working

on a third volume on the nineteenth- and twentieth-century British navy. Still useful, however, is William Laird Clowes, *The Royal Navy: A History from the Earliest Times to the Present*, 7 vols. (Boston: Little, Brown; London: Sampson Low, Marston, 1897–1903). For an introduction to the Dutch navy, see Jaap R. Bruijn, *The Dutch Navy of the Seventeenth and Eighteenth Centuries* (Columbia: University of South Carolina Press, 1993).

6. Rodger, *Command of the Ocean*, 6–19; Jones, *Anglo-Dutch Wars*, 128–29; Padfield, *Tide of Empires*, 225–29; Palmer, "The 'Military Revolution' Afloat."

7. For the final decades of the ship of the line, see Andrew Lambert, "Preparing for the Russian War: British Strategic Planning, March 1853–March 1854," in Richard Harding, ed., *Naval History, 1680–1850* (Burlington VT: Ashgate, 2006), 69–93; Lambert, *Battleships in Transition: The Creation of the Steam Battlefleet, 1815–1860* (Annapolis: Naval Institute Press, 1984), and Lambert, *The Last Sailing Battlefleet: Maintaining Naval Mastery, 1815–1850* (London: Conway Maritime Press, 1991), as well as David Lyon and Rif Winfield, *The Sail and Steam Navy List: All the Ships of the Royal Navy, 1815–1889* (London: Chatham, 2004).

8. This includes the weight of the wooden carriage on which it was mounted. The cannon itself weighed almost 7,200 pounds: Boudriot, *Seventy-four Gun Ship*, 4:120–21; Thomas Adams, "A Standard Caliber: The Genesis of the French 30-Pounder," in Edward Freeman, ed., *Les Empires en guerre et paix, 1793–1860: Journées franco-anglaises d'histoire de la Marine, Porsmouth, 23–26 mars 1988* (Vincennes: Service historique de la marine, 1990), 195. Gun ports were in common use by the middle of the sixteenth century, by which time cast-iron cannon (cheaper than brass cannon) were being manufactured: Glete, *Navies and Nations*, 1:25; Guilmartin, "Earliest Shipboard Gunpowder Ordnance," 664–65; Larrie D. Ferreiro, *Ships and Science: The Birth of Naval Architecture in the Scientific Revolution* (Cambridge: MIT Press, 2007), 196. Guilmartin, 649–69, and Glete, *Warfare at Sea*, 21–24, provide a good introduction to the beginning of ship cannon.

9. John B. Hattendorf, "Sir George Rooke and Sir Cloudesley Shovell, c1650–1709 and 1650–1707," in Peter Le Fevre and Richard Harding, eds.,

Precursors of Nelson: British Admirals of the Eighteenth Century (London: Chatham, 2000), 64. The difficulties that sailing ship admirals faced are discussed by N. A. M. Rodger, "Image and Reality in Eighteenth-Century Naval Tactics," in Harding, *Naval History*, 321–37, and by Michael A. Palmer, *Command at Sea: Naval Command and Control since the Sixteenth Century* (Cambridge: Harvard University Press, 2003), 1–209.

10. It was 2,617 tons compared with 1,522 tons: Lavery, *Ship of the Line*, 1:158, 187. For further details see Ehrman, *Navy in the War of William III*, 12.

11. Ehrman, *Navy in the War of William III*, 19–21, 36.

12. Archives de la Marine (kept at the Archives Nationales, Paris), series B^5, vol. 3, pages 2–4; Boudriot, *Seventy-four Gun Ship*, 4:40; Patrick Villiers, *Marine royale, corsaires et trafic dans l'Atlantique de Louis XIV à Louis XVI*, 2 vols. (Villeneuve d'Ascq: Presses universitaires du Septentrion, 2002), 1:29–30; Rodger, *Command of the Ocean*, 498–99. There are several dozen complete crew rosters in *Les Combattants français de la guerre américaine, 1778–1783: Listes établies d'après les documents authentiques déposés aux Archives Nationales et aux Archives du Ministère de la Guerre* (Paris: Quantin, 1903), 3–219.

13. E. H. Jenkins, *A History of the French Navy from Its Beginnings to the Present Day* (London: Macdonald and James, 1973), 73–75; Jonathan R. Dull, *The French Navy and American Independence: A Study of Arms and Diplomacy, 1774–1787* (Princeton: Princeton University Press, 1975), 374–75; "Comparison des forces navales en 1692 et 1779," Archives de la Marine, series B^5, box 12.

14. Glete, *Navies and Nations*, 1:190–92, 2:561.

15. Glete, *Navies and Nations*, 1:183, 189–90; R. E. J. Weber, "The Introduction of the Single Line Ahead as a Battle Formation by the Dutch, 1665–1666," in Glete, *Naval History*, 313–27.

2. Louis XIV and His Wars

1. John B. Wolf, *Louis XIV* (New York: W. W. Norton, 1968) is a perceptive and highly readable biography. Shorter studies with good accounts of war and diplomacy include Andrew Lossky, *Louis XIV and the French Monarchy* (New Brunswick: Rutgers University Press, 1994), and John A. Lynn, *The Wars*

of Louis XIV (New York: Longman, 1999). The superb diplomatic historian Ragnhild Hatton portrays Louis as generally moderate in his goals; see her essay "Louis XIV and His Fellow Monarchs" in an excellent collection of essays she edited, *Louis XIV and Europe* (Columbus: Ohio State University Press, 1976), 16–59. The same conclusion is reached by the renowned historian Emmanuel Le Roy Ladurie in his survey *The Ancien Régime: A History of France, 1610–1774*, trans. Mark Greengrass (Oxford: Blackwell, 1996), 264–76. On the other hand, Paul Sonnino, "The Origins of Louis XIV's Wars," in Jeremy Black, ed., *The Origins of War in Early Modern Europe* (Edinburgh: John Donald,.1987), 112–31, is quite critical of him. For a general history of French foreign policy, see Jeremy Black, *From Louis XIV to Napoleon: The Fate of a Great Power* (London: UCL Press, 1999).

2. An excellent survey, concentrating on the diplomatic and military aspects of the war, is C. V. Wedgwood, *The Thirty Years' War* (Garden City NY: Anchor Books, Doubleday, 1961). For the Spanish side of the war, consult J. H. Elliott, *The Count-Duke of Olivares: The Statesman in an Age of Decline* (New Haven: Yale University Press, 1986), 452–673; Stradling, *Armada of Flanders*, 39–150; Phillips, *Six Galleons*, 103–18; and R. C. Anderson, "The Thirty Years' War in the Mediterranean," in Glete, *Naval History*, 403–37. The French entry into the war is analyzed by David Parrott, "The Causes of the Franco-Spanish War of 1635–59," in Black, *Origins of War*, 72–111.

3. For the seventeenth-century French army, see John A. Lynn, *Giant of the Grand Siècle: The French Army, 1610–1715* (Cambridge: Cambridge University Press, 1997). There is a useful comparison of the strength of various seventeenth-century European armies in Glete, *War and the State*, 32–36, 155–57.

4. The debate between Richelieu and his chief rival, Michel de Marillac, an advocate of Louis XIII's focusing his efforts against his *internal* rivals, is discussed by J. Russell Major, *From Renaissance Monarchy to Absolute Monarchy: French Kings, Nobles, and Estates* (Baltimore: Johns Hopkins University Press, 1994), 263–67.

5. Pierre Goubert, *Louis XIV and Twenty Million Frenchmen*, trans. Anne Carter (New York: Vintage Books, 1970), 46.

6. See Alan James, *The Navy and Government in Early Modern France*

(Woodbridge, UK: Boydell Press for the Royal Historical Society, 2004), and Jenkins, *French Navy*, 32–37. Although quite cursory, Jenkins's book remains the best survey in English of the seventeenth- and eighteenth-century French navy. Philippe Masson, *Histoire de la marine*, vol. 1, *L'Ere de la voile* (Paris and Limoges: Charles Lavauzelle, 1981), is a lavishly illustrated French-language survey. A more detailed study is Charles de La Roncière, *Histoire de la marine française*, 6 vols. (Paris: E. Plon, Nourrit, 1899–1932), although it does not cover the period beyond 1715. A perceptive, although perhaps overly critical, survey in French of Louis XIV's navy is Daniel Dessert, *La Royale: Vaisseaux et marins du Roi-Soleil* (Paris: Fayard, 1996). An excellent recent study, covering most of the period before 1789, is Villiers, *Marine royale*; also useful is Michel Vergé-Franseschi, *La Marine française au XVIIIe siècle: Guerres-Administration-Exploration* (Paris: SEDES, 1996). For Colbert, see Inès Murat, *Colbert*, trans. Robert Francis Cooke and Jeannie Van Asselt (Charlottesville: University Press of Virginia, 1984).

7. Commandant Alain Demerliac, *La Marine de Louis XIV: Nomenclature des Vaisseaux du Roi-Soleil de 1661 à 1715* (Nice: Editions Omega, 1992), 5–11, 15, 22–23, 32–33; Glete, *Navies and Nations*, 1:191–92, 195, 198–99. The late Commandant Demerliac and his staff compiled five magnificent reference books on the warships of the French navy; the others will be cited in succeeding chapters. They are easily usable even for those who do not read French. Their British equivalent is a single-volume work, slightly less detailed but beautifully illustrated, by David Lyon, *The Sailing Navy List: All the Ships of the Royal Navy Built, Purchased, and Captured, 1688–1860* (London: Conway Maritime Press, 1993); it has been supplemented for part of the period by Rif Winfield, *British Warships in the Age of Sail, 1793–1815: Design, Construction, Careers, and Fates* (London: Chatham; Minneapolis: MBI, 2005) and *British Warships in the Age of Sail, 1714–1795: Design, Construction, Careers, and Fates* (London: Chatham, 2007). My book could not have been written without them; all naval historians are in their debt.

8. James Pritchard, *In Search of Empire: The French in the Americas, 1670–1730* (Cambridge: Cambridge University Press, 2004), 3–263. Pritchard's encyclopedic study is vital for the understanding of French colonial history.

9. Ehrman, *Navy in the War of William III*, 89, 212, 221, 636–37; Roger Morriss, *The Royal Dockyards during the Revolution and Napoleonic Wars* (Leicester: Leicester University Press, 1983), 108–9; Ann Coats, "Efficiency in Dockyard Administration, 1660–1800: A Reassessment," in Harding, *Naval History*, 413–29. There are wonderful illustrations of the dockyards opposite Ehrman, *Navy in the War of William III*, 88, and throughout Jonathan G. Coad, *The Royal Dockyards, 1690–1850: Architecture and Engineering Works of the Sailing Navy* (Aldershot, UK: Scolar Press, 1989). Nothing, however, can compare to the exquisite paintings of the French ports by the great Joseph Vernet, now at the Louvre and the Musée de la Marine in Paris. The best history of a French port is Martine Acerra, *Rochefort et la construction navale française, 1661–1815*, 4 vols. (Paris: Librairie de l'Inde, 1993). See also José P. Merino, "Graving Docks in France and Spain before 1800," in Harding, *Naval History*, 457–80.

10. For the growth of England's potential for making war, see John Brewer, *The Sinews of Power: War, Money, and the English State, 1688–1783* (New York: Alfred A. Knopf, 1989).

11. The finest account of life aboard warships in the age of sail is the masterpiece by N. A. M. Rodger, *The Wooden World: An Anatomy of the Georgian Navy* (London: Collins, 1986). Larrie D. Ferreiro's magnificent *Ships and Science* details the French navy's support of scientific research; for Bouguer's work on the metacenter, see 187–258. For French signaling, see Palmer, *Command at Sea*, 125–26; the related topic of a scientific approach to fleet tactics, which attracted both British and French theoreticians, is discussed by Michel Depeyre, *Tactiques et stratégies navales de la France et de Royaume-Uni de 1690 à 1815* (Paris: Economica, 1998). The delightful Janet MacDonald, *Feeding Nelson's Navy: The True Story of Food at Sea in the Georgian Era* (London: Chatham; Mechanicsburg PA: Stackpole Books, 2004); Ehrman, *Navy in the War of William III*, 120–22, 144–57; and Alain Clouet, "Se nourrir sur le gaillard d'avant au temps de la voile," *Neptunia*, no. 240 (December 2006): 12–19, all discuss diet; for the diet of seventeenth-century Spanish sailors, see Phillips, *Six Galleons*, 98–103, 163–72. The invention of canning is described by MacDonald, 171–72, and by Sue Shephard, *Pickled, Potted, and Canned: How the Art of Food Processing*

Changed the World (London: Simon and Schuster, 2000), 226–47. For the policies on shore leave and the various preventives for scurvy, see Boudriot, *Seventy-four Gun Ship*, 4:152, 182–83; Rodger, *Command of the Ocean*, 208–9, 318, 484–86, 499–500; MacDonald, 154–66; and Duncan Crewe, *Yellow Jack and the Worm: British Naval Administration in the West Indies, 1739–1748* (Liverpool: Liverpool University Press, 1993), 21. Other books discussing life at sea include Brian Lavery, ed., *Shipboard Life and Organisation, 1731–1815* (London: Naval Records Society, 1998); Nicholas Blake, *Steering to Glory: A Day in the Life of a Ship of the Line* (London: Chatham, 2005); Anthony Deane, *Nelson's Favourite: HMS Agamemnon at War, 1781–1809* (Annapolis: Naval Institute Press, 1996); and David Cordingly, *Billy Ruffian: The Bellerophon and the Downfall of Napoleon: The Biography of a Ship of the Line, 1783–1836* (London: Bloomsbury, 2003).

12. Jean Bérenger, "An Attempted *Rapprochement* between France and the Emperor: The Secret Treaty for the Partition of the Spanish Succession of 19 January 1668," in Hatton, *Louis XIV and Europe*, 133–52. For an example of Louis's considering Spain an inveterate French enemy, see his comment from 1669 quoted by Paul Sonnino, "What Kind of Idea Is the Idea of 'Balance of Power'?" in Peter Krüger and Paul W. Schröder, eds., *The Transformation of European Politics, 1763–1848: Episode or Model in Modern History?* (Munich: LIT, 2002), 68. A good introduction to the diplomacy of early modern Europe is Derek McKay and H. M. Scott, *The Rise of the Great Powers, 1648–1815* (London: Longman, 1983).

13. See Paul Sonnino, *Louis XIV and the Origins of the Dutch War* (Cambridge: Cambridge University Press, 1988).

14. Padfield, *Tide of Empires*, 2:22–63; Jones, *Anglo-Dutch Wars*, 145–78; Clowes, *Royal Navy*, 2:253–98, 424–37; P. G. Rogers, *The Dutch in the Medway* (London: Oxford University Press, 1970).

15. Jenkins, *French Navy*, 49; Jones, *Anglo-Dutch Wars*, 189–216; Rodger, *Command of the Ocean*, 80–85; Clowes, *Royal Navy*, 2:298–322; A. Van der Moer, "Michel Adrianszoon de Ruyter: Ornament of His Age (1607–1676)," in Sweetman, *Great Admirals*, 82–111; Peter Padfield, *Maritime Supremacy and the Opening of the Western Mind: Naval Campaigns That Shaped the Modern World, 1588–1782* (London: John Murray, 1999), 100–115, and *Tide*

of Empires, 2:80–117; Donald G. Schomette and Robert D. Haslach, *Raid on America: The Dutch Naval Campaign of 1672–1674* (Columbia: University of South Carolina Press, 1988).

16. Jenkins, *French Navy*, 55–64; Pritchard, *In Search of Empire*, 266–300; Wolf, *Louis XIV*, 213–65; Carl J. Ekberg, *The Failure of Louis XIV's Dutch War* (Chapel Hill: University of North Carolina Press, 1979); R. C. Anderson, "The Sicilian War of 1674–1678," *Mariner's Mirror* 57 (1971): 239–65.

17. Ehrman, *Navy in the War of William III*, 174–244, does a masterful job of tracing the evolution of British naval administration. See also Rodger, *Command of the Ocean*, 95–111, and C. S. Knighton, *Pepys and the Navy* (Stroud, UK: Sutton, 2003).

18. This description of the so-called Glorious Revolution of 1688 is based on Jonathan I. Israel, "The Dutch Role in the Glorious Revolution," in Jonathan I. Israel, ed., *The Anglo-Dutch Moment: Essays on the Glorious Revolution and Its World Impact* (Cambridge: Cambridge University Press, 1991), 105–62; Jonathan Israel and Geoffrey Parker, "Of Provident and Protestant Winds: The Spanish Armada of 1688 and the Dutch Armada of 1688," in Israel, 335–63; J. R. Jones, *The Revolution of 1688 in England* (London: Weidenfeld and Nicolson, 1972); Roger B. Manning, *An Apprenticeship in Arms: The Origins of the British Army, 1585–1702* (Oxford: Oxford University Press, 2006), 345–70; and John Carswell, *The Descent on England: A Study of the English Revolution of 1688 and Its European Background* (New York: John Day, 1969). For the unsuccessful efforts of James's fleet, see Ehrman, *Navy in the War of William III*, 201–44, and David Davies, "James II, William of Orange, and the Admirals," in Eveline Cruickshanks, ed., *By Force or by Default? The Revolution of 1688–1689* (Edinburgh: John Donald, 1989), 82–105. For the king, see Maurice Ashley, *James II* (Minneapolis: University of Minnesota Press, 1977), and for Herbert, see Ehrman, *Navy in the War of William III*, 274–77, and Peter Le Fevre, "Arthur Herbert, Earl of Torrington, 1648–1715," in Le Fevre and Harding, *Precursors of Nelson*, 19–41.

19. Figures are for 1 January 1689. The English total includes twenty-six of the 4th rate, carrying 48–50 cannon, while the French total includes only six of the 4th rate carrying 48–50 cannon: Lyon, *Sailing Navy List*,

11–13; Ehrman, *Navy in the War of William III*, 4; Demerliac, *La Marine de Louis XIV*, 5–12, 15–18, 22–26.

20. Geoffrey Symcox, *The Crisis of French Sea Power, 1688–1697: From the Guerre d'Escadre to the Guerre de Course* (The Hague: Martinus Nijhoff, 1974), 18–19; Donald Pilgrim, "The Colbert-Seignelay Naval Reforms and the Beginning of the War of the League of Augsburg," *French Historical Studies* 9 (1975–76): 235–62; Laurent Dingli, *Colbert, marquis de Seignelay: Le fils flamboyant* (Paris: Perroin, 1997), 238–363. For the naval side of the ensuing war, usually called the Nine Years' War or the War of the League of Augsburg, see, in addition to Symcox and Pilgrim, Edward B. Powley, *The Naval Side of King William's War, 16th/26th November 1688–14th June 1690* (Hamden CT: Archon Books, 1972); Ehrman, *Navy in the War of William III*, 245–553; Clowes, *Royal Navy*, 2:326–65, 461–97; Jenkins, *French Navy*, 69–92; Padfield, *Maritime Supremacy*, 119–56; Rodger, *Command of the Ocean*, 136–63, 211–12; A. N. Ryan, "William III and the Brest Fleet in the Nine Years' War," in Ragnhild Hatton and J. S. Bromley, eds., *William III and Louis XIV, 1680–1720: Essays by and for Mark A. Thomson* (Liverpool: Liverpool University Press, 1968), 49–67; C. D. Lee, "The Battle of Beachy Head: Lord Torrington's Conduct," and Peter Le Fevre, "'Mere Laziness' or Incompetence: The Earl of Torrington and the Battle of Beachy Head," *Mariner's Mirror* 80 (1994): 270–97; Philip Aubrey, *The Defeat of James Stuart's Armada, 1692* (Leicester: Leicester University Press, 1979); K. A. J. McLay, "Combined Operations and the European Theatre during the Nine Years' War, 1688–97," *Historical Research* 78 (2005): 506–39; and the excellent *Guerres maritimes (1688–1713)* (Vincennes: Service historique de la marine, 1996), which contains nine essays in English and seven in French.

21. Demerliac, *La Marine de Louis XIV*, 11–14, 16–19, 22–28; Lyon, *Sailing Navy List*, 11–13, 17–23; Glete, *Navies and Nations*, 1:209. The Dutch total, which is for 1695, includes ships of 44 or more cannon. The French navy's strength seems to have peaked in 1694 at 106 ships of the 1st to 3rd rates: Dessert, *La Royale*, 302.

22. For the size of the French army, see Lynn, *Giant of the Grand Siècle*, 55. Comparative naval strengths are given in Glete, *Navies and Nations*,

1:220–30. Budget figures are from Symcox, *Crisis of French Sea Power*, 146, 234; Ehrman, *Navy in the War of William III*, 460–90; Rodger, *Command of the Ocean*, 642; and Henri Legohérel, *Les Tréoriers généraux de la Marine (1517–1788)* (Paris: Cujas, 1965), table facing 180. For this period I have used an exchange rate of 13:1 as recommended by Rodger, *Command of the Ocean*, 669n.

23. Demerliac, *La Marine de Louis XIV*, 11–14, 17–20, 24–29.

24. For the naval side of the War of the Spanish Succession, see Rodger, *Command of the Ocean*, 164–80; Padfield, *Maritime Supremacy*, 157–69; Clowes, *Royal Navy*, 2:366–417, 500–534; La Roncière, *Histoire de la marine française*, 6:43–590; Jenkins, *French Navy*, 94–105; Phillips, *Treasure of the* San José; John B. Hattendorf, *England in the War of the Spanish Succession: A Study of the English View and Conduct of Grand Strategy, 1702–1712* (New York: Garland, 1987); J. H. Owen, *War at Sea under Queen Anne, 1702–8* (Cambridge: Cambridge University Press, 1938); and R. D. Merriman, ed., *Queen Anne's Navy: Documents Concerning the Administration of the Navy of Queen Anne, 1702–14* (London: Naval Records Society, 1961). There is an account of the Battle of Malaga in J. Creswell, *British Admirals of the Eighteenth Century* (London: Allen and Unwin, 1972), 52–62.

25. Villiers, *Marine royale*, 1:81; Legohérel, *Les Trésoriers généraux*, table facing 180; Rodger, *Command of the Ocean*, 642–43. As in the previous war, expenditures were greater than appropriations for both navies, but the overall pattern is similar. For expenditures, see Rodger, *Command of the Ocean*, 642–43, and Catherine M. Desbarets, "France in North America: The Net Burden of Empire during the First Half of the Eighteenth Century," *French History* 11 (1997): 1–28. The exchange rate varied considerably; I have used the average 1708–9 rate as computed from John J. McCusker, *Money and Exchange in Europe and America, 1600–1775: A Handbook* (Chapel Hill: University of North Carolina Press, 1978), 87, 91.

26. Hattendorf, *War of the Spanish Succession*, 312–13, 320–21; Symcox, *Crisis of French Sea Power*, 225–26; Pritchard, *In Search of Empire*, 358–401.

27. Owen, *War at Sea*, 158–92; Fernand Braudel, *The Identity of France*, vol. 1, *History and Environment*, trans. Siân Reynolds (London: Collins, 1988), 351–72; Ciro Paoletti, "Prince Eugene of Savoy, the Toulon Expedition of

1707, and the English Historians: A Dissenting View," *Journal of Military History* 70 (2006): 939–62; J. Meirat, "Le Siège de Toulon en 1707," *Neptunia*, no. 71 (Autumn 1963): 2–9.

28. There is an excellent recent biography of Philip V by Henry Kamen, *Philip V of Spain: The King Who Reigned Twice* (New Haven: Yale University Press, 2001). See also Kamen's *The War of Succession in Spain, 1700–15* (Bloomington: Indiana University Press; London: Weidenfeld and Nicolson, 1969).

3. Foolish Wars End an Age of Peace

1. Ehrman, *Navy in the War of William III*, 554–62; Crewe, *Yellow Jack and the Worm*; Christian Buchet, "The Royal Navy in the Caribbean, 1689–1763," *Mariner's Mirror* 80 (1994): 30–44; and Julian Gwyn, *Frigates and Foremasts: The North American Squadron in Nova Scotia Waters, 1749–1815* (Vancouver: University of British Columbia Press, 2003) and *Ashore and Afloat: The British Navy and the Halifax Yard before 1820* (Ottawa: University of Ottawa Press, 2004). The French established no dockyards in the Western Hemisphere until 1787, while in Europe they were at a serious disadvantage in the number of dry docks for cleaning and repairing warships: Daniel A. Baugh, "Naval Power: What Gave the British Naval Supremacy?" in Leandro Prados de la Escosura, ed., *Exceptionalism and Industrialization: Britain and Its European Rivals, 1688–1815* (Cambridge: Cambridge University Press, 2004), 235–57.

2. Not surprisingly, the British financial innovations during William and Mary's reign had Dutch antecedents: Manning, *Apprenticeship in Arms*, 428–29. For the English navy's use of the Bank of England and its early difficulties, see Ehrman, *Navy in the War of William III*, 540–44, 575–83, 591–93. The French failure is described in Colin Jones, *The Great Nation: France from Louis XV to Napoleon, 1715–99* (New York: Columbia University Press, 2002), 61–73.

3. Daniel Szechi, *1715: The Great Jacobite Rebellion* (New Haven: Yale University Press, 2006). George I is the subject of a brilliant biography, Ragnhild Hatton, *George I, Elector and King* (Cambridge: Harvard University Press, 1978). It was reissued in 2001 by Yale University Press under the

title *George I.* See also Joyce Marlow, *The Life and Times of George I* (London: Weidenfeld and Nicolson, 1973).

4. There are numerous biographies of the regent. A recent one that is concise and very readable is Christine Previtt, *Philippe, Duc d'Orléans, Regent of France* (New York: Atlantic Monthly Press, 1997). For an astute appraisal of the regency, see Le Roy Ladurie, *Ancien Régime,* 279–301.

5. Hatton, *George I,* 36–37, 184–90, 216–22; R. C. Anderson, *Naval Wars in the Baltic, 1522–1850* (London: Francis Edwards, 1969), 162–207; David Aldridge, "The Navy as Handmaid for Commerce and Foreign Policy, 1680–1720," in Jeremy Black and Philip Woodfine, eds., *The Navy and the Use of Naval Power in the Eighteenth Century* (Atlantic Highlands NJ: Humanities Press International, 1989), 64–66; and David Aldridge, "Sir John Norris, 1660?–1749," in Le Fevre and Harding, *Precursors of Nelson,* 138–44. For the importance of the Baltic region, see Ehrman, *Navy in the War of William III,* 51–65.

6. Hatton, *George I,* 230–35; Kamen, *Philip V,* 119–28; Clowes, *Royal Navy,* 3:30–40; John D. Harbron, *Trafalgar and the Spanish Navy* (Annapolis: Naval Institute Press, 1998), 29–32.

7. Although by now rather dated, the standard authority in English on Fleury is Arthur McCandless Wilson, *French Foreign Policy during the Administration of Cardinal Fleury, 1726–1743: A Study in Diplomacy and Commercial Development* (Cambridge: Harvard University Press; London: Humphrey Milford, Oxford University Press, 1936). See also Le Roy Ladurie, *Ancien Régime,* 337–72.

8. Using a fleet commanded by the superb sailor and diplomat Admiral Sir Charles Wager, Britain forced Russia to demobilize its Baltic fleet in 1726. This averted another crisis. Wager commanded off Gibraltar the following year: Anderson, *Naval Wars in the Baltic,* 211–12; Daniel A. Baugh, "Sir Charles Wager, 1666–1743," in Le Fevre and Harding, *Precursors of Nelson,* 113–15. For continuing colonial disputes, see Jeremy Black's introduction to his *Origins of War,* 14–15, and Max Savelle, *The Origins of American Diplomacy: The International History of Angloamerica, 1492–1763* (New York: Macmillan; London: Collier-Macmillan, 1967), 246–47, 279–85.

9. Wilson, *French Foreign Policy,* 294–317; Michael Jebb, "Economic

Policy and Economic Development," in Jeremy Black, ed., *Britain in the Age of Walpole* (Basingstoke, UK: Macmillan, 1984), 121–44.

10. Demerliac, *La Marine de Louis XIV*, 19–21, 29–31; Glete, *Navies and Nations*, 1:217–18, 224 (columns A through F); 2:576–77, 584–85; Harbron, *Trafalgar and the Spanish Navy*, 59; Lyon, *Sailing Navy List*, 107.

11. The *Royal Louis*, 106, *Parfait*, 72, *Lys*, 72, *Conquerant*, 70, *Invincible*, 68, *Henry*, 64, *Grafton*, 66, *Toulouse*, 62, *Achille*, 62, *Hercule*, 60, *Mercure*, 60, and *Oriflamme*, 60. This does not include two 50's, the *Protée* and *Français*, that were downgraded to frigates after the last war: Demerliac, *La Marine de Louis XIV*, 11–31, 35. Only one ship of the line, the *Content*, 56, was launched between 1715 and 1719: Alain Demerliac, *La marine de Louis XV: Nomenclature des navires français de 1715 à 1774* (Nice: Editions Omega, 1995), 48. During the previous six years only two ships of the line (the *Conquerant* in 1712 and the *Toulouse* in 1714) had been launched. I have counted only ships of the 1st through 3rd rates as ships of the line; the distinction between French 3rd rate ships of the line and 4th rate heavy frigates was based less on the number of guns (some 4th rates carrying as many as 50) than on the size of their guns; see Winfield, *50-Gun Ship*, 124–25.

12. Lyon, *Sailing Navy List*, 17–25, 33–36, 39, 45, 192; Glete, *Navies and Nations*, 1:226. This number includes ships of 50 cannon.

13. Demerliac, *La Marine de Louis XIV*, 11–14, and *La Marine de Louis XV*, 35, 37, 42–43, 48–50; Lyon, *Sailing Navy List*, 36, 40–41, 44–45. The new large ship was the *Foudroyant*, 110, launched in 1724 and demolished in 1742 without having been in action. The next large ships, the *Royal Louis*, 118 (accidentally destroyed in 1742 before launching) and the *Royal Louis*, 116 (1759–73) did not see action either: Demerliac, *La Marine de Louis XV*, 35.

14. Marc Egnal, *A Mighty Empire: The Origins of the American Revolution* (Ithaca: Cornell University Press, 1988), 56–57; Fred Anderson and Andrew Cayton, *The Dominion of War: Empire and Liberty in North America, 1500–2000* (New York: Viking, 2005), 85–103; David J. Weber, *The Spanish Frontier in North America* (New Haven: Yale University Press, 1992), 179–91; Jon Parmenter and Mark Power Robison, "The Perils and

Possibilities of Wartime Neutrality on the Edge of Empire: Iroquois and Acadians between the French and British in North America, 1744–1760," *Diplomatic History* 31 (2007): 167–206. There are numerous books on French and British relations with the Indians. The best, in my opinion, is Richard White, *The Middle Ground: Indians, Empires, and Republics in the Great Lakes Region, 1650–1815* (Cambridge: Cambridge University Press, 1991). For the construction of Fort St. Frédéric, see Russell P. Bellico, *Sails and Steam in the Mountains: A Maritime and Military History of Lake George and Lake Champlain* (Fleischmanns NY: Purple Mountain Press, 1992), 18–20. Fighting during the wars of Louis XIV is described in Gerald S. Graham, *Empire of the North Atlantic: The Maritime Struggle for North America* (Toronto: University of Toronto Press; London: Oxford University Press, 1958), 64–102.

15. Wilson, *French Foreign Policy*, 215–39; Jeremy Black, *The Collapse of the Anglo-French Alliance, 1727–1731* (Gloucester, UK: Alan Sutton; New York: St. Martin's Press, 1987). A defensive alliance meant that each party was obliged to assist militarily the other or others, but only if they were attacked. For a survey of British-French relations in the eighteenth century, see Jeremy Black, *Natural and Necessary Enemies: Anglo-French Relations in the Eighteenth Century* (London: Duckworth, 1986). I discuss the topic in "Great Power Confrontation or Clash of Cultures? France's War against Great Britain and Its Antecedents," in Warren Hofstra, ed., *Cultures in Conflict: The Seven Years' War in North America* (Lantham, Md.: Rowman and Littlefield, 2007), 61–77. The best biography of George II is Jeremy Black, *George II: Puppet of the Politicians?* (Exeter: University of Exeter Press, 2007). See, too, Brendan Simms, *Three Victories and a Defeat: The Rise and Fall of the First British Empire* (New York: Basic books, 2008).

16. Wilson, *French Foreign Policy*, 240–64; John L. Sutton, *The King's Honor and the King's Cardinal: The War of the Polish Succession* (Lexington: University Press of Kentucky, 1980); Jeremy Black, "British Neutrality in the War of the Polish Succession, 1733–1735," *International History Review* 8 (1986): 345–66.

17. The various negotiations were completed, however, only in May 1739, when the Russians signed: Wilson, *French Foreign Policy*, 263–71.

18. Demerliac, *La Marine de Louis XV*, 43, 49, 50; Lyon, *Sailing Navy List*, 40–41, 44–46.

19. Wilson, *French Foreign Policy*, 290–317.

20. The best source for the breakdown of relations between Great Britain and Spain is Philip Woodfine, *Britannia's Glories: The Walpole Ministry and the 1739 War with Spain* (Woodbridge, UK: Boydell Press for the Royal Historical Society, 1998). See also Woodfine's earlier summary, "The Anglo-Spanish War of 1739," in Black, *Origins of War*, 85–109, and Geoffrey Walker, *Spanish Politics and Imperial Trade, 1700–1789* (Bloomington: Indiana University Press, 1979).

21. Lyon, *Sailing Navy List*, 18, 20, 22, 24–25, 33–36, 39–41, 44–46; C. de Saint Hubert, "Ships of the Line of the Spanish Navy (1714–1825)," *Warship* 10 (1986): 129–33.

22. National Archives of the United Kingdom (Public Record Office), Kew, England, State Papers Foreign, series 42 (Secretary of State: State Papers Naval), vol. 116, unpaginated; Sir Herbert W. Richmond, *The Navy in the War of 1739–48*, 3 vols. (Cambridge: Cambridge University Press, 1920), 1:261–64.

23. The best study of the initial phase of the war is Richard Harding, *Amphibious Warfare in the Eighteenth Century: The British Expedition to the West Indies, 1740–1742* (Woodbridge, UK: Boydell Press for the Royal Historical Society, 1991). See also Baugh, "Sir Charles Wager, 1666–1743," 120–23, and Richard Pares, *War and Trade in the West Indies, 1739–1763* (Oxford: Clarendon Press, 1936), which is wonderfully written and full of insights.

24. The classic study of them is William Lytle Schurz, *The Manila Galleon* (New York: E. P. Dutton, 1939).

25. Richard Harding, "Edward Vernon, 1684–1757," in Le Fevre and Harding, *Precursors of Nelson*, 165–68. For the importance of Havana, see John Robert McNeill, *Atlantic Empires of France and Spain: Louisbourg and Havana, 1700–1763* (Chapel Hill: University of North Carolina Press, 1985), 35–45, 85–92, 190–201; C. Douglas Inglis, "The Spanish Naval Shipyard at Havana in the Eighteenth Century," in *New Aspects of Naval History: Selected Papers from the 5th Naval History Symposium* (Baltimore: Nautical

and Aviation Publishing Company of America, 1985), 47–58; Harbron, *Trafalgar and the Spanish Navy*, 51–75. Harbron, 164–73, reprints Saint Hubert, "Ships of the Line of the Spanish Navy," cited above.

26. Harding, *Amphibious Warfare*, 51, 85; Richmond, *Navy in the War of 1739–48*, 1:110n (with dates changed to the new style or Gregorian calendar); J. C. Oglesby, "Spain's Havana Squadron and the Preservation of the Balance of Power in the Caribbean, 1740–1748," *Hispanic-American Historical Review* 49 (1969): 476.

27. Harding, *Amphibious Warfare*, 91–93; Richmond, *Navy in the War of 1739–48*, 1:106–8; Wilson, *French Foreign Policy*, 322–24.

28. For the attack on Cartagena and subsequent British operations, see Harding, *Amphibious Warfare*, 83–149; Charles E. Nowell, "The Defense of Cartagena," *Hispanic American Historical Review* 42 (1962): 477–501, and Julián de Zulueta, "Health and Military Factors in Vernon's Failure at Cartagena," *Mariner's Mirror* 78 (1992): 127–41. The logistical challenges of amphibious operations are analyzed by Piers Mackesy, "Problems of an Amphibious Power: Britain against France, 1793–1815," Richard Harding, "Sailors and Gentlemen of Parade: Some Professional and Technical Problems Concerning the Conduct of Combined Operations in the Eighteenth Century," and David Syrett, "The Methodology of British Amphibious Operations during the Seven Years' and American Wars," all in Harding, *Naval History*, 117–26, 127–47, 309–20.

29. Wilson, *French Foreign Policy*, 279, 319–21; Rohan Butler, *Choiseul*, vol. 1, *Father and Son, 1719–1754* (Oxford: Clarendon Press, 1981), 220–27; Karl Roider, "The Perils of Eighteenth-Century Peacemaking: Austria and the Treaty of Belgrade, 1739," *Central European History* 5 (1972): 195–207.

30. There are two excellent general surveys in English of the ensuing War of the Austrian Succession: Reed Browning, *The War of the Austrian Succession* (New York: St. Martin's Press, 1993), and M. S. Anderson, *The War of the Austrian Succession, 1740–1748* (London: Longman, 1995). See also H. M. Scott, *The Birth of a Great Power System, 1740–1815* (Harlow, UK: Pearson/Longman, 2006), 39–71. Scott's survey of the diplomatic history of the period is particularly valuable for eastern Europe and has an excellent bibliography.

31. For the dispute between Belle-Isle and Fleury, see Wilson, *French Foreign Policy*, 327–47. For Fleury's long-standing fear of Francis's candidacy, see Jeremy Black, "French Foreign Policy in the Age of Fleury Reassessed," *English Historical Review* 103 (1988): 367.

32. Richmond, *Navy in the War of 1739–48*, 1:151–78.

33. Richmond, *Navy in the War of 1739–48*, 1:103–4, 153–54, 160–63.

34. Jonathan R. Dull, *The French Navy and the Seven Years' War* (Lincoln: University of Nebraska Press, 2005), 257, lists them.

35. The best account of the invasion attempt is in French, Jean Colin, *Louis XV et les Jacobites: Le Projet de débarquement en Angleterre de 1743–1744* (Paris: R. Chapelot, 1901). For British countermeasures, see Richmond, *Navy in the War of 1739–48*, 2:58–93, and Julian S. Corbett, *Some Principles of Maritime Strategy* (London: Longmans, Green, 1911), 239–40, 247–53.

36. For the ships lost at Dunkirk, see Colin, *Louis XV et les Jacobites*, 150–52, 170–71.

37. For the operations of the Toulon fleet and the Battle of Toulon, see Richmond, *Navy in the War of 1739–48*, 2:1–57; Clowes, *Royal Navy*, 3:92–106; Creswell, *British Admirals*, 66–80; Ruddock Mackay, *Admiral Hawke* (Oxford: Clarendon Press, 1965), 22–34.

38. Appropriations in 1745 were 4 to 5 million livres less than in 1744: Legohérel, *Les Trésoriers généraux*, table facing 180. For comparative Britain and French appropriations in this and the following two wars, see chapter 8, below.

39. Richmond, *Navy in the War of 1739–48*, 2:170–89; Bruce Lenman, *The Jacobite Risings in Britain, 1689–1746* (New York: Holmes and Meier; London: Eyre Methuen, 1980), 231–59, 287–89; F. J. McLynn, *France and the Jacobite Rising of 1745* (Edinburgh: University of Edinburgh Press, 1981); Christopher Duffy, *The '45* (London: Cassell, 2003), 370–73, 576–77.

40. Pritchard, *Louis XV's Navy*, 73–76; McNeill, *Atlantic Empires of France and Spain*, 82, 93, 107, 138; Jean-François Brière, "Pêche et politique à Terre-Neuve au XVIIIe siècle: La France veritable gagnante du traité d'Utrecht?" *Canadian Historical Review* 64 (1983): 168–87, and *La Pêche française en Amérique du Nord au XVIIIe siècle* (Saint-Laurent QC: Fides, 1990), 223; T. J. A. Le Goff, "Offre et productivité de la main-d'oeuvre

dans les armements français au XVIIIe siècle," *Histoire, économie et société* 2 (1983): 459, 462, 467, and "The Labor Market for Sailors in France," in Paul Van Royen, Jaap Bruijn, and Jan Lucassen, eds., *"Those Emblems of Hell"? European Sailors and the Maritime Labour Market, 1570–1870* (St. John's NF: International Maritime History Association, 1997), 300; Charles de la Morandière, *Histoire de la pêche française de la morue dans l'Amérique septentrionale*, 2 vols. (Paris: G. P. Maisonneuve et Larose, 1962), 2:999. Pritchard notes that dockyard workers, boys, elderly ex-sailors, and others were registered by the navy, creating an artificial number of more than 100,000 in 1758–59. The British had no system of registration, but a recent study estimates that by 1791 there were nearly 100,000 British seamen, almost double the number in 1738: David J. Starkey, "War and the Market for Seafarers in Britain, 1736–1792," in Harding, *Naval History*, 519–36. For other estimates, see Sarah Palmer and David M. Williams, "British Sailors, 1775–1840," in Von Royen et al., *"Those Emblems of Hell?"* 101–2, and Rodger, *Command of the Ocean*, 206, 319, 395.

41. Richmond, *Navy in the War of 1739–48*, 2:201–16; McNeill, *Atlantic Empires of France and Spain*, 11–26, 81–85, 94–97, 137–54; John A. Schutz, *William Shirley: King's Governor of Massachusetts* (Chapel Hill: University of North Carolina Press, 1961), 85–100; James A. Pritchard, *In Search of Empire*, 148–50, and *Anatomy of a Naval Disaster: The 1746 French Naval Expedition to North America* (Montreal and Kingston: McGill-Queen's University Press, 1995), 26–28; J. S. McLennan, *Louisbourg: From Its Foundation to Its Fall, 1713–1758* (London: Macmillan, 1918); Julian Gwyn, *An Admiral for America: Sir Peter Warren, Vice Admiral of the Red, 1703–1752* (Gainesville: University Press of Florida, 2004), 76–99.

42. There is an good account of the new Board of Admiralty in N. A. M. Rodger, *The Insatiable Earl: A Life of John Montagu, Fourth Earl of Sandwich, 1718–1792* (London: HarperCollins, 1993), 20–39. For a summary of Anson's career, see N. A. M. Rodger, "George, Lord Anson, 1697–1762," in Le Fevre and Harding, *Precursors of Nelson*, 177–99. The establishment and subsequent use of the Western Squadron are the subject of Michael Duffy, "The Establishment of the Western Squadron as the Linchpin of British Naval Strategy," in Michael Duffy, ed., *Parameters of British Naval Power,*

1650–1850 (Exeter: University of Exeter Press, 1992), 60–81 (reprinted in Harding, *Naval History*, 96–116), and Richard Middleton, "British Naval Strategy, 1755–62: The Western Squadron," *Mariner's Mirror* 75 (1989): 349–67. Such a squadron had been proposed in 1693: Ryan, "William III and the Brest Fleet," 59–60; see Duffy, "Establishment," 62, and Rodger, *Command of the Ocean*, 252, for earlier precedents.

43. McNeill, *Atlantic Empires of France and Spain*, 69; National Archives of the United Kingdom (Public Record Office), Admiralty Series 8 (List Books), vol. 25, lists of British ships in service on 1 January 1745 and 1 June 1746 (Old Style).

44. This story is recounted magnificently by Pritchard, *Anatomy of a Naval Disaster*. For the English side, see Richmond, *Navy in the War of 1739–48*, 41–45.

45. Richmond, *Navy in the War of 1739–48*, 3:3–5, 23–38, 43; Richard Harding, "The Expedition to Lorient, 1746," *Age of Sail* 1 (2002–3), 34–54.

46. Richmond, *Navy in the War of 1739–48*, 3:80–81, 178–225.

47. Richmond, *Navy in the War of 1739–48*, 3:83–94.

48. Richmond, *Navy in the War of 1739–48*, 3:102–11; Mackay, *Admiral Hawke*, 69–88.

49. The best English-language source for the peace negotiations still is Sir Richard Lodge, *Studies in Eighteenth-Century Diplomacy, 1740–1748* (London: J. Murray, 1930), 259–411. But see also Rodger, *Insatiable Earl*, 49–54, and Jack M. Sosin, "Louisbourg and the Peace of Aix-la-Chapelle, 1748," *William & Mary Quarterly*, 3rd ser., 14 (1957): 516–35.

50. For a more detailed analysis of the results of the war, see Dull, *French Navy and the Seven Years' War*, 5–9.

4. Sea Power and the Outcome of the Seven Years' War

1. For Albemarle's praise of Puyzieulx, see Black, *Natural and Necessary Enemies*, 52.

2. Black, *Natural and Necessary Enemies*, 36–63; Bob Harris, "War, Empire, and the 'National Interest' in Mid-Eighteenth-Century Britain," in Julie Flavell and Stephen Conway, eds., *Britain and France Go to War: The Impact of War and Warfare in Anglo-America, 1754–1815* (Gainesville: University Press of Florida, 2004), 13–40.

3. For the Board of Trade's opinion, see John Ehrman, *The Younger Pitt*, 3 vols. (New York: Dutton; Stanford: Stanford University Press, 1969–96), 1:342. The cost of Canada is discussed in Desbarets, "France in North America." The most thorough account of the work of the border commission is Enid Robbie, *The Forgotten Commissioner: Sir William Mildmay and the Anglo-French Commission of 1750–1755* (East Lansing: Michigan State University Press, 2003).

4. White, *Middle Ground*, 186–242; Michael N. McConnell, *A Country Between: The Upper Ohio Valley and Its Peoples, 1724–1774* (Lincoln: University of Nebraska Press, 1992), 61–88, 98–108; Francis Jennings, *Empire of Fortune: Crown, Colonies, and Tribes in the Seven Years' War in America* (New York: W. W. Norton, 1988), 24–57; W. J. Eccles, "The Fur Trade and Eighteenth-Century Imperialism," *William & Mary Quarterly*, 3rd ser., 40 (1983): 341–62.

5. There is a good account of these developments in Fred Anderson, *Crucible of War: The Seven Years' War and the Fate of Empire in British North America, 1754–1766* (New York: Alfred A. Knopf, 2000), 5–7, 42–65.

6. Dull, *French Navy and the Seven Years' War*, 258–60. This does not include a ship of the line that was wrecked upon launching.

7. Paul Mapp, "British Culture and the Changing Character of the Mid-Eighteenth-Century British Empire," in Hofstra, *Cultures in Conflict*, 33, 52; Lyon, *Sailing Navy List*, 17, 33, 39–47, 67, 72–73, 75–77; Clive Wilkinson, *The British Navy and the State in the Eighteenth Century* (Woodbridge, UK: Boydell Press in association with the National Maritime Museum, 2004), 77–80, 90–94; Saint Hubert, "Ships of the Line of the Spanish Navy," 133–34, 208–9. Ships of the line counted in this chapter include 50-gun ships.

8. Pritchard, *Louis XV's Navy*, 137–40. Pritchard's marvelous book is authoritative for every aspect of the French navy except strategy and operations, which it does not attempt to cover. For the interwar period, see also Pritchard's "Fir Trees, Financiers, and the French Navy during the 1750s," *Canadian Journal of History* 23 (1988): 337–54.

9. For Anson's work at the admiralty, see Richard Middleton, "Naval Administration in the Age of Pitt and Anson, 1755–1763," in Black and

Woodfine, *British Navy and the Use of Naval Power in the Eighteenth Century*, 109–28, and Rodger, "George, Lord Anson, 1697–1762."

10. The best account of the negotiations is T. R. Clayton, "The Duke of Newcastle, the Earl of Halifax, and the American Origins of the Seven Years' War," *Historical Journal* 24 (1981): 571–603.

11. For a detailed account of the frontier fighting, see Matthew C. Ward, *Breaking the Backcountry: The Seven Years' War in Virginia and Pennsylvania, 1754–1765* (Pittsburgh: University of Pittsburgh Press, 2003). For the expulsion of the Acadians, see John Mack Faragher, *"A Great and Noble Scheme": The Tragic Story of the Expulsion of the French Acadians from Their American Homeland* (New York: W. W. Norton, 2005).

12. There is a brilliant account of the campaign by Jacques Aman, *Une campagne navale méconnue à la veille de la guerre de Sept Ans: L'escadre de Brest en 1755* (Vincennes: Service historique de la marine, 1986).

13. The ships and their locations are listed in Dull, *French Navy and the Seven Years' War*, 261–71; for troop strength in 1759, see 144–45.

14. See particularly Herbert H. Kaplan, *Russia and the Outbreak of the Seven Years' War* (Berkeley: University of California Press, 1968). I have made a more detailed analysis of the French options and Newcastle's diplomacy in *French Navy and the Seven Years' War*, 36–45. Black, *George II*, 222–26, ascribes primary responsibility for the treaties to the king.

15. The most thorough account of the campaign and battle, as well as of Byng's execution, is Dudley Pope, *At Twelve Mr. Byng Was Shot* (Philadelphia: J. P. Lippincott, 1962). If not otherwise noted, my account of naval operations during the war is based on Dull, *French Navy and the Seven Years' War.*

16. William M. Fowler Jr., *Empires at War: The French and Indian War and the Struggle for North America, 1754–1763* (New York: Walker, 2005) is a good recent military history of operations in North America. For the naval side of the Oswego campaign, see Peter MacLeod, "The French Siege of Oswego in 1756: Inland Naval Warfare in North America," *American Neptune* 45 (1989): 262–71.

17. For Pitt's role in British strategy, see Richard Middleton, *The Bells of Victory: The Pitt-Newcastle Ministry and the Conduct of the Seven Years' War, 1757–1762* (Cambridge: Cambridge University Press, 1985). This excellent

book largely (but not completely) supersedes Sir Julian S. Corbett, *England in the Seven Years' War: A Study in Combined Strategy*, 2nd ed., 2 vols. (London: Longman, Green, 1918).

18. There are numerous books on Frederick's war with Austria, Russia, and Sweden. Good introductions are Dennis E. Showalter, *The Wars of Frederick the Great* (London: Longman, 1996), and Duffy, *Frederick the Great: A Military Life* (London: Routledge and Kegan Paul, 1985).

19. See Ian Steele's excellent campaign history, *Fort William Henry and the "Massacre"* (New York: Oxford University Press, 1990).

20. For the war in Germany from a British-Hanoverian perspective, see Sir Reginald Savory, *His Britannic Majesty's Army in Germany during the Seven Years' War* (Oxford: Clarendon Press, 1966). The most thorough study of French diplomacy and military operations (although it does not study the French navy in detail) is Richard Waddington's masterpiece, *La Guerre de Sept Ans: Histoire diplomatique et militaire*, 5 vols. (Paris: Firmin-Didot, 1899–1914).

21. The best account is Christopher Duffy, *Prussia's Glory: Rossbach and Leuthen 1757* (Chicago: Emperor's Press, 2003).

22. Dull, *French Navy and the Seven Years' War*, 80–81; T. J. A. Le Goff, "Problèmes de recrutement pendant la Guerre de Sept Ans," *Revue historique* 283 (January–June 1990): 226.

23. By 1758 nearly 20,000 French crewmen were in British prisons: Le Goff, "Problèmes de recrutement," 231. In 1758 Louis authorized about 42 million livres for the navy, while Parliament authorized almost £3.9 million (equivalent to about 90 million livres): Pritchard, *Louis XV's Navy*, 220; Rodger, *Command of the Ocean*, 644.

24. The only complete account is an unpublished 1969 doctoral dissertation by William Kent Hackmann, "English Military Expeditions to the Coast of France, 1757–1761," University of Michigan, Ann Arbor.

25. A. J. B. Johnston, *Endgame, 1758: The Promise, the Glory, and the Despair of Louisbourg's Last Decade* (Lincoln: University of Nebraska Press, 2007), 148–296; Dull, *French Navy and the Seven Years' War*, 105–8, 269–71. Johnston, *Endgame*, 186, 226, 291, gives the more accurate account of two of the ships, the *Brillant* and *Bizarre*.

26. Ian McCulloch, "'Like Roaring Lions Breaking from Their Chains': The Battle of Ticonderoga, 8 July 1758," in Donald R. Graves, ed., *Fighting for Canada: Seven Battles, 1758–1995* (Toronto: Robin Bass Studio, 2000), 23–80. See also René Chartrand, *Ticonderoga, 1758: Montcalm's Victory against All Odds* (Westport, Conn.: Praeger, 2004).

27. The most thorough account of the Quiberon campaign is Geoffrey Marcus, *Quiberon Bay* (Barre MA: Barre, 1963).

28. See Piers Mackesy, *The Coward of Minden: The Affair of Lord George Sackville* (London: Allen Lane, 1979).

29. Marshall Smelser, *The Campaign for the Sugar Islands, 1759: A Study in Amphibious Warfare* (Chapel Hill: University of North Carolina Press, 1955), gives an overview from a British perspective.

30. I previously wrote that La Clue's squadron had been ordered to Brest: Dull, *French Navy and the Seven Years' War*, 136–37. Professor Daniel Baugh has called my attention to an article that convincingly argues that La Clue was ordered to Cadiz and that, although Berryer favored sending him from there to Martinique, the Royal Council of State had not yet reached a decision on his final destination: —— Costet, "Une Erreur historique: La Destination de l'escadre de Toulon en 1759," *Revue maritime*, new series, no. 119 (November 1929): 637–41.

31. C. P. Stacey, *Quebec, 1759: The Siege and the Battle* (Toronto: Macmillan, 1959), remains the best study of the campaign, but see also Stephen Brumwell, *Paths of Glory: The Life and Death of General James Wolfe* (London: Hambledon Continuum, 2006), and Matthew C. Ward, *The Battle for Quebec 1759* (Stoud, UK: Tempus, 2005).

32. Dull, *French Navy and the Seven Years' War*, 275–80, gives orders of battle for the British and French navies. For the Genoese ships, see 171.

33. Dull, *French Navy and American Independence*, 79–80.

34. For a convincing reappraisal of Peter's foreign policy, see Carol S. Leonard, *Reform and Regicide: The Reign of Peter III of Russia* (Bloomington: Indiana University Press, 1993).

35. See Dull, *French Navy and the Seven Years' War*, 207–8, 278–79, 284.

36. David Syrett, ed., *The Siege and Capture of Havana, 1762* (London:

Navy Records Society, 1970); David F. Marley, "Havana Surprised: Prelude to the British Invasion, 1762," *Mariner's Mirror* 78 (1992): 293–305, and "A Fearful Gift: The Spanish Naval Build-up in the West Indies, 1759–1762," *Mariner's Mirror* 80 (1994): 403–17.

37. Nicholas Tracy, *Manila Ransomed: The British Assault on Manila in the Seven Years' War* (Exeter: Exeter University Press, 1995).

38. P. J. Marshall, ed., *The Oxford History of the British Empire*, vol. 2, *The Eighteenth Century* (Oxford: Oxford University Press, 1998), 487–551, and Vincent T. Harlow, *The Founding of the Second British Empire*, 2 vols. (London: Longmans, Green, 1952–64), 2:7–224, trace the beginnings of the British expansion. Particularly useful is P. J. Marshall, *The Making and Unmaking of Empires: Britain, India, and America, c. 1750–1783* (Oxford: Oxford University Press, 2005), which contrasts British success in India to the breakdown of the British relationship with its North American colonies.

39. Dull, *French Navy and the Seven Years' War*, 242.

5. Winners and Losers in the War of American Independence

1. There are a number of superb studies of postwar British diplomacy, including Michael Roberts, *British Diplomacy and Swedish Politics, 1758–1773* (Minneapolis: University of Minnesota Press, 1980) and *Splendid Isolation, 1763–1780* (Reading: University of Reading, 1970), as well as H. M. Scott, *British Foreign Policy in the Age of the American Revolution* (Oxford: Clarendon Press, 1990).

2. See McConnell, *A Country Between*, 135–206; Richard Middleton, *Pontiac's War: Its Causes, Course, and Consequences* (New York: Routledge, 2007); Gregory Dowd, *War under Heaven: Pontiac, the Indian Nations, and the British Empire* (Baltimore: Johns Hopkins University Press, 2002); and Colin G. Calloway, *The Scratch of a Pen: 1763 and the Transformation of North America* (Oxford: Oxford University Press, 2006), 66–91.

3. Marshall, *Making and Unmaking of Empires*, 278–79, 322; John Shy, *Toward Lexington: The Role of the British Army in the Coming of the American Revolution* (Princeton: Princeton University Press, 1965); John Murrin, "The French and Indian War, the American Revolution, and the Counterfactual Hypothesis: Reflections on Lawrence Henry Gipson and John Shy," *Reviews in American History* 1 (1973): 307–18.

4. Neil R. Stout, *The Royal Navy in America, 1760–1775: A Study of the Enforcement of British Colonial Policy in the Era of the American Revolution* (Annapolis: Naval Institute Press, 1973). There was a long history of tension between Americans and the British navy; see Denver Brunsman, "The Knowles Impressment Riots of the 1740s," *Early American Studies* 5 (2007), 324–66, and Jesse Lemisch, "Jack Tar in the Streets: Merchant Seamen in the Politics of Revolutionary America, *William & Mary Quarterly*, 3rd ser., 25 (1968): 371–401.

5. Scott, *British Foreign Policy*, 140–56; Nicholas Tracy, *Navies, Deterrence, and American Independence: Britain and Seapower in the 1760s and 1770s* (Vancouver: University of British Columbia Press, 1988); Julius Goebel Jr., *The Struggle for the Falkland Islands: A Study in Legal and Diplomatic History* (New Haven: Yale University Press, 1927). France had one great triumph: the acquisition of Corsica. See Geoffrey W. Rice, "Deceit and Distraction: Britain, France, and the Corsican Crisis of 1768," *International History Review* 28 (2006): 287–315.

6. Wilkinson, *British Navy and the State*, 105–212, and "The Earl of Egmont and the Navy, 1763–6," in Harding, *Naval History*, 377–92.

7. For the increased national debt, see Brewer, *Sinews of Power*, 30, 39–40.

8. Dull, *French Navy and the Seven Years' War*, 214. For details, see Edmond Dziembowski, *Un nouveau Patriotism français, 1750–1770: La France face à la puissance anglaise à l'époque de la guerre de Sept Ans* (Oxford: Voltaire Foundation, 1998), 458–72.

9. Raymond A. Abarca, "Classical Diplomacy and Bourbon 'Revanche' Strategy, 1763–1770," *Review of Politics* 32 (1970): 313–37; H. M. Scott, "The Importance of Bourbon Naval Reconstruction to the Strategy of Choiseul after the Seven Years' War," *International History Review* 1 (1979): 17–35.

10. Dull, *French Navy and the Seven Years' War*, 245–50, and *French Navy and American Independence*, 351. Ship of the line totals in this chapter include 50-gun ships. A recent article argues that at a late stage in the crisis Choiseul, believing war inevitable, decided to support Spain's demands: H. M. Scott, "Choiseul et le Troisième Pacte de Famille," in Lucien Bély, ed., *Le Présence des Bourbons en Europe XVIe–XXIe siècle* (Paris: Presses Universitaires de France, 2003), 207–20.

11. Albert Sorel, *Europe and the French Revolution*, vol. 1, *The Political Traditions of the Old Régime*, trans. Alfred Cobban and J. W. Hunt (Garden City, N.Y.: Doubleday, Anchor Books, 1971), 244–45. A good biography, albeit sometimes unduly apologetic of the king's failings, is John Hardman, *Louis XVI* (New Haven: Yale University Press, 1993). There is no adequate biography of Louis XV in English; the best one in French is Michel Antoine, *Louis XV* (Paris: Fayard, 1989). James Pritchard gives an astute appraisal of Louis XV, however, in "The French Navy, 1748–1762: Problems and Perspectives," in Harding, *Naval History*, 215.

12. See H. M. Scott, *The Emergence of the Eastern Powers, 1756–1775* (London: Cambridge University Press, 2001).

13. Jonathan R. Dull, "France and the American Revolution Seen as Tragedy," in Ronald Hoffman and Peter J. Albert, eds., *Diplomacy and Revolution: The Franco-American Alliance of 1778* (Charlottesville: University Press of Virginia, 1981), 83–84.

14. Dull, *French Navy and the Seven Years' War*, 253–54.

15. M. S. Anderson, "Great Britain and the Russian Fleet, 1769–70," *Slavonic and East European Review* 31 (1952–53): 148–63; Michael Roberts, "Great Britain and the Swedish Revolution, 1772–73," *Historical Journal* 7 (1964): 1–46.

16. Dull, *French Navy and American Independence*, 30–44. If not otherwise noted, the present chapter is based on that book.

17. Daniel A. Baugh, "The Politics of British Naval Failure, 1775–1777," *American Neptune* 52 (1991): 221–46.

18. For the meeting in Philadelphia, see Leonard W. Labaree et al., eds., *The Papers of Benjamin Franklin*, 39 vols. to date (New Haven: Yale University Press, 1959–), 22:310–18. Brian N. Morton and Donald C. Spinelli, *Beaumarchais and the American Revolution* (Lanham MD: Lexington Books, 2003), is the best study of Beaumarchais's role.

19. Dull, *French Navy and American Independence*, 351, 360.

20. The best military history of the war from a British perspective is Piers Mackesy, *The War for America, 1775–1783* (Cambridge: Harvard University Press, 1965). Mackesy is an incomparable military historian and a first-rate naval historian. Several of his books are cited in other chapters;

all are superb. For British naval operations, see Creswell, *British Admirals*, 120–77; Daniel A. Baugh, "Why Did Britain Lose Command of the Sea during the War for America?" in Black and Woodfine, *British Navy and the Use of Naval Power*, 149–69; W. M. James, *The British Navy in Adversity: A Study of the War of American Independence* (New York: Longmans, Green, 1926); Rodger, *Insatiable Earl*; David Syrett, *The Royal Navy in American Waters, 1775–1783* (Aldershot, UK, and Brookfield VT: Scolar Press, 1989), *The Royal Navy in European Waters during the American Revolutionary War* (Columbia: University of South Carolina Press, 1998), and *Admiral Lord Howe: A Biography* (Annapolis: Naval Institute Press, 2006), 49–108; John A. Tilley, *The British Navy and the American Revolution* (Columbia: University of South Carolina Press, 1987); and Peter Trew, *Rodney and the Breaking of the Line* (Barnsley, UK: Pen and Sword, 2006).

21. Rodger, *Command of the Ocean*, 335–36, 341–42. See also Jonathan R. Dull, "Mahan, Sea Power, and the War for American Independence," *International History Review* 10 (1988): 59–67, and David Syrett, "Home Waters or America? The Dilemma of British Naval Strategy in 1778," *Mariner's Mirror* 77 (1991): 365–77.

22. Dull, *French Navy and American Independence*, 359–60.

23. Jonathan R. Dull, "Was the Continental Navy a Mistake?" *American Neptune* 44 (1984): 167–70.

24. For the Spanish contribution to American independence, see Thomas E. Chávez, *Spain and the Independence of the United States: An Intrinsic Gift* (Albuquerque: University of New Mexico Press, 2002).

25. See A. Temple Patterson, *The Other Armada: The Franco-Spanish Attempt to Invade Britain in 1779* (Manchester: University of Manchester Press, 1960).

26. Dull, *French Navy and American Independence*, 176n, 361–68; Lavery, *Nelson's Navy*, 70, 82–84, 173–75, 222; Rodger, *Command of the Ocean*, 375, 420–21; Padfield, *Maritime Supremacy*, 237, 250–52; John E. Talbott, *The Pen and Ink Sailor: Charles Middleton and the King's Navy, 1778–1813* (Portland OR: Frank Cass, 1998), 45–72, 104–14; M. Maurer, "Coppered Bottoms for the Royal Navy: A Factor in the Maritime War of 1778–1783," *Military Affairs* 14 (1950): 57–61; R. J. B. Knight, "The Introduction of Copper Sheathing

in the Royal Navy, 1779–1786," in Harding, *Naval History*, 481–91, and "The Fleets at Trafalgar: The Margin of Superiority," in David Cannadine, ed., *Trafalgar in History: A Battle and Its Afterlife* (Basingstoke, UK: Palgrave Macmillan, 2006), 66; and Roger Morriss, "Charles Middleton, Lord Barham, 1726–1813," in Le Fevre and Harding, *Precursors of Nelson*, 310–13. Rodger estimates that coppering added a knot's speed to ships whose top combat speed was 5 to 6 knots: *Command of the Ocean*, 344.

27. Dull, *French Navy and American Independence*, 199–201, 297–98, 345–50.

28. Dull, *French Navy and American Independence*, 213–14; Richard Buel Jr., *In Irons: Britain's Naval Supremacy and the American Revolutionary Economy* (New Haven: Yale University Press, 1998).

29. Syrett, *Royal Navy in European Waters*, 95–132; Dull, *French Navy and American Independence*, 369–72.

30. Roderick Cavaliero, *Admiral Satan: The Life and Campaigns of Suffren* (London: I. B. Tauris, 1994), is the best account of Suffren's exploits.

31. Labaree et al., *Papers of Benjamin Franklin*, 34:434n.

32. John Walton Caughey, *Bernardo de Gálvez in Louisiana, 1776–1783* (Berkeley: University of California Press, 1934); Francisco Morales Padrón, ed., *Journal of Don Francisco Saavedra de Sangronis during the Commission He Had in His Charge from 25 June 1780 until the 20th of the Same Month of 1783*, trans. Aileen Moore Topping (Gainesville: University of Florida Press, 1989). The city of Galveston is named after him.

33. Buel, *In Irons*, 213–17; Trew, *Rodney*, 112–34; Kenneth Breen, "Graves and Hood at the Chesapeake," *Mariner's Mirror* 66 (1980): 53–65; J. A. Sulivan, "Graves and Hood," *Mariner's Mirror* 69 (1983): 175–94. The best overall account of the Yorktown campaign is William B. Willcox, *Portrait of a General: Sir Henry Clinton in the War of Independence* (New York: Alfred A. Knopf, 1964), 392–494.

34. Figures are for 1 April: Dull, *French Navy and American Independence*, 373–76. My list of British ships fails to include the *Bristol*, 50, en route to the Indian Ocean, for which see Cavaliero, *Admiral Satan*, 137.

35. Dull, *French Navy and American Independence*, 144n, 256n, 278–79. For the auxiliary officers, see Jacques Aman, *Les Officiers bleus dans la marine*

française au XVIIIe siècle (Geneva: Droz, 1976). The number of crewmen is discussed below in chapter 8.

36. See Trew, *Rodney*, 135–72, 190–92, and J. D. Spinney, "Rodney and the Saints: A Reassessment," *Mariner's Mirror* 68 (1982): 377–89.

37. Dull, *French Navy and American Independence*, 352–55.

38. For the negotiations, see Labaree et al., *Papers of Benjamin Franklin*, vols. 37–38; Dull, *French Navy and American Independence*, 292–335; Harlow, *Founding of the Second British Empire*, 1:223–407; Ronald Hoffman and Peter J. Albert, eds., *Peace and the Peacemakers: The Treaty of 1783* (Charlottesville: University Press of Virginia, 1986); and Andrew Stockley, *Britain and France at the Birth of America: The European Powers and the Peace Negotiations of 1783* (Exeter: University of Exeter Press, 2001).

6. Change and Continuity during the French Revolution

1. The most thorough modern account of the commercial treaty is an unpublished 1970 doctoral dissertation, Marie Martenis Donaghey, "The Anglo-French Negotiations of 1786–1787," University of Virginia, Charlottesville, but there is a perceptive analysis in Jeff Horn, *The Path Not Taken: French Industrialization in the Age of Revolution, 1750–1830* (Cambridge: MIT Press, 2006), 51–88. The best study of British diplomacy during the period and particularly of British relations with France is Jeremy Black, *British Foreign Policy in an Age of Revolutions, 1783–1793* (Cambridge: Cambridge University Press, 1994). For the Crimean crisis, see Alan W. Fisher, *The Russian Annexation of the Crimea, 1772–1783* (Cambridge: Cambridge University Press, 1970).

2. Dull, *French Navy and the Seven Years' War*, 254. For an analysis of the impact of the three great wars of 1740–83, see Joël Félix, "The Financial Origins of the French Revolution," in Peter D. Campbell, ed., *The Origins of the French Revolution* (Basingstoke, UK: Palgrave Macmillan, 2006), 35–62. See also the final chapter of the present book for naval expenses during the wars and the exchange rate I've used.

3. The first volume of Ehrman's superb *Younger Pitt* provides a thorough account of Pitt's program, while Calonne's is discussed in E. N. White, "Was There a Solution to the Ancien Régime's Financial Dilemma?" *Journal of Economic History* 49 (1989): 545–68.

4. Dull, *French Navy and American Independence*, 378, and *French Navy and the Seven Years' War*, 254; C. Hippeau, *Le Gouvernement de Normandie au XVIIe et au XVIIIe siècle: Documents tirés des archives du château d'Harcourt*, 9 vols. (Caen: Goussiaume de Laporte, 1863–70), 3:153–490; Alain Demerliac, *La Marine de Louis XVI: Nomenclature des navires français de 1774 à 1792* (Nice: Editions Omega, 1996), 44–46, 49–57, and *La Marine de la Révolution: Nomenclature des navires français de 1792 à 1799* (Nice: Editions Omega, 1999), 19–29; Saint Hubert, "Ships of the Line of the Spanish Navy," 211, 283; Lyon, *Sailing Navy List*, 63–66, 68–75, 77–78, 109; P. L. C. Webb, "The Rebuilding and Repair of the Fleet, 1783–93," in Harding, *Naval History*, 503–18.

5. Matthew Z. Mayer, "The Price for Austria's Security," *International History Review* 26 (2004): 257–99, 473–514; T. C. W. Blanning, "An Old but New Biography of Leopold II," in T. C. W. Blanning and David Cannadine, eds., *History and Biography: Essays in Honor of Derek Beales* (Cambridge: Cambridge University Press, 1996), 53–71; Ehrman, *Younger Pitt*, 1:520–42. For the collapse of France's system of international security, see Orville T. Murphy, *The Diplomatic Retreat of France and Public Opinion on the Eve of the French Revolution, 1783–1789* (Washington DC: Catholic University of America Press, 1998); Bailey Stone, *The Genesis of the French Revolution: A Global-Historical Interpretation* (Cambridge: Cambridge University Press, 1994) and *Re-Interpreting the French Revolution: A Global-Historical Perspective* (Cambridge: Cambridge University Press, 2002); Jeremy Whiteman, *Reform, Revolution and French Global Policy, 1787–1791* (Burlington VT: Ashgate, 2003); and Munro Price, "The Dutch Affair and the Fall of the *Ancien Régime*," *Historical Journal* 38 (1995): 875–905. The most comprehensive survey in English of European diplomacy during this period is Paul W. Schroeder, *The Transformation of European Politics, 1763–1848* (Oxford: Clarendon Press, 1994). Although well informed on eastern Europe, it needs to be used with extreme caution when it deals with French history. For those who read French, there is a masterpiece of wisdom, empathy (except for the *sans-culottes*, the workers and shopkeepers of Paris), and erudition: Albert Sorel, *L'Europe et la Révolution française*, 8 vols. (Paris: Plon-Nourrit, 1887–1904); unfortunately, only the first volume has been

translated into English (as *The Political Traditions of the Old Régime*, cited above, chapter 5).

6. For introductions to the crisis and ensuing revolution, see Michel Vovelle, *The Fall of the French Monarchy, 1787–1792*, trans. Susan Burke (Cambridge: Cambridge University Press; Paris: La Maison des sciences de l'homme, 1984); D. M. G. Sutherland, *France, 1789–1815: Revolution and Counterrevolution* (London: Fontana-Collins, 1985) and *The French Revolution and Empire: The Quest for a Civic Order* (Maldon MA: Blackwell, 2003); and William Doyle, *Origins of the French Revolution*, 2nd ed. (Oxford: Oxford University Press, 1988) and *The Oxford History of the French Revolution*, 2nd ed. (Oxford: Oxford University Press, 2002).

7. For the royal family's attempts to escape, see Munro Price, *The Road from Versailles: Louis XVI, Marie Antoinette, and the Fall of the French Monarchy* (New York: St. Martin's Press, 2002), and Timothy Tackett, *When the King Took Flight* (Cambridge: Harvard University Press, 2003). For the king's rejection of the Revolution, see Munro Price, "Mirebeau and the Court: Some New Evidence," *French Historical Studies* 29 (2006): 37–75. Louis XIV and his mother had fled Paris with Mazarin during the Fronde: Wolf, *Louis XIV*, 38–41.

8. In a French population of about 28.5 million, between 100,000 and 400,000 were nobility: Julian Swann, "The French Nobility, 1715–1789," in H. M. Scott, ed., *The European Nobilities in the Seventeenth and Eighteenth Centuries*, 2 vols. (London: Longman, 1995), 1:143–44.

9. William S. Cormack, *Revolution and Political Conflict in the French Navy, 1789–1794* (Cambridge: Cambridge University Press, 1995), 158–59.

10. For these officials, see Cormack, *Revolution and Political Conflict*, 22n, 98n, 126–27, 141n; Sorel, *L'Europe et la Révolution française*, 2:321–22; and Martine Acerra and Jean Meyer, *Marines et Révolution* (Rennes: Editions Ouest-France, 1988), 268. For the denunciation of Fleurieu, see Clive H. Church, *Revolution and Red Tape: The French Ministerial Bureaucracy, 1770–1850* (New York: Oxford University Press, 1981), 53–54.

11. Black, *British Foreign Policy*, 255–56; Ehrman, *Younger Pitt*, 1:313, 554–71; Paul Webb, "The Naval Aspects of the Nootka Sound Crisis," *Mariner's Mirror* 61 (1975): 133–54; Carla Rahn Phillips, "'The Life Blood of the

Navy': Recruiting Sailors in Eighteenth-Century Spain," *Mariner's Mirror* 87 (2001): 439.

12. See Michael J. Sydenham, *The Girondins* (London: University of London, Athlone Press, 1961). As usual, Sorel's appraisal is sensible and balanced. He praises the Girondins' idealism, while regretting their lack of common sense: *L'Europe et la Révolution française*, 2:301–4, 395–96, 409–10.

13. There is an excellent summary of the war crisis in T. C. W. Blanning, *The Origins of the French Revolutionary Wars* (London: Longman, 1986), 69–130.

14. Blanning, *Origins*, 131–72; Ehrman, *Younger Pitt*, 2:206–13, 233–58.

15. For useful accounts of French naval operations from 1789 through 1792, see William S. Cormack, "Legitimate Authority in Revolution and War: The French Navy in the West Indies, 1789–1793," *International History Review* 18 (1996): 1–27, and Léon Guérin, *Histoire de la marine contemporaine de France: Depuis 1784 jusqu'à 1848* (Paris: Adolphe Delahayes, 1855), 159–240.

16. See Samuel Scott, *The Response of the Royal Army to the French Revolution: The Role and Development of the Line Army, 1787–93* (Oxford: Clarendon Press, 1978).

17. Archives Nationales, M^{iv} 662, Affaires Maritimes, No. 9–9b^{is}.

18. Aman, *Les Officiers bleus*; Dessert, *La Royale*, 219–35, 353; Symcox, *Crisis of French Sea Power*, 23–32; Michel Vergé-Franceschi, "Les compagnons d'armes de Tourville à Barfleur-La Hougue," in Martine Acerra, ed., *L'invention du vaisseau de ligne, 1450–1700* (Paris: S. P. M., 1997), 237–40; Dull, *French Navy and American Independence*, 145, 317n; Auguste Thomazi, *Les Marins de Napoléon* (Paris: Jules Tallandier, 1957). Vergé-Franceschi is the author of a seven-volume study of the admirals of the French navy during the reign of Louis XV, *Les Officiers généraux de la marine royal (1715–1774): Origines-conditions-services* (Paris: Librairie de l'Inde, 1990).

19. National Archives of the United Kingdom (Public Record Office), Admiralty Series 8 (List Books), vol. 70; Lyon, *Sailing Navy List*, 62–79, 109, 203, 214–16; Winfield, *British Warships in the Age of Sail, 1793–1815*;

William James, *The Naval History of Great Britain from the Declaration of War by France in 1793 to the Accession of George IV*, rev. ed., 6 vols. (London: Richard Bentley & Son, 1878), 1:445–46; Norman Hampson, *La Marine de l'an II: Mobilisation de la flotte de l'océan, 1793–1794* (Paris: Marcel Rivière, 1959), 241–55. James's figures are generally higher than those I've used based on Admiralty Series 8, as apparently he includes ships not fully manned.

20. Cormack, *Revolution and Political Conflict*, 215–41; Hampson, *La Marine de l'an II*, 124–25; Syrett, *Howe*, 122–26; Clowes, *Royal Navy*, 4:200–202; Roger Morriss, ed., *The Channel Fleet and the Blockade of Brest, 1793–1801* (Burlington VT: Ashgate Publishing for the Navy Records Society, 2001), 23.

21. For British war strategy during 1793 see Ehrman, *Younger Pitt*, 2:261–326.

22. Still useful is Robert R. Palmer, *Twelve Who Ruled: The Year of the Terror in the French Revolution* (Princeton: Princeton University Press, 1941). A brilliant introduction to the French Revolutionary Army is Jean-Paul Bertaud, *The Army of the French Revolution: From Citizen Soldiers to Instruments of Power*, trans. R. R. Palmer (Princeton: Princeton University Press, 1988). A good brief introduction to French military operations is Steven T. Ross, *Quest for Victory: French Military Strategy, 1792–1799* (South Brunswick NJ: A. S. Barnes; London: Thomas Yoseloff, 1973). For the Federalist revolt, see Alan Forrest, *Paris, the Provinces, and the French Revolution* (London: Arnold, 2004), and Paul R. Hanson, *The Jacobin Republic under Fire: The Federalist Revolt in the French Revolution* (University Park: Penn State University Press, 2003).

23. Sutherland, *French Revolution and Empire*, 214; Ehrman, *Younger Pitt*, 2:282–94; Alfred H. Burne, *The Noble Duke of York: The Military Life of Frederick, Duke of York and Albany* (London: Staples Press, 1949), 35–97; Michael Duffy, "'A Particular Service': The British Government and the Dunkirk Expedition of 1793," *English Historical Review* 91 (1976): 529–54.

24. Cormack, *Revolution and Political Conflict*, 173–214, 250; Ehrman, *Younger Pitt*, 298, 303–18; David G. Chandler, *The Campaigns of Napoleon*

(New York: Macmillan, 1966), 20–29; Malcolm Crook, *Toulon in War and Revolution: From the Ancien Régime to the Restoration, 1750–1820* (Manchester: Manchester University Press, 1991), 148. For an introduction to the British navy during the wars of 1793–1815, see Lavery, *Nelson's Navy*. In addition to James, *Naval History*, a number of works deal with British naval operations during the period, including Rodger, *Command of the Ocean*, 426–72, 528–74; Clowes, *Royal Navy*, 4:196–561, and throughout vol. 5; and Nicholas Tracy, ed., *The Naval Chronology: The Contemporary Record of the Royal Navy at War*, 5 vols. (London: Chatham, 1998–99). See also Winfield, *British Warships in the Age of Sail, 1793–1815*.

25. Hampson, *La Marine de l'an II*, 126–59; Cormack, *Revolution and Political Conflict*, 242–75; Otto von Pivka [Digby Smith], *Navies of the Napoleonic Era* (Newton Abbot, UK: David and Charles; New York: Hippocrene Books, 1980), 160–69. British figures are for April and do not include several ships of the line and several 50's serving as guard ships, prison ships, or hospital ships.

26. Syrett, *Howe*, 128–35; Clowes, *Royal Navy*, 4:216–40; Oliver Warner, *The Glorious First of June* (New York: Macmillan, 1961); Michael Duffy and Roger Morriss, eds., *The Glorious First of June: A Naval Battle and Its Aftermath* (Exeter: University of Exeter Press, 2001); Creswell, *British Admirals*, 197–213. Laurence Evans, "The Convoy, the Grain, and Their Influence on the French Revolution," *Northern Mariner/Le Marin du nord* 5 (1995): 45–51, argues convincingly that the grain convoy was a stopgap measure to appease the Parisians. For the 1693 convoy, see Symcox, *Crisis of French Sea Power*, 141–42.

27. Michael Duffy, *Soldiers, Sugar, and Seapower: The British Expedition to the West Indies and the War against Revolutionary France* (Oxford: Clarendon Press, 1987), 115–125, a superb book.

28. For the French offensive and the British counteroffensive, see Duffy, *Soldiers*, 141–47, 159–240. For French privateering, see H. J. K. Jenkins, "The Heyday of French Privateering from Guadeloupe, 1796–1798," *Mariner's Mirror* 64 (1978): 245–50.

29. The best account of the faltering British war effort is Ehrman, *Younger Pitt*, 2:327–81. For Spencer's replacement of Chatham and its

consequences see Ehrman, 2:379, 417; Talbott, *Pen and Ink Sailor*, 136–44; and Andrew Lambert, "William, Lord Hotham, 1736–1813," in Peter Le Fevre and Richard Harding, eds., *British Admirals of the Napoleonic Wars: The Contemporaries of Nelson* (London: Chatham; St. Paul MN: MBI, 2005), 23–44. For the British blockade of Brest, see Morriss, *Channel Fleet*, and Richard Saxby, "The Blockade of Brest in the French Revolutionary War," *Mariner's Mirror* 78 (1992): 25–35.

30. For this period see Andrew Lambert, "Sir William Cornwallis, 1744–1819," in Le Fevre and Harding, *Precursors of Nelson*, 360–62, and "Hotham" in Le Fevre and Harding, *British Admirals*, 26–41; Clowes, *Royal Navy*, 4:252–79; Louis-Edouard Chevalier, *Histoire de la Marine française sous la première république* (Paris: L. Hachette, 1886), 164–219. Chevalier's work is still the best study of the French navy for the period after 1 June 1794 (pending the promised sequel to Cormack's book). The debacle at Quiberon is treated by Maurice Hutt, *Chouannerie and Counter-Revolution: Puisaye, the Princes, and the British Government in the 1790s*, 2 vols. (Cambridge: Cambridge University Press, 1983), 2:269–323; and Tom Wareham, "'This Disastrous Affair': Sir John Borlase Warren and the Expedition to Quiberon Bay, 1795," *Age of Sail* 2 (2003–4): 9–27.

31. Demerliac, *La Marine de la Révolution*, 19–29, 59–64; Lyon, *Sailing Navy List*, 62–79, 109, 203, 214–16: James, *Naval History*, 1:447.

32. For the Thermidorians and the Directory, see Schroeder, *Transformation of European Politics*, 157–207; Georges Lefebvre, *The Thermidorians and the Directory: Two Phases of the French Revolution*, trans. Robert Baldick (New York: Random House, 1964); Denis Woronoff, *The Thermidorian Regime and the Directory, 1794–1799*, trans. Julian Jackson (Cambridge: Cambridge University Press; Paris: La Maison des sciences de l'homme, 1984); Martyn Lyons, *France under the Directory* (Cambridge: Cambridge University Press, 1975); and C. H. Church, "In Search of the Directory," in J. F. Bosher, ed., *French Government and Society, 1500–1850: Essays in Memory of Alfred Cobban* (London: Athlone Press, 1973), 261–94.

33. Ehrman, *Younger Pitt*, 2:500–501.

34. Glete, *Navies and Nations*, 2:400, 641; Kevin D. McCranie, *Admiral Lord Keith and the Naval War against Napoleon* (Gainesville: University Press

of Florida, 2006), 42–52. For Austria's decision to continue fighting, see Karl A. Roider Jr., *Baron Thugut and Austria's Response to the French Revolution* (Princeton: Princeton University Press, 1987), 170–88.

35. The confusing campaigns in St. Domingue are admirably covered by David Patrick Geggus, *Slavery, War, and Revolution: The British Occupation of Saint-Domingue, 1793–1798* (Oxford: Oxford University Press, 1982), and Laurent Dubois, *Avengers of the New World: The Story of the Haitian Revolution* (Cambridge: Belknap Press of Harvard University Press, 2004). See also Madison Smartt Bell, *Toussaint Louverture* (New York: Pantheon Books, 2007).

36. Sorel, *L'Europe et la Révolution française*, 5:140–66; Demerliac, *La Marine de la Révolution*, 64–66.

37. Saint Hubert, "Ships of the Line of the Spanish Navy," 133–34, 208–11, 283–85; Cesário Fernández Duro, *Armada española desde la unión de los Reinos de Castilla y de Aragón*, 9 vols. (Madrid: Tipográfico "Succesores de Rivadeneyra," 1895–1903), 8:59; Julián de Zulueta, "Trafalgar—The Spanish View," *Mariner's Mirror* 66 (180): 297.

38. Eunice H. Turner, "The Russian Squadron with Admiral Duncan's North Sea Fleet," *Mariner's Mirror* 49 (1963): 212–22; J. David Davies, "Adam, Viscount Duncan, 1731–1804," in Le Fevre and Harding, *British Admirals*, 51–55; Norman E. Saul, *Russia and the Mediterranean, 1797–1807* (Chicago: University of Chicago Press, 1970). For the Russian navy, see also Glete, *Navies and Nations*, 2:390–92, 398, 403–4; Lavery, *Nelson's Navy*, 292–94; Pivka, *Navies of the Napoleonic Era*, 194–98; Blanning, *Origins*, 188, 191; Anderson, *Naval Wars in the Baltic*, 297–300.

39. National Archives of the United Kingdom (Public Record Office), Admiralty Series 8 (List Books), vol. 72. This does not include three Dutch ships recently captured near the Cape of Good Hope, the *Dordrecht*, 64, the *Revolutie* (ex-*Prins Frederik*), 66, and the *Tromp*, 54: Winfield, *British Warships in the Age of Sail, 1793–1815*, 105–7, 114.

40. Clowes, *Royal Navy*, 4:297–305; H. Stuart Jones, *An Invasion That Failed: The French Expedition to Ireland, 1796* (Oxford: Basil Blackwell, 1950); Edouard Desbrière, *1739–1805: Projets et tentatives de débarquement aux îles Britanniques*, 4 vols. (Paris: R. Chapelot, 1900–1902), 1:135–232. Also two

frigates were used to escort 1,200 irregular troops who landed in Wales in early 1797 but quickly surrendered: H. Stuart Jones, *The Last Invasion of Britain* (Cardiff: University of Wales Press, 1950). For the mutinies, see Conrad Gill, *The Naval Mutinies of 1797* (Manchester: Manchester University Press, 1913); James Dugan, *The Great Mutiny* (New York: G. P. Putnam's Sons, 1965); G. C. Manwaring and Bonamy Dobree, *The Floating Republic* (New York: Harcourt, Brace, 1935); and Anthony G. Brown, "The Naval Mutinies—Sedition or Ships' Biscuits: A Reappraisal," *Mariner's Mirror* 92 (2006): 60–74.

41. See Colin White, *1797, Nelson's Year of Destiny: Cape St. Vincent and Santa Cruz de Tenerife* (Stroud, UK: Sutton, 1998), 27–86, and M. A. J. Palmer, "Sir John's Victory: The Battle of Cape St. Vincent Reconsidered," *Mariner's Mirror* 77 (1991): 31–46.

42. Marcel Reinhard, "Les Négociations de Lille et le crise de 18 Fructidor d'après la correspondance inédite de Colchen," *Revue d'Histoire moderne et contemporaine* 5 (1958): 39–56. For British assistance to moderates and royalists who wished to gain power by electoral means, see Harvey Mitchell, *The Underground War against Revolutionary France: The Missions of William Wickham, 1794–1800* (Oxford: Clarendon Press, 1965), 140–216. Truguet was removed under pressure from the moderates, but to their dismay he was replaced by the directors' choice, Pléville Le Pelley: Mitchell, 191–92. For Barthélemy's escape, see Elizabeth Sparrow, *Secret Service: British Agents in France, 1792–1815* (Woodbridge, UK: Boydell Press, 1995), 132, 137.

43. Sorel, *L'Europe et la Révolution française*, 5:392–401, describes the murders.

44. For summaries of the Battle of Camperdown, see Davies, "Duncan," in Le Fevre and Harding, *British Admirals*, 57–63, and Clowes, *Royal Navy*, 4:324–33.

45. Desbrière, *Projets et tentatives*, 2:69–132; Thomas Pakenham, *The Year of Liberty: The Great Irish Rebellion of 1798* (Englewood Cliffs NJ: Prentice-Hall, 1969); A. B. Rodger, *The War of the Second Coalition, 1798–1801: A Strategic Commentary* (Oxford: Clarendon Press, 1964), 41; Chevalier, *La Marine sous la première république*, 401–2; Jonathan North, "French Invasion of Ireland," *Military History Quarterly* 15 (2002–3): 68–77.

46. See Juan Cole, *Napoleon's Egypt: Invading the Middle East* (Basingstoke, UK: Palgrave Macmillan, 2007).

47. An astute analysis of the campaign is provided by Rodger, *War of the Second Coalition*, 1–73. The naval side is ably covered by Brian Lavery, *Nelson and the Nile: The Naval War against Bonaparte, 1798* (London: Chatham, 1998), and Michèle Battesti, *La Batalle d'Aboukir, 1798: Nelson contrairie la stratégie de Bonaparte* (Paris: Economica, 1998). See also Chevalier, *La Marine sous la première république*, 338–93; Ehrman, *Younger Pitt*, 3:138; Chandler, *Campaigns of Napoleon*, 205–27; Michael Duffy, "British Naval Intelligence and Bonaparte's Egyptian Expedition of 1798," *Mariner's Mirror* 84 (1998): 278–90; and Oliver Warner, *The Battle of the Nile* (New York: Macmillan, 1960) and *Nelson's Battles* (London: B. T. Batsford, 1965), 27–76. For the burning of the *Orient*, see Roger Knight, *The Pursuit of Victory: The Life and Achievement of Horatio Nelson* (New York: Basic Books; London: Penguin Books, 2005), 294–96. Knight's is the best to date of the many biographies of Nelson. Oddly, the first paperback edition did not include its splendid footnotes.

48. Rodger's *War of the Second Coalition* is an excellent introduction to the campaigns of 1799 and 1800. The British role is ably discussed in Ehrman, *Younger Pitt*, 3:197–257, 317–411, and in Piers Mackesy, *Statesmen at War: The Strategy of Overthrow, 1798–1799* (New York: Longman, 1974) and *War without Victory: The Downfall of Pitt, 1799–1802* (Oxford: Clarendon Press; New York: Oxford University Press, 1984). Paul I's policies are treated by Roderick E. McGrew, *Paul I of Russia, 1754–1801* (Oxford: Clarendon Press, 1992), and Saul, *Russia and the Mediterranean*. See also Schroeder, *Transformation of European Politics*, 204–7. The captured Dutch ships are listed in Lyon, *Sailing Navy List*, 240–42.

49. Mackesy, *Statesmen at War*, 97–101, 168–69; Chevalier, *La Marine sous la première république*, 408–16; McCranie, *Admiral Lord Keith*, 1–2, 66–77; Christopher Lloyd, ed., *The Keith Papers*, vol. 2 (London: Naval Records Society, 1950), 30–58.

50. Rodger, *War of the Second Coalition*, 249–74; Piers Mackesy, *British Victory in Egypt, 1801* (London: Routledge, 1995); Brendan P. Ryan, "Aboukir Bay, 1801," in Merrill L. Bartlett, ed., *Assault from the Sea: Essays on the*

History of Amphibious Warfare (Annapolis: Naval Institute Press, 1983), 69–73; Edward Ingram, *Commitment to Empire: Prophecies of the Great Game in Asia, 1797–1800* (Oxford: Clarendon Press, 1981), 336–37.

51. Rodger, *War of the Second Coalition*, 219–26; Clowes, *Royal Navy*, 4:458–70; Louis-Edouard Chevalier, *Histoire de la marine française sous le consulat et l'empire* (Paris: L. Hachette, 1886), 38–43, 50–63; David Greenwood, "James, Lord de Saumarez, 1757–1836," and Colin White, "Sir Richard Goodwin Keats, 1756–1834," in Le Fevre and Harding, *British Admirals*, 255–61, 354–56; Lee Bienkowski, *Admirals in the Age of Nelson* (Annapolis: Naval Institute Press, 2003), 214–16, 231–34.

52. Ehrman, *Younger Pitt* , 3:345–58, 366–72.

53. Ehrman, *Younger Pitt*, 3:393–400; Schroeder, *Transformation of European Politics*, 217–21; McGrew, *Paul I*, 282–357; Ole Feldbæk, *Denmark and the Armed Neutrality, 1800–1801: Small Power Policy in a World War*, trans. Jean Lundskær-Nielsen (Copenhagen: Akademisk Forlag Universitesforlaget i København, 1980) and *The Battle of Copenhagen, 1801: Nelson and the Danes*, trans. Tony Wedgwood (Barnsley, UK: Leo Cooper, 2002); Dudley Pope, *The Great Gamble: Nelson at Copenhagen* (London: Chatham, 2001); James J. Kenney Jr., "Lord Whitworth and the Conspiracy against Tsar Paul I: The New Evidence of the Kent Archive," *Slavic Review* 36 (1977): 205–19.

54. Ehrman, *Younger Pitt*, 3:495–523. Piers Mackesy's analysis is similar: *War without Victory*, 168–201. Both authors also discuss the decline of Pitt's health and morale. For varying assessments of Addington's government, compare Charles John Fedorak, *Henry Addington, Prime Minister, 1801–1804: Peace, War, and Parliamentary Politics* (Akron: University of Akron Press, 2002); C. D. Hall, "Addington's War: Unspectacular but Not Unsuccessful," *Historical Research* 61 (1988): 306–15; and John R. Breihan, "The Addington Party and the Navy in British Politics, 1801–1806," in Craig L. Symonds, ed., *New Aspects of Naval History: Selected Papers Presented at the Fourth Naval History Symposium, United States Naval Academy, 25–26 October 1979* (Annapolis: Naval Institute Press, 1981), 167–89, with Ehrman, *Younger Pitt*, 3:552–662.

55. Sorel, *L'Europe et la Révolution française*, 6:181–213; Ehrman, *Younger Pitt*, 3:469–71.

7. The Role of the Navies in the Napoleonic War

1. Commandant Alain Demerliac, *La Marine du consulat et du premier empire: Nomenclature des navires et guerre française de 1800 à 1815* (Nice: ANCRE, 2003), 12–18, 73, 82.

2. Lyon, *Sailing Navy List*, 62–79, 105–10, 115, 214, 236–41; James, *Naval History*, 3:504; Lavery, *Nelson's Navy*, 223.

3. Dubois, *Avengers of the New World*, 280–301; Michael Zuckerman, *Almost Chosen People: Oblique Biographies in the American Grain* (Berkeley: University of California Press, 1993), 175–218.

4. Guérin, *Histoire de la marine contemporaine*, 683; Demerliac, *La Marine du consulat*, 16.

5. Bell, *Toussaint Louverture*, 219–22; John Kukla, *A Wilderness So Immense: The Louisiana Purchase and the Destiny of America* (New York: Alfred A. Knopf, 2003), 216.

6. Schroeder, *Transformation of European Politics*, 231–45, provides an overview of European diplomacy, although a rather biased one. Isser Woloch, *Napoleon and His Collaborators: The Making of a Dictatorship* (New York: W. W. Norton, 2001), is balanced and scholarly. For other views of Napoleon's rule, see Steven Englund, *Napoleon: A Political Life* (New York: Scribner, 2004); Charles J. Esdaile, *The Wars of Napoleon* (London: Longman, 1995); Louis Bergeron, *France under Napoleon*, trans. R. R. Palmer (Princeton: Princeton University Press, 1981); J. David Markham, *Napoleon's Road to Glory: Triumphs, Defeat, and Immortality* (London: Brassey, 2003); and Howard G. Brown, *Ending the French Revolution: Violence, Justice, and Repression from the Terror to Napoleon* (Charlottesville: University of Virginia Press, 2006). For the brief interwar period, see John D. Grainger, *The Amiens Truce: Britain and Bonaparte, 1801–1803* (Woodbridge, UK: Boydell Press, 2004), but it should be used with caution, as it downplays British responsibility for the outbreak of the new war. Frank McLynn, *Napoleon: A Biography* (London: Jonathan Cape, 1997), 263–67, is more evenhanded.

7. Sorel, *L'Europe et la Révolution française*, 6:211; Desbrière, *Projets et tentatives*, 3:36–40; Demerliac, *La Marine du consulat*, 12–16, 66–75, 82–83; Harold C. Deutsch, *The Genesis of Napoleonic Imperialism* (Cambridge:

Harvard University Press; London: Humphrey Milford, Oxford University Press, 1938), 121.

8. National Archives of the United Kingdom (Public Record Office), Admiralty Series 8 (List Books), vol. 87; Lyon, *Sailing Navy List*, 105–6, 110–13, 115; Breihan, "Addington Party," 165–81; Rodger, *Command of the Ocean*, 476–80, 615–17; Roger Morriss, "St. Vincent and Reform, 1801–1804," *Mariner's Mirror* 69 (1983): 268–90; James, *Naval History*, 3:506.

9. Demerliac, *La Marine du consulat*, 140; Demerliac, *La Marine de Louis XV*, 77; Dull, *French Navy and the Seven Years' War*, 135. For a description and critique of the new generation of prames, see Alan Schom, *Trafalgar: Countdown to Battle, 1803–1805* (New York: Atheneum, 1990), 75.

10. Demerliac, *La Marine du consulat*, 3, 140–43; Schom, *Trafalgar*, 70–116, 122–27; Chevalier, *La Marine sous le consulat et l'empire*, 86–124, 157–63.

11. Schom, *Trafalgar*, 136–41; Rodger, *Command of the Ocean*, 531.

12. For the decision to seize the Spanish ships, see Ehrman, *Younger Pitt*, 3:702–5, for Melville's resignation and Barham's appointment, see 752–66. A good source for the continental war of 1805 is Frederick W. Kagan, *The End of the Old Order: Napoleon and Europe, 1801–1805* (Cambridge: Da Capo Press, 2006), the first of a planned four-volume series. See also Chandler, *Campaigns of Napoleon*, 381–439.

13. For perceptive comparisons of the huge differences between Napoleon and Hitler, see Steven Englund, "Napoleon and Hitler," *Journal of the Historical Society* 6 (2006): 151–67, and *Napoleon: A Political Life*, 464–67; and Woloch, *Napoleon and His Collaborators*, 238–39. The assassination attempt on Napoleon that came closest to success is described by Michael J. Sydenham, "The Crime of 3 Nivôse (24 December 1800)," in Bosher, *French Government and Society*, 295–320.

14. National Archives of the United Kingdom (Public Record Office), Admiralty Series 8 (List Books), vol. 89; Knight, "Fleets at Trafalgar," 68–74; Glete, *Navies and Nations*, 2:400, 641; Saint Hubert, "Ships of the Line of the Spanish Navy," 133, 208–11, 283–85; René Maine, *Trafalgar: Napoleon's Naval Waterloo* (New York: Charles Scribner's Sons, 1957), 109.

15. Rodger, *Command of the Ocean*, 532–6; Schom, *Trafalgar*, 168–207, arrives at the same total.

16. For the expedition to Naples, see Kagan, *End of the Old Order*, 313–21, 327–29; William Henry Flaghart III, *Counterpart to Trafalgar: The Anglo-Russian Invasion of Naples, 1805–1806* (Columbia: University of South Carolina Press, 1992); Piers Mackesy, *The War in the Mediterranean, 1803–1810* (Cambridge: Harvard University Press, 1957), 67–93.

17. There are numerous accounts of the campaign. The most detailed are Edouard Desbrière, *The Naval Campaign of 1805*, trans. Constance Eastwick, 2 vols. (Oxford: Clarendon Press, 1933) and Julian S. Corbett, *The Campaign of Trafalgar* (London: Longmans, Green, 1910). More recent accounts include Knight, *Pursuit of Victory*, 478–524, Harbron, *Trafalgar and the Spanish Navy*, 115–50, and Schom, *Trafalgar*. An especially perceptive analysis of the battle is Michael Duffy, ". . . All Was Hushed Up: The Hidden Trafalgar," *Mariner's Mirror* 91 (2005): 216–40. Tim Clayton and Phil Craig, *Trafalgar: The Men, the Battle, the Storm* (London: Hodder and Stroughton, 2004), is a vivid account. The roles of Cornwallis, Barham, and Calder are discussed in Lambert, "Cornwallis," 366–73; I. Lloyd Phillips, "Lord Barham at the Admiralty, 1805–6," *Mariner's Mirror* 64 (1978): 217–33; and Nicholas Tracy, "Sir Robert Calder, 1745–1810," in Le Fevre and Harding, *British Admirals*, 197–217, and "Sir Robert Calder's Action," *Mariner's Mirror* 77 (1991): 259–69. For the ships that participated in the battle, see Goodwin, *Ships of Trafalgar*.

18. Steven T. Ross, *European Diplomatic History, 1789–1815: France against Europe* (Garden City, N.Y.: Anchor Books, Doubleday, 1969), 277.

19. Chevalier, *La Marine sous le consulat et l'empire*, 246–60; Maurice Dupont, *L'Amiral Willaumez* (Paris: Tallandier, 1987), 281–313.

20. Sutherland, *French Revolution and Empire*, 341–46, 371; Horn, *Path Not Taken*, 216–40, 277–88; François Crouzet, "War, Blockade, and Economic Change in Europe, 1792–1815," in Harding, *Naval History*, 149–70, and *L'Economie britannique et le blocus continental (1806–1813)*, 2 vols. (Paris: Presses Universitaires de France, 1958); Lance E. Davis and Stanley L. Engerman, *Naval Blockades in Peace and War: An Economic History since 1750* (Cambridge: Cambridge University Press, 2006), 29–52; Gavin Daly, "Napoleon and the 'City of Smugglers,' 1810–1814," *Historical Journal* 50 (2007): 333–52.

21. Richard Glover, "The French Fleet, 1807–14: Britain's Problem and Madison's Opportunity," *Journal of Modern History* 39 (1967): 233–52. See also Lawrence S. Kaplan, *Entangling Alliances with None: American Foreign Policy in the Age of Jefferson* (Kent: Kent State University Press, 1987); Clifford L. Egan, *Neither Peace nor War: Franco-American Relations, 1803–1812* (Baton Rouge: Louisiana State University Press, 1983), and Peter P. Hall, *Napoleon's Troublesome Americans: French-American Relations, 1804–1815* (Washington: Potomac Books, 2005).

22. Demerliac, *La Marine du consulat*, 3, 12–16, 66–85; Sorel, *L'Europe et la Révolution française*, 7:245, 452, 518; Lyon, *Sailing Navy List*, 62–75, 104–6, 109–15, 214, 236–41, 267–70; Clowes, *Royal Navy*, 5:10; James, *Naval History*, 4:478, 5:456; Rodger, *Command of the Ocean*, 645; Chevalier, *La Marine sous le consulat et l'empire*, 400; Winfield, *British Warships in the Age of Sail, 1793–1815*; Robert W. Daly, "Operations of the Russian Navy during the Reign of Napoleon I," *Mariner's Mirror* 34 (1948): 182. The French total includes fourteen ships of the line acquired from the Netherlands and four from Venice, but does not include two in the Neapolitan navy. The British total includes two dozen or so ships of the line in ordinary (not in service). I have used an exchange rate of 18:1 based on Owen Connelly, ed., *Historical Dictionary of Napoleonic France, 1799–1815* (Westport CT: Greenwood Press, 1985), 174.

23. See Christopher D. Hall, *British Strategy in the Napoleonic War, 1803–15* (Manchester: Manchester University Press; New York: St. Martin's Press, 1992); Richard Woodman, *The Victory of Seapower: Winning the Napoleonic War, 1806–1814* (London: Chatham, 1998); Roy Adkins and Lesley Adkins, *The War for All the Oceans: From Nelson at the Nile to Napoleon at Waterloo* (London: Little, Brown, 2006); and the somewhat breathless Paul Fregosi, *Dreams of Empire: Napoleon and the First World War, 1792–1815* (London: Hutchinson, 1989), 254–352.

24. For South American operations, see Deane, *Nelson's Favourite*, 222–90; Rudy Bauss, "Rio de Janeiro: Strategic Base for the Global Designs of the British Royal Navy, 1777–1815," in Symonds, *New Aspects*, 83–87; Vincent P. O'Hara, "The Battles of Buenos Aires," *Military History Quarterly* 17, no. 4 (Summer 2005): 42–51; John D. Grainger, "The Navy in

the River Plate, 1806–1808," *Mariner's Mirror* 81 (1995): 287–96; and John D. Grainger, ed., *The Royal Navy in the River Plate, 1806–1807* (Brookfield VT: Ashgate for the Navy Records Society, 1996). The attack on Egypt is covered by Mackesy, *War in the Mediterranean*, 182–99, and John Marlowe, *Perfidious Albion: The Origins of Anglo-French Rivalry in the Levant* (London: Elek Books, 1971), 99–122.

25. On 1 January 1813 the British had a dozen ships of the line in North American waters. National Archives of the United Kingdom (Public Record Office), Admiralty Series 8 (List Books), vol. 100. Jon Latimer offers a survey of the war from a British perspective in *1812: War with America* (Cambridge: Belknap Press of Harvard University Press, 2007). Naval dimensions of the war are treated in Graham, *Empire of the North Atlantic*, 240–61; Robert Gardiner, ed., *The Naval War of 1812* (London: Chatham, 1998); and Wade G. Dudley, *Splintering the Wooden Wall: The British Blockade of the United States, 1812–1815* (Annapolis: Naval Institute Press, 2005). Reginald Horsman, *The War of 1812* (New York: Alfred A. Knopf, 1969), and Donald R. Hickey, *The War of 1812: A Forgotten Conflict* (Urbana: University of Illinois Press, 1989), are good introductions to its military side; see also Hickey's *Don't Give Up the Ship! Myths of the War of 1812* (Urbana: University of Illinois Press, 2006). For the political background, see J. C. A. Stagg, *Mr. Madison's War: Politics, Diplomacy, and Warfare in the Early American Republic, 1783–1830* (Princeton: Princeton University Press, 1983).

26. MacDonald, *Feeding Nelson's Navy*, 46, 53–60.

27. For the attack on the Danes, see Clowes, *Royal Navy*, 5:209–15, and A. N. Ryan, "Causes of the British Attack on Copenhagen, 1807," *English Historical Review* 68 (1953): 37–55. The Danish prizes are listed in Lyon, *Sailing Navy List*, 267–70.

28. James, *Naval History*, 4:298–303; Clowes, *Royal Navy*, 5:247–50; Raymond Carr, "Gustavus IV and the British Government, 1804–9," *English Historical Review* 60 (1945): 36–66; Sven G. Trulsson, *British and Swedish Policies and Strategy after the Peace of Tilset in 1807* (Lund, Sweden: C. W. K. Gleesup, 1976).

29. For the Russian fleet at the Tagus, see Clowes, *Royal Navy*, 5:231,

233–34, 246–47, and Christopher D. Hall, *Wellington's Navy: Sea Power and the Peninsular War, 1809–1814* (London: Chatham; Mechanicsburg PA: Stackpole Books, 2004), 18–19, 36–37.

30. For Saumarez and British operations in the Baltic, see Rodger, *Command of the Ocean*, 560–61; A. N. Ryan, "An Ambassador Afloat: Vice-Admiral Sir James Saumarez and the Swedish Court, 1808–1812," in Black and Woodfine, eds., *British Navy and the Use of Naval Power*, 237–58, and "The Defense of British Trade with the Baltic, 1808–1813," in Harding, *Naval History*, 45–68; A. N. Ryan, ed., *The Saumarez Papers: Selections from the Baltic Correspondence, 1808–1812* (London: Naval Record Society, 1968); Greenwood, "Saumarez," and Michael Duffy, "Sir Samuel Hood, 1762–1814," in Le Fevre and Harding, *British Admirals*, 249–69, 337–38, and Anderson, *Naval Wars in the Baltic*, 322–45.

31. Modern biographies of Collingwood are Oliver Warner, *The Life and Letters of Vice-Admiral Lord Collingwood* (London: Oxford University Press, 1968); Max Adams, *Trafalgar's Lost Hero: Admiral Lord Collingwood and the Defeat of Napoleon* (New York: John Wiley, 2005); and Hugh Owen, "Cuthbert, Lord Collingwood, 1748–1810," in Le Fevre and Harding, *British Admirals*, 139–63. For samples of his correspondence see Warner, *Collingwood*, and C. H. H. Owen, ed., "Letters from Vice-Admiral Lord Collingwood," in Michael Duffy, ed., *The Naval Miscellany, vol. VI* (Burlington VT: Ashgate for the Navy Records Society, 2003), 149–220. For the 1808 crisis, see Warner, *Collingwood*, 193–205; Mackesy, *War in the Mediterranean*, 230–58; and Chevalier, *La Marine sous le consulat et l'empire*, 281–84. See also Lawrence Sondhaus, "Napoleon's Shipbuilding Program in Venice and the Struggle for Mastery in the Adriatic," *Journal of Military History* 53 (1989): 349–62.

32. Gordon Bond, *The Grand Expedition: The British Invasion of Holland in 1809* (Athens: University of Georgia Press, 1979); Carl Christie, "The Royal Navy and the Walcheron Expedition of 1809," in Symonds, *New Aspects*, 190–200.

33. For British naval and military operations in Spain and Portugal, see Hall, *Wellington's Navy*; Rory Muir, *Britain and the Defeat of Napoleon, 1807–1815* (New Haven: Yale University Press, 1996); Charles Esdaile, *The*

Peninsular War: A New History (London: Allen Lane, 2002); and Michael Glover, *The Peninsular War, 1807–1814: A Concise Military History* (Newton Abbot: David and Charles, 1974). The deterioration of Franco-Russian relations is described in vol. 7 of Sorel, *L'Europe et la Révolution française.*

34. For the campaigns and diplomacy of 1813–14, see Chandler, *Campaigns of Napoleon*, 865–1004; Sorel, *L'Europe et la Révolution française*, 8:1–353; Schroeder, *Transformation of European Politics*, 396–516; Henry A. Kissinger, *A World Restored: Metternich, Castlereagh, and the Problems of Peace, 1812–20* (Boston: Houghton Mifflin; Cambridge: Riverside Press, 1957).

8. The Ingredients of Supremacy in the Age of Sail

1. Quoted in Ehrman, *Younger Pitt*, 2:412. In 1499 Louis XII of France was warned that the three things necessary to make war were money, more money, and still more money: Glete, *War and the State*, 126. This still had a substantial element of truth three centuries later. For perceptive analyses of British and French government finances, see Martin Daunton, "The Fiscal-Military State and the Napoleonic Wars: Britain and France Compared," in Cannadine, *Trafalgar in History*, 18–43, and Peter Mathias and Patrick O'Brien, "Taxation in Britain and France, 1715–1810: A Comparison of the Social and Economic Incidence of Taxes Collected for the Central Government," *Journal of European Economic History* 5 (1976): 601–50.

2. For a recent example of such an approach, see Adam Nicolson, *Men of Honour: Trafalgar and the Making of the English Hero* (London: HarperCollins, 2005). The American edition has been renamed *Seize the Fire: Heroism, Duty, and the Battle of Trafalgar.*

3. Dull, *French Navy and American Independence*, 304.

4. Brewer, *Sinews of Power*; Dull, *French Navy and the Seven Years' War*, 46–47; Mathias and O'Brien, "Taxation in Britain and France," 610–11; P. K. O'Brien, "Public Finance in the Wars with France, 1797–1815," in H. T. Dickinson, ed., *Britain and the French Revolution* (Basingstoke: Macmillan Education, 1989), 165–87; Richard Bonney, "Toward the Comparative Fiscal History of Britain and France during the 'Long' Eighteenth Century," in Prados de la Escosura, ed., *Exceptionalism and Industrialisation*, 191–215. By the mid-eighteenth century, France had a population of about 22 million, about three times that of England, Scotland, and Wales: A. Goodwin,

ed., *The New Cambridge Modern History*, vol. 8, *The American and French Revolutions* (Cambridge: Cambridge University Press, 1965), 714–15. On the eve of the French Revolution, French foreign trade exceeded British by more than 30 percent: Horn, *Path Not Taken*, 76.

5. The French figures are from Legohérel, *Les Trésoriers généraux*, table facing 180; Pritchard, *Louis XV's Navy*, 218; Dull, *French Navy and American Independence*, 350. British figures are from Rodger, *Command of the Ocean*, 643–44. I have rounded the figures and converted livres to pounds at 23.5:1, a common exchange rate for the period; see McCusker, *Money and Exchange*, 96–97. An eighteenth-century livre was roughly equivalent in purchasing power to at least $5 (twenty-first century).

6. Dull, *French Navy and the Seven Years' War*, 87, and *French Navy and American Independence*, 144n; Rodger, *Command of the Ocean*, 638. See also Stephen F. Gradish, *The Manning of the British Navy during the Seven Years' War* (London: Royal Historical Society, 1980). When Spain joined the Seven Years' War in late 1761, it could muster only 26,000 crewmen: Marley, "A Fearful Gift," 414.

7. For example, François Crouzet, "The Second Hundred Years' War: Some Reflections," *French History* 10 (1996): 432–50.

8. See Andrew Lambert, "The Magic of Trafalgar: The Nineteenth-Century Legacy," in Cannadine, *Trafalgar in History*, 155–74, and Kennedy, *Rise and Fall of British Naval Mastery*, 149–237.

9. For a different view stressing the differences between England and France, see Frank O'Gorman, "Eighteenth-Century England as an *Ancien Régime*," in Stephen Taylor, Richard Connors, and Clyve Jones, eds., *Hanoverian Britain and Empire: Essays in Memory of Philip Lawson* (Woodbridge, UK: Boydell Press, 1998), 23–36.

10. "La politique de toutes les puissances est dans leur géographie": Napoleon to Frederick William III, 10 November 1804, quoted in Sorel, *L'Europe et la Révolution française*, 6:400–401.

11. Henri Doniol, *Politiques d'autrefois: Le Comte de Vergennes et P. M. Hennin* (Paris: Armand Colin, 1898), 103–4. The English translation is mine.

Index

Studies in War, Society, and the Military

Military Migration and State Formation
The British Military Community in Seventeenth-Century Sweden
Mary Elizabeth Ailes

The State at War in South Asia
Pradeep P. Barua

An American Soldier in World War I
George Browne
Edited by David L. Snead

Imagining the Unimaginable
World War, Modern Art, and the Politics of Public Culture in Russia, 1914–1917
Aaron J. Cohen

The Rise of the National Guard
The Evolution of the American Militia, 1865–1920
Jerry Cooper

The Thirty Years' War and German Memory in the Nineteenth Century
Kevin Cramer

Political Indoctrination in the U.S. Army from World War II to the Vietnam War
Christopher S. DeRosa

In the Service of the Emperor
Essays on the Imperial Japanese Army
Edward J. Drea

The Age of the Ship of the Line
The British and French Navies, 1650–1815
Jonathan R. Dull

You Can't Fight Tanks with Bayonets
Psychological Warfare against the Japanese Army in the Southwest Pacific
Allison B. Gilmore

A Strange and Formidable Weapon
British Responses to World War I Poison Gas
Marion Girard

Civilians in the Path of War
Edited by Mark Grimsley and Clifford J. Rogers

I Die with My Country
Perspectives on the Paraguayan War, 1864–1870
Edited by Hendrik Kraay and Thomas L. Whigham

North American Indians in the Great World War
Susan Applegate Krouse
Photographs and original documentation by Joseph K. Dixon

Citizens More than Soldiers
The Kentucky Militia and Society in the Early Republic
Harry S. Laver

Soldiers as Citizens
Former German Officers in the Federal Republic of Germany, 1945–1955
Jay Lockenour

Army and Empire
British Soldiers on the American Frontier, 1758–1775
Michael N. McConnell

The Militarization of Culture in the Dominican Republic, from the Captains General to General Trujillo
Valentina Peguero

Arabs at War
Military Effectiveness, 1948–1991
Kenneth M. Pollack

The Politics of Air Power
From Confrontation to Cooperation in Army Aviation Civil-Military Relations
Rondall R. Rice

Andean Tragedy
Fighting the War of the Pacific, 1879–1884
William F. Sater

The Grand Illusion
The Prussianization of the Chilean Army
William F. Sater and Holger H. Herwig

Sex Crimes under the Wehrmacht
David Raub Snyder

The Paraguayan War
Volume 1: Causes and Early Conduct
Thomas L. Whigham

The Challenge of Change
Military Institutions and New Realities, 1918–1941
Edited by Harold R. Winton and David R. Mets